The
ARMCHAIR
ECONOMIST

Economics and Everyday Life
Revised and Updated for the 21st Century

STEVEN E. LANDSBURG

SIMON &
SCHUSTER

London · New York · Sydney · Toronto · New Delhi

A CBS COMPANY

First published in Great Britain in 2009 by Simon & Schuster UK Ltd
This edition published in 2012 by Simon & Schuster UK Ltd
A CBS COMPANY

ISBN: 978-1-47110-131-1

Designed by Jill Putorti

Printed and bound by CPI Group (UK) Ltd, Croydon, CR0 4YY

TABLE OF CONTENTS

PREFACE TO
THE SECOND EDITION

One day in 1991, I walked into a medium-size bookstore and counted over 80 titles on quantum physics and the history of the universe. A few shelves over I found Richard Dawkins's bestseller *The Selfish Gene*, along with dozens of others explaining Darwinian evolution and the genetic code.

In the best of these books, I discovered natural wonders, confronted mysteries, learned new ways of thinking, and felt I had shared in a great intellectual adventure founded on ideas that are dazzling in their scope and their simplicity.

Economics too is a great intellectual adventure, but in 1991 I could find not a single book that proposed to share that adventure with the general public. There was nothing that revealed the economist's unique way of thinking, using a few simple ideas to illuminate the whole range of human behavior, shake up our preconceptions, and jolt us into new ways of seeing the world.

I resolved to write that book. *The Armchair Economist* was published in 1993 and attracted a large and devoted following. In the intervening 20 years, it has earned much high praise. But what I take most pride in is that *The Armchair Economist* is still widely recognized among economists as the book to give your mother when she wants to understand what you do all day.

A lot has changed in that 20 years. Today no bookstore patron could complain about a paucity of titles in the popular economics section. Some of the new titles are quite good. Several, I daresay, were inspired by *Armchair*. The most well-known of the recent titles is Levitt and Dubner's *Freakonomics*, which I think is a rollicking good read (and I said so when I reviewed it for the *Wall Street Journal*). But for all its merits, *Freakonomics* is more a collection of wonderful and enlightening anecdotes than a guide to understanding economics. *Freakonomics* is out to dazzle you with facts; *The Armchair Economist* is out to dazzle you with logic.

Logic matters. It leads us from simple ideas to surprising conclusions. A simple idea is that people respond to incentives. A surprising conclusion is that when drivers are protected by air bags, they drive more recklessly and have more accidents. A simple idea is that when the price of something goes down, suppliers provide less of it. A surprising conclusion is that recycling programs, which reduce the price of timber, ensure that fewer trees are planted and forests shrink. A simple idea is that monopolists charge whatever price the market will bear for their output. A surprising conclusion is that when oil supplies are interrupted, steep price hikes are evidence of competition, not monopoly; a monopoly oil company wouldn't wait for a supply interruption to raise the price.

Evidence matters too, but logic can be powerful all on its own. Take, for example, the argument about recycling and the size of forests. If I wrote that the reason we have large cattle herds in this country is that people eat a lot of meat, few readers would demand detailed numerical evidence to support that conclusion. The idea itself is too powerful and too compelling. It's instructive, then, to realize that the same powerful and compelling idea tells us that one reason we have large cultivated forests is that people use a lot of paper. Of course, ideas can always be misleading—but then so can numbers. Still, we advance by learning new ways to think, even if those ways are not infallible.

Much else has changed since 1991. When I wrote *The Armchair Economist*, I envisioned a "computer game of life," where nobody ever tells you whether you won or lost. You live and you die, and if you play well you collect rewards. If you decide it's not worth the trouble to play well, that's fine too. Today that game exists, and over 20 million people have played it. It's called Second Life. In 1991, when I wanted an example of a crazy entrepreneurial wild goose chase, I invented a story about a CEO who wanted to build a computer you could carry in your pocket. Perhaps you're now reading these words on that computer.

There's also much that hasn't changed. The basic principles of economics continue to surprise, delight, and edify, and they're much the same as they were in 1991, though there are always new applications.

In updating *The Armchair Economist* for the 21st century, I've culled the Internet, the media, and my own experience of life for good contemporary applications of the eternal ideas of economic theory. As a result, some chapters—those where the examples were starting to seem a little musty—have been almost entirely rewritten. Others have been updated to put more emphasis on today's concerns. I've excised all references to cassette tapes, Polaroid film, and Walter Mondale.

This edition has also benefited enormously from the critical eye of Lisa Talpey, who read multiple drafts of every chapter and wouldn't let me stop revising until I'd met her extremely high standards for clarity. Until Lisa got her hands on this manuscript, I'd had no idea how much room there was for improvement.

One other thing has changed since 1991: The world has become a more ideological place. Nowadays it's almost impossible to explain a noncontroversial bit of economic reasoning without being suspected of some ulterior ideological agenda. So let me be up-front about this: I do have opinions. Speaking very broadly, I tend to be optimistic about the power of markets to do good, and skeptical of the power of governments to do better. And I am sure there's an occasional passage in this book where I've failed to restrain myself from betraying those prejudices. But this book is not a work of ideology. It is, with rare exceptions, about the basic principles that guide the work of almost all economists, regardless of where they lie on the political spectrum. There is some disagreement among economists about which of these ideas are most important, but very little disagreement that they are basically correct. Economists from the far left to the far right have praised *The Armchair Economist* for its accurate portrayal of the ideas we all have in common, and in this new edition I've aimed to continue deserving that praise.

INTRODUCTION

Shortly after I arrived at the University of Chicago to begin my graduate studies, the *Wall Street Journal* published a list of "ways to stump an economist." It was written by a man named John Tracy McGrath, who raised a series of embarrassingly simple questions about everyday life that he thought economists would be unable to answer: Why does a pack of cigarettes bought from a cigarette machine cost more than a pack of cigarettes bought from the man at the candy store? Why can't racetracks make change in less than 20-cent increments? Why does orange soda cost four times as much as gasoline?

That night over dinner, my friends and I—first-year graduate students all—had quite a laugh at McGrath's expense. With just a little knowledge of economics, all of his questions seemed easy.

Today, with over 30 years of additional knowledge, I think that all of McGrath's questions are both fascinating and difficult. In my recollection, the answers that came so easily over dinner consisted of nothing more than refusals to take the questions seriously. I believe that we dismissed most of them with the phrase "supply and demand," as if that meant something. Whatever we thought it meant, we were sure that it was what economics was about.

Here is what I *now* think economics is about. First, it is about observing the world with genuine curiosity and admitting that it is full of mysteries. Second, it is about trying to solve those mysteries in ways that are consistent with the general proposition that human behavior is usually designed to serve a purpose. Sometimes the mysteries themselves—like McGrath's—are hard to solve, so we practice by trying to solve similar mysteries in fictional worlds that we invent and call models. If the goal is to understand why orange soda costs more than gasoline, we might begin by thinking about a world where the only things that anybody ever buys are orange soda and gasoline. If the goal is to understand why particular constituencies want to outlaw silicone breast implants, we might begin by thinking about a world where men choose their marriage partners exclusively on the basis of breast size.

We think about models not because they are realistic, but because thinking about models is a good warm-up exercise for thinking about the world we live in. The goal, always, is to understand our own world. The first step toward understanding—and the step that we had not yet taken when we started graduate school—is to admit that the world is not always easy to understand.

This book is a compendium of essays about how economists think. It is about the things that we find mysterious, why we find them mysterious, and how we try to understand them. It describes some mysteries that I think are solved and others that I think are not. There are a lot of good reasons to learn about economics, but the reason I have tried to stress in this book is that economics is a tool for solving mysteries, and solving mysteries is fun.

For most of my adult life, I have had the splendid privilege of eating lunch every day with an extraordinary group of economic detectives who never fail to inspire me with their incisiveness, their whimsy, and their capacity for wonder. Almost daily someone arrives at lunch with a new mystery to solve, a dozen brilliant and original solutions are proposed, and a dozen devastating objections are raised and occasionally overcome. We do it for sheer joy.

This book is largely a chronicle of what I have learned at lunch. I am sure that some of the ideas are original with me, but I am no longer sure which ones. Many others I learned from Mark Bils, John Boyd, Marvin Goodfriend, Bruce Hansen, Hanan Jacoby, Jim Kahn, Ken McLaughlin, Alan Stockman, and the others who have come and gone over the years. With profound thanks for taking me along on their roller-coaster ride, this book is dedicated to the lunch group.

A NOTE ON THE CHAPTERS

These chapters give a sampling of how economists see the world. For the most part, they can be read in any order. Some chapters refer to ideas from earlier chapters, but these references are never essential to the flow of things.

The ideas expressed in this book are intended to give a fair representation of how mainstream economists think. Of course, there is room for disagreement over specifics, and any particular economist would surely want to dissent from some of the things that I say. But I believe that most economists who read this book will agree that it accurately reflects their general viewpoint.

Attentive readers will observe that this book applies economic reasoning to a vast array of human (and sometimes nonhuman) behavior. They will note also that when a question arises regarding the range of applicability of an economic principle, the author always prefers to risk error in the direction of being overly inclusive. I believe that the laws of economics are universal; they are blind to race and blind to gender. I am therefore confident that no attentive reader will mistake my occasional use of the generic pronouns "he," "him," and "his" for the exclusively masculine pronouns with the same spellings and pronunciations.

I

What Life Is All About

CHAPTER I

THE POWER OF INCENTIVES

How Seat Belts Kill

Most of economics can be summarized in four words: "People respond to incentives." The rest is commentary.

"People respond to incentives" sounds innocuous enough, and almost everyone will admit its validity as a general principle. What distinguishes the economist is his insistence on taking the principle seriously at all times.

I am old enough to remember the late 1970s and waiting half an hour to buy a tank of gasoline at a federally controlled price. Virtually all economists agreed that if the price were allowed to rise freely, people would buy less gasoline. Many noneconomists believed otherwise. The economists were right: When price controls were lifted, the lines disappeared.

Perhaps each generation has to learn this lesson anew. When gas prices spiked in the summer of 2008, journalists predicted that petroleum-addicted Americans would pay any price necessary to maintain their old habits. Economists were certain that gas consumption would fall. Once again the economists were right. By August 2008, gas consumption had fallen by about 8.5 percent, which (not coincidentally) was just about exactly the consensus forecast among economists.

The economist's faith in the power of incentives serves him well, and he trusts it as a guide in unfamiliar territory. Back when seat belts (or air bags or antilock brakes) were first introduced, any economist could have predicted one of the consequences: The number of car accidents increased. That's because the threat of being killed in an accident is a powerful incentive to drive carefully. But a driver with a seat belt or an air bag faces less of a threat. Because people respond to incentives, drivers are less careful. The result is more accidents.

The governing principle is precisely the same one that predicts behavior at the gas pump. When the price of gasoline is low, people choose to buy more gasoline. When the price of accidents (e.g., the probability of being killed or the expected medical bill) is low, people choose to have more accidents.

You might object that accidents, unlike gasoline, are not in any sense a "good" that people would ever choose to purchase. But speed and recklessness are goods in the sense that people seem to want them. Choosing to drive faster or more recklessly is tantamount to choosing more accidents, at least in a probabilistic sense.

An interesting question remains: How big is the effect in question? How many additional accidents are caused by seat belts, air bags, and other safety equipment? Here is a striking way to frame the question: Seat belts tend to *reduce* the number of driver deaths by making it easier to survive an accident. At the same time, seat belts tend to *increase* the number of driver deaths by encouraging reckless behavior. Which effect is the greater? Is the net effect to decrease or to increase the number of driver deaths?

This question can't be answered by pure logic. One must look at actual numbers. The first person to do that was Sam Peltzman of the University of Chicago. He found that the two effects are of approximately equal size and therefore cancel each other out. When seat belts were first introduced (along with padded dashboards and collapsible steering columns) there were more accidents and fewer driver deaths per accident, but the total number of driver deaths remained essentially unchanged. Pedestrian deaths, however, appear to have increased—pedestrians, after all, are not equipped with padded dashboards. Subsequent studies have found comparable results for air bags and antilock brakes.

I have discovered that when I tell noneconomists about Peltzman's results, they find it almost impossible to believe that people would drive less carefully simply because their cars are safer. Economists, who have learned to respect the principle that people respond to incentives, do not have this problem.

If you find it hard to believe that people drive less carefully when their cars are safer, consider the proposition that people drive *more* carefully when their cars are more dangerous. This is, of course, just another way of saying the same thing, but somehow people find it easier to believe. If I took the seat belts out of your car, wouldn't you be more cautious when driving? What if I took the doors off?

Carrying this logic to its extreme, we could probably cut the accident rate dramatically by requiring each new car to have a spear mounted on the steering wheel, pointing directly at the driver's heart. I predict there would be a lot less tailgating.

At the other extreme, NASCAR drivers have cars so safe that they can generally crash into concrete walls at high speeds and walk away with no injuries. How do they respond to all that safety? In the words of the economists Russell Sobel and Todd Nesbit, "They race them at 200 miles per hour around tiny oval racetracks only inches away from other automobiles—and have lots of wrecks." And when the cars get safer, they have even more wrecks. NASCAR introduces hundreds of safety-related rule changes every year, which has allowed Sobel, Nesbit, and others to test and confirm this prediction.

One of the most dramatic rule changes followed the tragic crash that killed Dale Earnhardt Sr. at the Daytona 500 in 2001. Drivers are now required to wear a head and neck restraining system, or HANS device, which affords considerable protection in the event of a crash. According to the economists Adam Pope and Robert Tollison, the HANS device has increased the frequency of crashes by roughly 2 percent. Driver deaths and injuries are down, but pit crew injuries are up.

It is in no sense foolhardy to take more risks when you have a seat belt. Driving recklessly has its costs, but it has its benefits too. You get where you are going faster, and you can often have a lot more fun along the way. "Recklessness" takes many forms: It can mean passing in dangerous situations, but it can also mean letting your mind wander or fiddling with your iPod. Any of these activities might make your trip more pleasant, and any of them might be well worth a slight increase in accident risk. So it would be a mistake to conclude that seat belts are counterproductive. They're definitely good for drivers, just not necessarily in the way you might expect.

Occasionally people are tempted to respond that nothing—or at least none of the things I've listed—is worth any risk of death. Economists find this objection particularly frustrating, because neither those who raise it nor anybody else actually believes it. All people risk death every day for relatively trivial rewards. Driving to Starbucks for a Mocha Frappuccino involves a clear risk that could be avoided by staying home, but people still drive to Starbucks. We need not ask whether small pleasures are worth *any* risk; the answer is obviously yes. The right question is *how much* risk those small pleasures are worth. It is perfectly rational to say, "I am willing to fiddle with my iPod while driving if it leads to a one-in-a-million chance of death, but not if it leads to a one-in-a-thousand chance of death." That is why more people fiddle with their iPods at 25 miles per hour than at 70.

Peltzman's observations reveal that driving behavior is remarkably sensitive to changes in the driver's environment. This affords an opportunity for some drivers to influence the behavior of others. Fans of *The Simpsons* might recall that Homer and Marge once posted a "Baby on Board" sign in their rear window so that other drivers would stop intentionally ramming their car. Even outside cartoons, people use those signs to signal other drivers to use extraordinary care. I know drivers who find these signs insulting because of the implication that they don't *already* drive as carefully as possible. Economists will be quite unsympathetic to this feeling, because they know that nobody *ever* drives as carefully as possible (do you have new brakes installed before each trip to the grocery store?) and because they know that most drivers' watchfulness does vary markedly with their surroundings. Virtually all drivers would be quite unhappy to injure the occupants of another car; many drivers would be especially unhappy if that other car contained a baby. That group *will* choose to drive more carefully when alerted to a baby's presence and *will* be glad to have that presence called to their attention.

This, incidentally, suggests an interesting research project. Economics suggests that many drivers are more cautious in the presence of a Baby on Board sign. The project is to find out *how much* more cautious by observing accident rates for cars with and without the signs. Unfortunately, accident rates can be misleading for at least three reasons. First, those parents who post signs are probably unusually cautious; they have fewer accidents just because they themselves are exceptionally careful drivers, independently of how their sign affects others. Second (and introducing a bias in the opposite direction), those parents who post signs know that the sign elicits caution from others, and they can therefore afford to be less vigilant themselves. This would tend to involve them in *more* accidents and at least partially cancel the effects of other drivers' extra care. Third, if Baby on Board signs really work, there is nothing to stop childless couples from posting them dishonestly. If drivers are aware of widespread deception, they will tend to suppress their natural responses.

This means that raw accident statistics cannot reveal how drivers respond to Baby on Board signs. The problem is to find a clever statistical technique to make all the necessary corrections. I do not propose to solve that problem here, but I offer it as an example of a typical difficulty that arises in empirical economic research. Many research projects in economics revolve around creative solutions to just such difficulties.

After this slight digression into the challenges of empirical research, let me return to my main topic: the power of incentives. It is the economist's second nature to account for that power. Will the invention of a better birth control technique reduce the number of unwanted pregnancies? Not necessarily: The invention reduces the "price" of sexual intercourse (unwanted pregnancies being a component of that price) and thereby induces people to engage in more of it. The percentage of sexual encounters that lead to pregnancy goes down, the number of sexual encounters goes up, and the number of unwanted pregnancies can go either down or up. Will energy-efficient cars reduce our consumption of gasoline? Not necessarily: An energy-efficient car reduces the price of driving, and people will choose to drive more. Statin drugs like Lipitor lower the price of being a couch potato and could therefore lead to more heart attacks. Low-tar cigarettes could increase the incidence of lung cancer. Better football helmets can mean more football injuries. Low-calorie synthetic fats could partly account for the obesity epidemic.

Criminal law is a critical area for understanding how people respond to incentives. To what extent do harsh punishments deter criminal activity? The death penalty is of particular interest. The deterrent effect of the death penalty has been studied intensely by innumerable government commissions and academic scholars. Often their studies consist of nothing more than examining murder rates in states with and without capital punishment laws. Economists tend to be harshly critical of these studies because they fail to account for other important factors that help to determine murder rates. (Often they fail even to account for how stringently the death penalty is enforced, although this varies appreciably from state to state.) On the other hand, the refined statistical techniques collectively known as *econometrics* are designed precisely to measure the power of incentives. This makes it natural to apply econometrics in examining the effect of the death penalty. One of the leaders in this effort has been Isaac Ehrlich of the State University of New York at Buffalo, whose pioneering research led him to a striking conclusion: During the 1960s (the last decade before the U.S. Supreme Court declared a moratorium on the death penalty), each execution prevented approximately eight murders. After the death penalty was reinstated, subsequent research found comparable numbers for more recent periods.

The details of Ehrlich's methods have been widely criticized by other economists, but it is possible to make too much of this. Most of the criticisms involve esoteric questions of statistical technique. Such questions are important. But there is widespread agreement in the economics profession that the *sort* of empirical study that Ehrlich undertook is capable of revealing important truths about the effect of capital punishment.*

Edward Leamer of the University of California at Los Angeles

---

* In the classroom, I use these studies to illustrate several points, not the least of which is that we can agree on matters of fact yet still differ on matters of policy. Isaac Ehrlich, the man who convinced much of the economics profession that capital punishment is a highly effective deterrent to murder, remains a passionate opponent of capital punishment.

once published an amusing article titled "Let's Take the Con out of Econometrics," in which he warned that the prejudices of the researcher can substantially affect his results. He showed that a simple econometric test, with a pro–death penalty bias built in, could demonstrate that each execution prevents as many as 13 murders. The same test, with an anti–death penalty bias built in, could demonstrate that each execution actually *causes* as many as 3 additional murders. Still, unless one goes very far in the direction of building in a bias against the death penalty, most econometric research reveals a substantial deterrent effect of capital punishment. Murderers respond to incentives.

How can this be? Are not many murders crimes of passion or acts of irrationality? Perhaps so. But there are two responses to this objection. First, Ehrlich's results indicate that each execution prevents eight murders; it does not indicate *which* eight murders are prevented. As long as some murderers can be deterred, capital punishment can be a deterrent. The second response is this: Why should we expect that people engaged in crimes of passion would fail to respond to incentives? We can imagine a man who hates his wife so much that under ordinary circumstances he would do her in if he thought he had a 90 percent chance of escaping execution. Perhaps in a moment of rage, he becomes so carried away that he will kill her even if he has only a 20 percent chance of escaping execution. Then even in the moment of rage, it matters very much whether he perceives his chances to be 15 percent or 25 percent.

(Let me mention a third response as well. Ehrlich did not just make up the number eight; he arrived at it through a sophisticated analysis of data. Skepticism is fine, but it is incumbent on the serious skeptic to examine the research with an open mind and to pinpoint what step in the reasoning, if any, he finds suspicious.)

There *is* evidence that people respond significantly to incentives even in situations where we don't usually imagine their behavior to be calculated or even rational. Apparently psychologists have discovered that if you hand people unexpectedly hot cups of coffee, they typically drop the cup if they believe it's cheap but manage to hang on if they believe the cup is valuable.

Due to some combination of arthritis (which makes it difficult for me to turn my head to the right) and irresponsibility, I had a years-long habit of backing the right rear corner of my car into lampposts, trees, and other stationary obstructions. Often enough so the body shop owner joked about giving me a quantity discount, I paid $180 to get my bumper repaired, and I came to think of this as an unavoidable expense. Then in 2002 I got a new car with a fiberglass bumper, backed it into a tree, and discovered that this repair was going to cost me over $500. I have not backed into anything since. Even economists respond to incentives.

Indeed the response to incentives may be as innate as any other instinctive behavior. In a series of experiments at Texas A&M University, researchers allowed rats and pigeons to "purchase" various forms of food and drink by pushing various levers. Each item has its price, such as 3 lever pushes for a drop of root beer or 10 for a piece of cheese. The animals are given "incomes" equal to a certain number of pushes per day; after the income is exhausted the levers become inoperable. In some versions of the experiments the animals can earn additional income by performing various tasks. They earn additional lever pushes at a fixed wage rate for each task they perform.

The researchers have found that rats and pigeons respond appropriately to changes in prices, changes in income, and changes in wage rates. When the price of root beer goes up, they buy less root beer. When wage rates go up, they work harder—unless their incomes are already very high, in which case they choose to enjoy more leisure. These are precisely the responses that economists expect and observe among human beings.

Incentives matter. The literature of economics contains tens of thousands of empirical studies verifying this proposition, and not one that convincingly refutes it. Economists are forever testing the proposition (while perhaps secretly hoping to make names for themselves by being the first to overturn it) and forever expanding the domain of its applicability. Whereas we used to think only about shoppers responding to the price of meat, we now think about drivers responding to seat belts, murderers responding to the death penalty, and rats and pigeons responding to wage, income, and price changes. Economists have studied how people choose marriage partners, family sizes, levels of religious activity, and whether to engage in cannibalism. (This trend has gone so far that the *Journal of Political Economy* published a satirical article on the economics of toothbrushing, which "predicted"—on the basis of certain assumptions about how the cleanliness of your teeth affects your wages—that people spend exactly half their waking hours brushing their teeth. "No sociological model," boasted the author, "can yield such a precise conclusion.") Through all the variations, one theme recurs: Incentives matter.

CHAPTER 2

RATIONAL RIDDLES

Why U2 Concerts Sell Out

Economics begins with the assumption that all human behavior is rational. Of course, this assumption is not always literally true; most of us can think of exceptions within our immediate families.

But the literal truth of assumptions is never a prerequisite for scientific inquiry. Ask a physicist how long it will take a bowling ball to land if you drop it from the roof of your house. He will happily assume that your house is located in a vacuum, and then proceed to calculate the right answer. Ask an engineer to predict the path of a billiard ball after it is struck at a certain angle. He will assume that there is no such thing as friction, and the accuracy of his prediction will give him no cause for regret. Ask an economist to predict the effects of a rise in the gasoline tax. He will assume that all people are rational and give you a pretty accurate response.

Assumptions are tested not by their literal truth but by the quality of their implications. By this standard, rationality has a pretty good track record. It implies that people respond to incentives, a proposition for which there is much good evidence. It implies that people will be willing to pay more for a 26-ounce box of cereal than for an 11-ounce box, that highly skilled workers will usually earn more than their unskilled counterparts, that people who love life will not jump off the Golden Gate Bridge, and that hungry babies will cry to announce their needs. All of these things are usually true.

When we assume that people are rational, we emphatically do *not* assume anything about their preferences. *De gustibus non disputandum est*—there's no accounting for tastes—is one of the economist's guiding principles. Some musical theatergoers prefer brilliant scores, exquisite lyrics, dazzling performances, memorable characters, celebrations of life, and new ways to see the world. Others find it more satisfying to hear a Muppet say "Fuck." We pronounce neither group irrational. Nor do we pronounce it irrational when people attend their second-, third-, or last-choice show to please a companion or to impress a friend. When we assert that people are rational, we mean only this: By and large, people who prefer to see *Avenue Q*, and who are not attempting to compromise, and who feel no urge to deceive anyone about their theatrical tastes, and who have no other good reason to buy a ticket for *A Little Night Music* instead of *Avenue Q*, will not buy tickets for *A Little Night Music* instead of *Avenue Q*. And most of the time, this is true.

Likewise, when a woman pays $1 for a lottery ticket that gives her one chance in 10 million of winning $5 million, we see no evidence of irrationality. Neither do we see irrationality in her twin sister, who chooses not to play. People have different attitudes toward risk, and their behavior appropriately differs. If a lottery player chose to play for $5 million instead of $8 million in another lottery with identical odds, *then* we would call her irrational. Our expectation is that such behavior is rare.

Still, much human behavior appears on the face of it to be irrational. When a celebrity endorses a product, sales increase even though the endorsement appears to convey no information about quality. Rock concerts and Broadway shows predictably sell out weeks in advance, and would still sell out even if the promoters raised ticket prices, but the prices aren't raised. Sales of earthquake insurance increase following an earthquake, even though the probability of a *future* earthquake may be no different than it was before. People take time off to vote in presidential elections, even though there is no perceptible chance that one vote will affect the outcome.

How should we respond to such phenomena? One eminently sensible response is to say, Well, people are often rational, but not always. Economics applies to some behavior, but not to all behavior. These are some of the exceptions.

An alternative response is to stubbornly maintain the fiction that all people are rational at all times, and to insist on finding rational explanations, no matter how outlandish, for all of this apparently irrational behavior.

Economists choose the latter course.

Why?

Imagine a physicist, well versed in the laws of gravity, which he believes to be excellent approximations to the ultimate truth. One day he encounters his first helium-filled balloon, a blatant challenge to the laws he knows so well. Two courses are open to him. He can say, "Well, the laws of gravity are usually true, but not always; here is one of the exceptions." Or he can say, "Let me see if there is any way to explain this strange phenomenon without abandoning the most basic principles of my science." If he takes the latter course, and if he is sufficiently clever, he will eventually discover the properties of objects that are lighter than air and recognize that their behavior is in perfect harmony with existing theories of gravity. In the process he will not only learn about helium-filled balloons; he will also come to a deeper understanding of how gravity works.

Now it might very well be that there are real exceptions to the laws of gravity, and that our physicist will one day encounter one. If he insists on looking for a good explanation without abandoning his theories, he will fail. If there are enough such failures, new theories will eventually arise to supplant the existing ones. Nevertheless the wise course of action, at least initially, is to see whether surprising facts can be reconciled with existing theories. The attempt itself is a good mental exercise for the scientist, and there are sometimes surprising successes. Moreover, if we are too quick to abandon our most successful theories, we will soon be left with nothing at all.

So economists spend a lot of time challenging each other to find rational explanations for seemingly irrational behavior. When two or more economists meet for lunch, the chances are excellent that one of these riddles will come up for discussion. I've been at countless such lunches myself and have a few examples I'd like to share.

Rock concerts starring major attractions sell out far in advance; tickets go on sale, and there's a brief window before they're gone. To get a ticket you've got to hop on the Internet at exactly the right moment and then keep refreshing your browser until you get lucky. If the price were higher, the window of availability might widen, but the tickets would still sell out. So why doesn't the promoter raise the price?

This particular question is a perennial among economists. The most common answer is that stories about the difficulty of procuring tickets are a form of free advertising, keeping the band in the public eye and prolonging its popularity. Promoters don't want to sacrifice the long-term value of this publicity for the short-term advantage of raising prices.

I personally find this story unsatisfying. It seems to me that there is also valuable publicity to be had from letting it be known that you've sold out a concert hall at $300 a ticket. Why should quick sellouts be better advertising than high-priced sellouts?

The best answer I've heard came from my friend Ken McLaughlin, and here it is: The promoters don't want *rich* audiences; they want *fanatic* audiences, the kind of audiences who won't leave the concert hall without loading up on CDs, T-shirts, and other merchandise. By and large, those are the sort of people who follow the band closely enough to know when tickets go on sale, and then rearrange their schedules to be online at the right time. In other words, they're people who will jump through hoops to get into a U2 concert. Low prices mean quick sellouts, and quick sellouts guarantee an audience that jumped through a lot of hoops.

This story rings true and provides a rational explanation of the promoters' behavior. Unfortunately, I think it fails to explain other similar phenomena: Hit Broadway shows seem to sell out predictably without prices being raised, as do blockbuster movies in their first week or two.* Can some variant of the same story work? I don't know.

Finding a theory like McLaughlin's is one goal of the game we play. There is also another goal. The unwritten rules specify that a theory must come packaged with a nontrivial prediction. In principle, the prediction could be used to test the theory. In this case, we predict low ticket prices and brief windows of availability for performers who sell a lot of music and T-shirts; high prices and easy availability for those who don't. I do not know whether this prediction is borne out, but I am eager to learn.

My next riddle is about product endorsements. It isn't hard to understand why people might be more attracted to movies that have been endorsed by Roger Ebert, whose career depends on his reputation for accuracy. That's why he gets quoted in movie ads.

But a lot of products are endorsed by celebrities with no particular expertise in the product and who are obviously being paid

---

* In the case of Broadway shows, it appears that prices are set in such a way that the best seats usually sell out before the cheaper ones do. I suspect this is to prevent people from paying for cheap seats and then moving to unsold expensive ones.

for their testimony. Well-known actors endorse Internet service providers; ex-politicians endorse prescription medicines. Pope Leo XIII once endorsed a cocaine-based patent medicine. Even Nobel prize–winning economists have gotten in on the act. People respond to these ads, and sales increase.

What useful information can there be in knowing that your luggage provider paid a six-figure fee to feature a famous person in a viral video? How can it be rational to choose your luggage on this basis?

Let me suggest an answer. A lot of people make luggage, and they pursue different formulas for success. Some go for the quick killing, turning out a cheap product and expecting to leave the market when its low quality becomes widely recognized. Others have a long-term strategy: Produce quality goods, let the market learn about them, and reap the eventual rewards. Those in the latter group want to be sure that consumers know who they are.

One way for a firm to do this is to very publicly post a bond to guarantee its continued existence: It places $500,000 on account in a bank and is allowed to recover $100,000 per year for five years; if the firm goes out of business in the interim, the owners sacrifice the bond. Only the high-quality firms would be willing to post these bonds. The rational consumer would prefer to patronize those firms.

Hiring a celebrity to endorse your product is like posting a bond. The firm makes a substantial investment up front and reaps returns over a long period of time. A firm that expects to disappear in a year won't make such an investment. When I see a celebrity endorsement, I know that the firm has enough confidence in the quality of its product to expect to be around a while.

This theory also makes a testable prediction: Celebrity endorsements will be more common for goods whose quality is not immediately apparent.

The same reasoning can explain why bank buildings tend to

have marble floors and Greek columns, particularly those that were built in the days before federal deposit insurance. Imagine a frontier con man who moves from town to town setting up banks and absconding with the money after a few months. Unlike the Wells Fargo Company, which plans to be in business permanently, he cannot afford to construct a magnificent building every place he goes. Other things being equal, rational townsfolk choose the bank with the nicer building—and a rational Wells Fargo company invests in a flamboyant display of its permanence.

This explains why banks have fancier architecture than grocery stores. It's a lot more important to know that your banker will be there next week than that your grocer will.

Here's an old favorite: Why are so many items sold for $2.99 and so few for $3.00? There is an enormous temptation to attribute this phenomenon to a mild form of irrationality in which consumers notice only the first digit of the price and are lulled into thinking that $2.99 is "about $2.00" instead of "about $3.00." In fact, this explanation seems so self-evident that even many economists believe it. For all I know, they could be right. Perhaps someday a careful analysis of such behavior will form the basis for a modified economics in which people are assumed to depart from rationality in certain systematic ways.* But before we abandon the foundations of all our knowledge, it might be instructive to consider alternatives.

As it happens, there is at least one intriguing alternative available. The phenomenon of "99-cent pricing" seems to have first become common in the 19th century, shortly after the invention of the cash register. The cash register was a remarkable innovation; not only did it do simple arithmetic, it also kept a record of every sale.

---

* The subject of *behavioral economics*, now in its infancy, aims to fill this role.

That's important if you think your employees might be stealing from you. You can examine the tape at the end of the day and know how much money should be in the drawer.

There is one small problem with cash registers: They don't actually record *every* sale; they record only those sales that are rung up. If a customer buys an item for $1 and hands the clerk a dollar bill, the clerk can neglect to record the sale, slip the bill in his pocket, and leave no one the wiser.

On the other hand, when a customer buys an item for 99 cents and hands the clerk a dollar bill, the clerk has to make change. This requires him to open the cash drawer, which he cannot do without ringing up the sale. Ninety-nine-cent pricing forces clerks to ring up sales and keeps them honest.

There are still some problems. Clerks could make change out of their own pockets or ring up the wrong numbers. But a customer waiting for change might notice either of these strange behaviors and alert the owner.

The real problem with this explanation is that it ignores the existence of sales taxes. In a state with a 7 percent sales tax, the difference between 99 cents and $1 on the price tag is the difference between $1.06 and $1.07 on the checkout line; the likelihood of needing change is about the same either way. Might it be that in states with different sales taxes, prices differ by a penny or two so that the price at the register comes out uneven in every state? This, at least, is a testable prediction. Here is another: 99-cent pricing should be less common in stores where the owners work the cash register.

Much primitive agriculture shares a strange common feature. There are very few large plots of land; instead each farmer owns several small plots scattered around the village. (This pattern was endemic in medieval England and exists today in parts of the Third World.) Historians have long debated the reasons for this scattering, which is believed to be the source of much inefficiency. Perhaps it arises from inheritance and marriage: At each generation, the family plot is subdivided among the heirs, so that plots become tiny; marriages then bring widely scattered plots into the same family. This explanation suffers because it seems to assume a form of irrationality: Why don't the villagers periodically exchange plots among themselves to consolidate their holdings?

Inevitably this problem attracted the attention of the economist and historian Deirdre McCloskey, whose instinct for constructing ingenious economic explanations is unsurpassed. Instead of asking "What social institutions led to such irrational behavior?" McCloskey asked, "Why is this behavior rational?" Careful study led her to conclude that it is rational because it is a form of insurance. A farmer with one large plot is liable to be completely ruined in the event of a localized flood. By scattering his holdings, the farmer gives up some potential income in exchange for a guarantee that he will not be wiped out by a local disaster. This behavior is not even exotic. Every modern insured homeowner does the same thing.

One way to test McCloskey's theory is to ask whether the insurance "premiums" (that is, the amount of production that is sacrificed by scattering) are commensurate with the amount of protection being "purchased," using as a yardstick the premiums that people are willing to pay in more conventional insurance markets. By this standard, it holds up well.

On the other hand, a very serious criticism is this: If medieval peasants wanted insurance, why didn't they buy and sell insurance policies, just as we do today? My own feeling is that this is like asking why they didn't keep their business records on personal computers. The answer is simply that nobody had yet figured out how to do it. Designing an insurance policy requires at least a minor act of genius, just like designing a computer. But there are those, more exacting than I, who think that McCloskey's theory will not be complete until this objection is answered. And they are absolutely right in demanding that we try to answer it. Theories should be tested to their limits.

There are a lot of riddles. Why does the business world reward good dressers to such an extent that there are best-selling books on how to "dress for success"? I suspect that fashionable and attractive dressing is a skill that those of us who incline toward jeans and T-shirts tend to underrate. The good dresser must be innovative without transcending the limits set by fashion; knowing the limits requires alertness and an eye for evolving patterns. These traits are valuable in many contexts, and it can be rational for firms to seek employees who exhibit evidence of them.

Why do men spend less on medical care than women do? Possibly because men are more likely than women to die violent deaths. The value of protecting yourself against cancer is diminished if you have a high probability of being hit by a truck. It is therefore rational for men to purchase less preventive care than women.

Why do people choose to bet on the same sports team they feel fond of? By betting against the team you like, you could guarantee yourself a partially good outcome no matter how the game turns out. In other areas of life we choose to hedge, but in sports betting we seem to put all our eggs in one basket. What explains the difference? Are we insuring ourselves against an expensive urge to celebrate in the event of a home team victory?

When two people share a hotel room in Britain, they often pay twice the single-room rate; in the United States they usually pay much less than that. What accounts for the difference? A noneconomist might be satisfied with an answer based on tradition. The economist wants to know why this pricing structure is rational and profit-maximizing. If any reader has a suggestion, I'd be pleased to hear it.

Economists are mystified by a lot of behavior that others take for granted. I have no idea why people vote. One hundred thirty million Americans cast votes for president in 2008. I wager that not one of those 130 million was naive enough to believe that he was casting the decisive vote in an otherwise tied election.

It is fashionable to cite George Bush's razor-thin 537-vote margin over Al Gore in the decisive state of Florida in 2000. But 537 is not the same as 1, even by the standards of precision that are conventional in economics. The probability of a one-vote margin under similar circumstances is still effectively zero. Unless you happen to be a Supreme Court Justice, your vote will never decide a presidential election.

It is equally fashionable to observe that "if everyone else thought that way and stayed home, then my vote would be important," which is as true and as irrelevant as the observation that if voting booths were spaceships, voters could travel to the moon. Everyone else does *not* stay home. The only choice that an individual voter faces is whether or not to vote, *given* that tens of millions of others are voting. At the risk of shocking your ninth-grade civics teacher, I am prepared to offer you an absolute guarantee that if you stay home next time around, your indolence will not affect the outcome.*

Some say that people vote out of a sense of "civic duty." But that ignores the fact that voting takes time away from other, more productive acts of civic duty. You can spend 15 minutes casting an

---

* André Weil, one of the greatest mathematicians of the past century, once wrote, "I could not count the times (for example, when I tell people that I never vote in elections) that I have heard the objection: 'But if everyone were to behave like you . . . '—to which I usually reply that this possibility seems to me so implausible that I do not feel obligated to take it into account."

essentially meaningless vote, or you can spend the same 15 minutes returning shopping carts from the parking lot to the front of the grocery store. In the second case, you'll have actually made the world a better place.

So why do people vote? I don't know.

I am not sure why people give each other store-bought gifts instead of cash, which is never the wrong size or color. Some say that we give gifts because it shows that we took the time to shop. But we could accomplish the same thing by giving the cash value of our shopping time, showing that we took the time to earn the money.

My friend David Friedman suggests that we give gifts for exactly the opposite reason: because we want to announce that we did *not* take much time to shop. If I really care for you, I probably know enough about your tastes to have an easy time finding the right gift. If I care less about you, finding the right gift becomes a major chore. Because you know that my shopping time is limited, the fact that I was able to find something appropriate reveals that I care. I like this theory.

I do not know why people leave anonymous tips in restaurants, and the fact that I leave them myself in no way alleviates my sense of mystery.

When we raise questions about activities like voting or gift giving or anonymous tipping, it is never our intention to be critical of them. Quite the opposite: Our working assumption is that whatever people do, they have excellent reasons for doing it. If we as economists can't see their reasons, then it is we who have a new riddle to solve.

CHAPTER 3

TRUTH OR CONSEQUENCES

How to Split a Check or Choose a Movie

If you're a nonsmoker in the market for life insurance, you should be thankful for cigarettes. They help keep your rates down.

That's because there are two types of people in this world. Actually, there are as many types of people in this world as there are people in this world, but let me simplify to make a point. There are the cautious and the reckless. The cautious exercise at health clubs, drink in moderation, drive defensively, and never ever smoke. The reckless snack on cotton candy, keep late hours, ride motorcycles without helmets, and smoke a great deal.

If the insurance companies had no way of telling us apart, the cautious would be forced to subsidize the immoderation of their reckless neighbors. And sometimes that's exactly what happens.

But if insurance companies can set premiums separately for each type of customer, then the reckless bear the full costs of their lifestyle. The trick for the insurance company is to determine who is who.

Smoking habits are a quick and easy indicator of general health consciousness. They reveal your type in a publicly observable way. Insurance companies use that information by offering lower premiums to nonsmokers. If you take advantage of such an offer, your discount reflects more than just the health benefits of not smoking. It reflects also that, as a nonsmoker, you are more likely than average to be watching your cholesterol.

Insurance companies know that people cheat, and they account for that when they set the nonsmoking premiums. If you are truly a nonsmoker, you pay a little more because some "nonsmokers" are sneaking cigarettes where the insurance company can't see them. But do not jump to the conclusion that if cigarettes were banned, your insurance rates would fall. As a *voluntary* nonsmoker, you implicitly notify your insurance company that you are probably cautious in a lot of ways they can't observe. As a nonsmoker in a world without cigarettes, you might be indistinguishable from everybody else, and be charged accordingly.

Advocates of mandatory helmet laws for motorcyclists argue that a rider without a helmet raises everyone's insurance premiums. The opposite might very well be true. Those who choose helmets reveal a general safety consciousness that helps to keep their premiums down. Mandatory helmets deprive safe drivers of a mechanism for advertising their character.

If the insurance company can offer discount rates to helmeted riders, those rates account not just for the safety characteristics of the helmet itself but for additional safety characteristics of the sort of rider who is likely to choose a helmet: a disinclination to weave in and out of traffic or to drive under the influence of alcohol. If all riders are helmeted by law, premiums continue to account for the benefits of the helmet but not for the rider's cautious personality. When helmets become mandatory, the careful rider's premiums are liable to rise.

Insurance markets are odd, because the buyer almost invariably has better information than the seller. If you wire your den with extension cords and cover them with paneling, you know exactly what you've done, but your insurance agent does not. He is left to wonder why you suddenly want to triple your fire insurance. Asymmetric information typically yields surprising outcomes, driven by one party's efforts to guess what the other party knows.

In some cases, asymmetric information threatens to drive insurance markets entirely out of existence. Rank policyholders' risk levels from 1 to 10, with 5 being the average. If the insurance company sets rates that reflect that average risk level, the 1s, 2s, and 3s might feel overcharged and drop out of the market. Now the average risk level is no longer 5 but 7. The company raises rates to compensate, which causes the 4s and 5s to drop out, which raises the average risk level to 8, which necessitates yet another rate increase. The vicious cycle can continue until everyone is uninsured.

If the insurance company could observe individual risk levels, it would charge each policyholder an appropriate premium and the problem would disappear. If policyholders could *not* observe their *own* risk levels, the 1s, 2s, and 3s would not drop out of the market and again the problem would disappear. It is the *asymmetry* of the situation—policyholders knowing more about themselves than the insurance company knows—that can break down the market.

To make matters still worse, people are likely to take on additional risks just *because* they are insured. Insured homeowners forgo security systems, and insured drivers drive faster. In the presence of full information, insurance companies could prohibit such behavior and discontinue coverage for the disobedient. Because insurers are not omniscient, they explore alternatives.

One alternative is for the insurance company to help its customers avoid risk. Your car insurance company might be willing to subsidize your purchase of an antitheft device; your health insurance company will undoubtedly provide you with free information on the benefits of diet and exercise; your fire insurance company can give you a free fire extinguisher. But there are limits to what can be accomplished. If you weren't inclined to buy a fire extinguisher to begin with, and if you get one for free from your insurance company, it might turn up at a garage sale.

Employers typically have less than perfect information about what their employees are up to. This makes it hard to get incentives right. You can't reward productivity that you can't observe.

Labor markets abound with mechanisms designed to address the incentive problem. The university where I teach "gives" me an office but does not allow me to sell that office to the highest bidder. In many cases, that rule is inefficient. I have colleagues who do all of their work at home and in the library and would gladly accept a lower salary in exchange for the right to convert their office to a Burger King (or, if Burger Kings are disallowed because of their boisterous clientele, then a computer store). The university would save money and productivity would not suffer. Presumably that outcome would be agreeable all around except for one little hitch. Even the professoriate harbors unscrupulous individuals, and some of those who *do* use their offices effectively would be willing to sacrifice some productivity in exchange for the right profit opportunity. If the university could identify and punish productivity declines, then the problem would vanish. In reality, information is asymmetric—*we* know whether we're producing, but we don't always tell the dean—so we end up accepting an imperfect rule.

Many firms provide their employees with more health coverage than is required by law, essentially giving an extra $500 worth of medical insurance instead of an extra $500 in wages. At first this seems mysterious: Why not give employees the cash and let them spend it as they want? A partial answer—and perhaps the entire answer—is that employees prefer nontaxable benefits to taxable wages. But another possible answer is that good health care enhances productivity. If productivity were easily observed and rewarded, there would be no issue here, because employees would have ample incentives on their own to acquire adequate health care. But in a world of imperfect information, employee benefit packages can be the best way to enforce good behavior.

If you are employed by, say, the General Electric Company, it is not unlikely that sooner or later you will discover something that can save the company $100. If that something requires a little effort on your part, and if that effort is invisible to your supervisor, you might choose to let it slide.

The company wants your incentives to be right and seeks appropriate mechanisms. One mechanism is profit sharing among employees. But in a company with half a million employees, profit sharing is not a very good incentive. If employees share equally in 100 percent of the company's profits, your $100 contribution adds only about ⅟₅₀ of a cent to your own income. Unless GE can observe its employees perfectly, only one mechanism gets the incentives exactly right: Each employee receives as his annual salary 100 percent of the corporate profits. If GE's profits are $1 billion this year, then *everybody*—from the chairman of the board down to the night janitor—earns exactly $1 billion. Now each dollar that you save the company is a dollar in your own pocket. You have just the right incentive to take every cost-justified measure to improve corporate productivity.

One tiny problem with this scheme is that if there is more than one employee, the books don't balance. A single billion in profits does not suffice to pay a billion each to 500,000 workers. But that's easy to handle. At the beginning of the year, each worker *purchases* his job by putting a large sum of money into a fund that is earmarked to make up the difference between the company's profits and its wage obligations. The price of a job can be set so that the books balance in an average year. Over time the revenue from job sales just covers the discrepancy between profits and wages.

This arrangement is the ideal solution to a very substantial problem, yet it strikes everybody who hears it as completely ludicrous. What is less clear is *why* it strikes us as ludicrous. The fact that no major corporation has implemented such an arrangement is good evidence that it is unworkable. But that is hardly enough reason to stop thinking about it. If we are to design better mechanisms in the future, we should pause to ask just where this one went wrong.

The most obvious answers are wholly inadequate. The usual first objection comes in the form of a question: "Where is an assembly-line worker going to come by $1 billion to buy his job?" The response is that he is going to borrow it. The counterresponse is that he is unlikely to have access to quite that good a line of credit.

At first glance the counterresponse seems devastating, but on closer inspection it is completely insubstantial. If workers can't borrow enough to finance the program in its entirety, they can at least borrow enough to finance a fraction of it. If GE can't sell you your job for $1 billion and give you the entire company profits at the end of the year, it can at least sell you your job for a *fraction* of $1 billion and give you the same *fraction* of the company profits at the end of the year. This is a poor approximation to the ideal, but it's better than no approximation at all.

If your theory is that the program is derailed by borrowing constraints, then your theory predicts that workers would be enrolled in a partial program that expands until every worker has borrowed every cent that he possibly can. But most workers have *not* borrowed every cent they possibly can. Your prediction is wrong, so your theory is wrong also.

Here is a another difficulty, less obvious but also harder to dismiss: The buy-your-job program gets the incentives just right for workers but gets them exactly wrong for stockholders. Once the workers have bought their jobs, stockholders root for financial disaster. With half a million employees, every dollar of earnings generates half a million dollars in wage obligations. If the company earns nothing, no wages need be paid.

Insofar as stockholders can influence corporate decision making, the consequences of this incentive structure are plainly disastrous. Nobody would be willing to buy a job at a firm where wages depend on profits and managers are doing everything possible to keep profits low. Conceivably this problem could be averted by a novel corporate structure that prevented stockholders from participating in any management decisions at any level. But the incentive would remain for unscrupulous stockholders to approach key workers and bribe them to work mischief in the plants.

There is a moral here: The system that you construct to solve one problem can be the source of another. It is true that stockholders cannot completely observe the behavior of workers but equally true that workers cannot completely observe the behavior of stockholders. When information is distributed unequally, we need to watch for unexpected consequences.

The buy-a-job program has a nice parallel in the form of a riddle. Ten people go out to eat at a restaurant that refuses to issue separate checks. Desserts are expensive, and nobody considers them worth the price. Unfortunately each diner reasons separately that if he orders dessert he'll pay for only a tenth of it, and each diner orders dessert on that basis. Everybody gets dessert, so everybody pays for shares of ten desserts. The cost to each diner is equal to the high price that he was initially unwilling to pay. How can this tragic outcome be avoided?

The solution is for each diner to pay the entire bill. Now ordering a $10 dessert increases your share not by $1 but by $10, and you don't order unless you're really willing to pay that much. The restaurant, of course, earns an enormous profit by collecting the bill 10 times over. Therefore the manager pays you to come to the restaurant in the first place. The bribe to enter is set so that on average it just exhausts the excess profits. (If it didn't just exhaust the excess profits, competing restaurants would offer better deals.)

A perfect solution? Almost, but not quite. As one of your party returns from the rest room, the manager quietly steers him aside and offers him $20 to order dessert.

Why are executive salaries so high? Why do stockholders approve annual compensation packages of $40 million and more for some of the highest-paid corporate officers? And more disturbingly, why do so many of those compensation packages include "golden parachute" clauses that seem designed to reward failure?

When the Harvard economists Michael Jensen and Kevin Murphy examined these issues back in the 1990s, they were led to reformulate the question to something more like "Why are executive salaries so *low*?"

At that time, Jensen and Murphy found evidence that executive salaries were tied only very loosely to corporate performance, so that when an executive managed to increase earnings by $1,000, he could expect only a $3.25 reward. They argued that stockholders might be far better off paying salaries that were higher on average but more dependent on accomplishments.

To some extent, Jensen and Murphy got their wish. CEO pay has multiplied sixfold over the past 30 years. Much of that additional compensation has come in the form of either stock options or grants of restricted stock (that is, stock that the executive is required to hold onto for a long period), so that at least in those respects, the value of compensation has become more closely tied to performance. But there's still a huge gap. The reward for saving the company $1,000 (or the punishment for costing the company $1,000) has roughly doubled, from $3.25 to about $6.50.

This raises two questions: Why have salaries grown so much, and why are rewards still so decoupled from performance?

First, the salaries: Some observers see the compensation explosion as evidence of corporate cronyism. They point out that executive pay packages are typically set by the executives' friends on the compensation committee, who might value their friendships more than they value their duty to the stockholders. One problem with this theory is that it can't explain why CEO pay packages have increased. Why should corporate cronyism have been any less a problem in 1990 than it is today?

Other observers have pointed out that the sixfold increase in CEO pay has been matched by a sixfold increase in firm size. It seems quite plausible that an exceptionally good decision maker is six times as valuable, and so able to command six times as much compensation, when his decisions affect an operation that is six times as big.

It's also been argued that the rise of globalization has intensified competition and so made managerial skills more valuable. And indeed, there is evidence that pay levels increase the most when firms face more competition from imports.

But what about the disconnect between executive performance and executive pay? One possible explanation is that stockholders are making a bad mistake. But to accept that explanation would be to lose our economic bearings. Even in a world where people make bad mistakes all the time, no economist should ever be satisfied with a theory that says something happened because somebody erred. The game is to see what we can learn by *assuming* that human behavior serves human purposes and then trying to divine what those purposes might be.

Here is the best answer I know of: To the stockholder, the executive is just another employee, and like any employee he must be prodded to perform. One area where a little extra prodding might be called for is in the area of risk taking. Stockholders are generally favorable to risky projects with high potential rewards. That's because stockholders are usually well diversified. If the project fails, their stock could become worthless, but that can be an acceptable risk when the stock represents only a small fraction of your entire portfolio.

Executives, by contrast, typically have large parts of their careers riding on the fortunes of a particular company and accordingly tread gingerly when risky projects come their way. From the stockholder's viewpoint, this is bad behavior and should be discouraged. The most direct form of discouragement is to monitor the executive's behavior and punish excessive caution. But if the stockholders were going to monitor every executive decision, they wouldn't need to hire an executive. In practice, stockholders don't have enough information to enforce their preferences directly.

This observation might go a long way toward explaining the uncoupling of rewards from performance. When the president of Nike green-lights a project to develop a rocket-powered running shoe, and when the project fails and loses millions, stockholders can't easily distinguish between two theories: Either the idea was asinine from the outset, or it was a sensible risk that happened to fail. Because the first theory might be correct, they want to fire the president. Because the second might be correct, they don't want to punish him too severely—that would send the wrong message to future presidents. So failed corporate officers are retired with enormous pensions. That practice is often derided in the popular press as a simple failure of common sense, but the economist's insistence on looking for method within apparent madness yields more insight than the journalist's resort to ridiculing that which he cannot immediately understand.

So the tension regarding risky projects goes a long way toward explaining those golden parachutes. It might also go a long way to answering my earlier question: Why are executive salaries so high? Remember that stockholders want executives to take more risks. One way to encourage a person to take risks is to make him wealthy. Other things being equal, multimillionaires are a lot mellower about losing their jobs than people who are worried about how to put their children through college. If you want your corporate president to be receptive to the rocket-powered running shoe project, you need to encourage that kind of mellowness. A high salary helps a lot in that direction.

The general level of executive salaries is as much a topic of journalistic scorn as the "inadequate" punishment of failed executives. I am appalled by the anti-intellectualism that underlies such scorn. All that separates us from the beasts is our ability to wonder *why* things are as they are. In the realm of economics, the answer to *why* often begins with the observation that information is asymmetrically distributed. The executive knows his own basis for making decisions, but stockholders can only guess. They are forced to mold his behavior through imperfect incentives. There are good reasons to think that a high salary, through its encouragement of risk taking, is a component of the optimal incentive scheme. This is hardly a complete analysis of the problem, but it is an indication that analysis is *possible*, and worth pursuing.

There is a class of logic puzzles in which the speaker visits an island populated entirely by liars and truth tellers. Liars always lie and truth tellers always tell the truth. Unfortunately the two are indistinguishable. The problem is usually to draw some inference from the utterances of various islanders or to formulate a question that will elicit some hidden information. The simplest problem is: When you meet an islander, what single question enables you to identify whether he is a liar? "Are you a liar?" doesn't work, because truth tellers and liars both answer "No." A common solution is to ask, "How much is 2 plus 2?"

When I tried this problem on my four-year-old daughter, her solution was to say, "I won't be your friend if you don't tell me the truth." I concluded that she was too young for logic puzzles.

When the person you are dealing with knows more than you do, there are two general approaches to mitigating your disadvantage. One is to design mechanisms that elicit appropriate *behavior*: Give insurance discounts to nonsmokers, or give out free fire extinguishers, or design pay packages that get the incentives right. The other is to design mechanisms that elicit the *information itself*. In recent years, economists have discovered that, contrary to all intuition, there are a fantastic number of mechanisms that can often induce people to reveal everything they know.

In Joseph Conrad's novel *Typhoon*, a number of sailors store gold coins in private boxes kept in the ship's safe. The ship hits stormy weather, the boxes break open, and the coins are hopelessly mixed. Each sailor knows how many coins he started with, but nobody knows what anybody *else* started with. The captain's problem is to return the correct number of coins to each sailor.

Does the problem seem intractable? Here is a simple solution: Have each sailor write down the number of coins he is entitled to. Collect the papers and distribute the coins. Announce in advance that if the numbers on the papers don't add up to the correct total, you will throw all of the coins overboard.

That solution is a simple manifestation of an elaborate theory whose slogan might be "Truth is accessible." In this instance the captain has a key piece of information: He knows the total number of coins. It turns out that even when a decision maker has *no information at all* he can frequently design a mechanism that elicits absolute truth from all concerned.

Last night my wife and I could not decide which movie to see. One of us (I can't remember which) preferred *The English Patient*, while the other leaned more toward *Sorority Babes in the Slimeball Bowl-o-rama*. We agreed that the person with the stronger preference—expressed in dollar terms—should prevail. The problem was to determine whose preference was the stronger. The problem was compounded because we were both perfectly willing to lie to get our way.

Here is what we did. We each wrote our bid on a piece of paper. The high bidder got to choose the movie but was required to make a charitable contribution equal to the *loser's* bid.

It was worth exactly $8 to me to get my way. Because winning meant paying the amount of my wife's bid, I wanted to win if my wife bid less than $8 and to lose if she bid more. I was able to ensure this outcome by bidding exactly $8. In other words, my own purely selfish motives led me to make an honest revelation. My wife did the same, and the person with the stronger preference won.

This worked so well that we are planning to use it regularly. Rather than make charitable contributions, however, we are going to make our payments to an economist couple we know. They are going to do the same, making their payments to us. On average, over time, we expect that the payments in one direction will be about as great as those in the other, so that nobody stands to lose financially from our arrangement.

An economist is somebody who thinks it is worth wondering why not everyone chooses movies in exactly this way.

CHAPTER 4

THE INDIFFERENCE PRINCIPLE

Who Cares If the Air Is Clean?

Would you rather live in San Francisco or in Lincoln, Nebraska? San Francisco offers extraordinary shopping districts, world-class museums, a temperate climate, and Golden Gate Park. Lincoln offers magnificent old houses that can be had for the price of a San Francisco studio apartment. You can have the world's finest seafood or you can have wall space.

Every few years the *Places Rated Almanac* issues its report on the best places to live in America. San Francisco gets credit for its cosmopolitan charms, and Lincoln gets credit for the allure of its housing market. Weighing the importance of education, climate, highways, bus systems, safety, and recreation, researchers rank cities in order of overall desirability. The implicit assumption is that the researchers have identified features that most people care about, and that we all pretty much agree about their relative importance.

If that assumption is correct, and if your tastes are not atypical, you can save yourself the expense of buying the almanac. When all factors are accounted for, all inhabited cities must be equally attractive. If they weren't, nobody would live in any but the best.

If San Francisco is better than Lincoln, Lincolnites move to San Francisco. Their exodus bids up housing prices in San Francisco, bids down housing prices in Lincoln, and thereby magnifies Lincoln's relative advantages. Before long, either the two cities become equally attractive or Lincoln becomes completely deserted.

Now in fact there are plenty of people who would rather live in San Francisco and plenty of others who would rather live in Lincoln. That's because, contrary to the implicit assumption of the *Places Rated Almanac*, different people care about different things. If you have an unusual taste for walking up steep hills, you're likely to be happier in San Francisco. But if you have a *commonly shared* taste for walking up steep hills, there's no reason, on that account, to choose one city over the other, because the many others who share your tastes will flock to San Francisco and bid up rents to a point that just cancels out the city's topographical advantages.

Call it the Indifference Principle: *Unless you're unusual in some way, nothing can ever make you happier than the next best alternative.* You might prefer cheddar cheese to provolone, but if all your neighbors share your preference, then the price of cheddar cheese must rise to the point where you're just as happy to buy the provolone. Fortunately most of us *are* unusual in a great variety of ways, which is what allows us to benefit from choosing one activity over another. The Indifference Principle calls our attention to the fact that the greatest gains in life come in the areas where we're most unusual.

Would you rather spend a bright summer day at the shopping mall or the Renaissance Fair? If you and your many neighbors all have similar preferences, then both choices must be equally attractive. If the Fair is more fun than the mall, people flock to the Fair, building up the crowd size until it's *not* more fun than the mall.

Would you rather spend a *rainy* summer day at the shopping mall or the Renaissance Fair? Once again, if you share your neighbors' preferences, both choices must be equally attractive. This leads to a startling conclusion: If the mall is just as good on rainy days as it is on sunny days, then the Renaissance Fair must also be just as good on rainy days as it is on sunny days! The disadvantages of getting wet must be exactly outweighed by the advantages of a smaller crowd.

Again, none of this applies to people with unusual preferences. If you are the one person in your neighborhood who likes getting wet, you'll want to go to the Fair on a rainy day. On the other hand, if *everyone* likes getting wet, then rain can't make the Fair more attractive—instead it draws a crowd big enough to offset its own allure. *In order for one activity to make you happier than another, you must be unusual in some way.*

Just as unusual preferences pay off, so do unusual talents. Tim Lincecum makes a lot of money not because he's a good pitcher but because he's a better pitcher than almost anybody else. On the flip side, widely shared talents reap few rewards. In the Woody Allen film *Radio Days*, a character with no particular skills contemplates a career in gold engraving, anticipating great wealth because he plans to hoard the shavings. What he overlooks is that the opportunity to hoard shavings, if it's real, must draw others like him into the engraving industry, bidding down wages and/or working conditions until gold engraving is no more attractive than the next best alternative.

What's more profitable: a motel or a gas station? In most cases, they must be about equally profitable. Otherwise motels would convert to gas stations (or vice versa) until profits in the two industries became equal.* This argument assumes (probably correctly) that most people can run gas stations about as well as they can run motels. The argument probably does not apply to Paul Greene and William Becker, the entrepreneurs who founded the Motel 6

---

* If gas stations are more profitable than motels, then motels start converting to gas stations. As the number of gas stations grows and the number of motel rooms shrinks, the price of gas falls and the price of a motel room rises, driving profits down for gas stations and up for motels. The process continues until profits are the same in both industries.

chain. Nor does it apply to the occasional motel operator with an unusual knack for making travelers happy or for keeping laundry costs down—provided that knack is somehow untransferable to the gas station business. Nor would it apply in an area where stringent licensing requirements restrict the number of motels. But in every one of those exceptional cases, the extra profits flow to someone with an unusual skill or an unusual resource: a unique vision, an uncommon talent, or a scarce motel license.

What's better: running for president or not running for president? There must always be candidates who are just on the fence. If everyone running had a strong preference to be in the race, then others like them would jump in, driving down the chance of winning until the latest entrant is just about indifferent. (This is part of why there are always big-name politicians who spend a long time testing the waters before deciding whether to plunge.)

Sex scandals have become a routine feature of the modern political campaign. Even candidates who have not yet been publicly humiliated must suffer sleepless nights wondering which details of their own private lives will remain private. Commentators argue, plausibly but incorrectly, that this development is clearly damaging to the candidates. They overlook the fact that *something* has to make potential candidates indifferent about running for office. Without sex scandals, more candidates would enter, to the detriment of everyone who is already in the race.*

When the police predictably crack down on drug dealers or prostitutes every few months, who is hurt? Not drug dealers or prostitutes. Most drug dealers have no extraordinary skills, and must therefore be indifferent between drug dealing and, say, street sweeping. Drug crackdowns don't change the desirability of street

---

* The argument fails to apply to candidates who are extraordinary in some relevant dimension, such as having unusually much or unusually little to hide.

sweeping, so they can't change the desirability of drug dealing. Instead they induce just enough exit from the drug industry, and therefore just enough in the way of higher prices and additional profit, to compensate for the prospect of a certain amount of jail time. The big losers are not the suppliers of drugs, but the demanders who pay those higher prices.*

When a barber's license requires thousands of dollars of mandatory training, who bears the cost? Not barbers, who must be indifferent between cutting hair and the next best alternative. By discouraging some potential barbers, training fees keep prices just high enough to maintain that indifference. The burden therefore falls entirely on the customers.

An organization called the Brotherhood for the Respect, Elevation, and Advancement of Dishwashers encourages restaurant patrons to deviate from tradition and tip the busboy. If the organization succeeds in changing public attitudes, who benefits? The answer is certainly not busboys. Busboys can never be happier than janitors, and janitors' fortunes do not change. When busboys start collecting tips, janitors start becoming busboys. Wages respond, and busboys' paychecks shrink. The janitors keep coming until everything the busboy gains at the restaurant table is lost at the payroll office.

Well, then, who benefits? If busboys' wages fall, you might guess that the big winner is the owner of the restaurant. But that can't be right either, because restaurant owners can never be happier than shoe store owners, and shoe store owners' fortunes do not change. When busboys' wages fall and restaurant profits increase, shoe stores start converting to restaurants. Menu prices fall and profits

---

* If you are very clever you might have thought that as drug dealers become street sweepers, the wages of street sweepers are bid down. This is almost surely false, as drug dealers move into a great variety of alternative occupations, so their influence on wages in any one of them is likely to be insignificant.

shrink. The shoe store owners keep coming until everything the owner saves in busboys' wages is lost at the cash register.

If each diner leaves a $5 tip for the busboy, then busboys' wages must fall by $5 per meal, and then the price of a meal must fall by $5. If it fell by less, restaurant owners would be ahead of the game, and that isn't possible as long as there are shoe stores waiting in the wings to become restaurants. So who benefits? Nobody. Diners' tips are returned to them in the form of lower menu prices. Nobody's wealth has changed. Diners might genuinely want to be generous to busboys, but the Indifference Principle intervenes.

Only the owner of a resource in fixed supply can avoid the consequences of the Indifference Principle. An increased demand for actors cannot benefit actors, because new entrants are drawn to the profession. But an increased demand for Ben Stiller *can* benefit Ben Stiller, because Ben Stiller is a fixed resource. There is only one of him. As Ben's earnings reach several million dollars per movie, starving actors strive to emulate his features, but their best efforts are imperfect. When scientists develop the ability to convert one person to a carbon copy of another, there will be just enough Ben Stiller clones to make being Ben Stiller a matter of indifference.

The Indifference Principle guarantees that *all economic gains accrue to the owners of fixed resources*. The busboy whose atypically pleasant personality generates more than the ordinary level of tipping can benefit from a change in tipping customs. His personality is a fixed resource. If *many* potential busboys had the same personality, it would generate no economic reward.

In the United States of America, we have a Clean Air Act that regulates the emissions from smokestacks and tailpipes. In March 2011 the Environmental Protection Agency, which administers those regulations, released a report on their estimated future costs and benefits. According to the EPA, by the year 2020 the Clean Air Act will cost American businesses (that is, owners, suppliers, employees, and customers) about $65 billion a year—roughly $450 per American family. If that estimate holds up, that's what the average family will lose through lower profits, lower wages, and higher prices. On the other hand, the EPA estimates that by 2020 the *benefits* of the Clean Air Act will soar to $2 trillion a year (mostly in the form of improvements in health), utterly dwarfing those costs. An uncritical observer might expect that those benefits would be shared by everyone who breathes, which is to say everyone. But the ability to breathe is not a fixed resource. Universal skills do not ordinarily reap great rewards.

If breathers do not benefit from clean air, then who does? Theory tells us to look for the owners of fixed resources. The most obvious candidates are urban landowners, who are able to charge higher rents after the smog lifts.

The Clean Air Act is a fantastically complicated piece of legislation imposed on a fantastically complicated economy, and to trace every one of its effects in detail would be a fantastically complicated task. But as Aesop discovered some time ago, the details of reality can disguise essential truths that are best revealed through simple fictions. Aesop called them fables, and economists call them models. Let me share one.

FABLE 1: A TALE OF TWO CITIES

Somewhere in the heart of the Rust Belt are two small cities: Cleanstown and Grimyville. All of the activities of daily life—shopping, working, going to the park—are equally pleasant in both cities, with one exception: breathing. The Grimyville Steel Company accounts for that. No Grimyvillian ever wakes up and fills his lungs with the crisp morning air that Cleanstowners take for granted. Not only do the residents of Grimyville find breathing relatively unpleasant; they also do less of it. Life expectancy is 10 years lower in Grimyville than in Cleanstown.

Why would anyone live in Grimyville? For one reason: It's cheaper. A house that rents for $10,000 a year in Cleanstown can be had for $5,000 in Grimyville. That $5,000 difference is just enough to keep folks in Grimyville. If it weren't, people would leave Grimyville and rents would fall even further. Young people deciding where to settle are indifferent between the two towns. They like the atmosphere in Cleanstown, but they like the housing prices in Grimyville.

Last week the Grimyville Council passed a Clean Air Act that requires Grimyville Steel to adopt extensive antipollution measures. Soon the air in Grimyville will be as pure as the purest air in Cleanstown. And when that happens, the rents in Grimyville will rise to Cleanstown levels.

Eventually renters in Grimyville will be living in a clone of Cleanstown. Is this an improvement for them? Evidently not, because if they'd preferred to live in Cleanstown, they would have lived there in the first place.

Those young people deciding where to settle gain nothing from the Clean Air Act. Earlier they had a choice between Cleanstown and Grimyville, and they were indifferent. Now they have a choice between two Cleanstowns. They're no worse off than they were before, but no better off either.

The only people who stand to gain from this entire affair are the property owners of Grimyville, who can now command higher rents than they did before. The Clean Air Act is equivalent to a tax on Grimyville Steel with the proceeds distributed entirely to Grimyville landowners.

The conclusion is stark, but, to be fair, the discussion is oversimplified. When we say that people are indifferent between Cleanstown and Grimyville, we implicitly assume that everyone shares identical circumstances. In actuality the world is more complicated. There might be people with special reasons to want to live in Grimyville, and among those there might be some who consider cleaner air in exchange for higher rents a bargain. Such people win when the Clean Air Act is passed. On the other hand, there could just as well be others who considered the old Grimyville a bargain, because they are less disturbed by pollution than their neighbors are. Those people are net losers when Grimyville turns into Cleanstown. An unusual preference is a fixed resource, which renders its owner liable to share in economic gains *and* losses.

So if there are important differences among nonlandowners, then the Clean Air Act affects some of them positively and some negatively, with no clear presumption about which effects dominate. On the other hand, if the *Grimyville Press* was right when it editorialized that "clean air is something whose value we can all appreciate equally," then only landowners stand to gain. If clean air is worth $5,000 a year to everyone, then clean air legislation raises rents by $5,000 a year, making no net difference to anyone but the landlord.

The Grimyville Clean Air Act is expected to cost $10 million per year. It is an invisible tax, and to a first approximation the proceeds are distributed entirely to the landowners of Grimyville. Of course, it is a strange kind of tax, because the proceeds available for distribution need not be related in any direct way to the revenues collected. Land rents could rise by either more or less than $10 million.

It seems an odd public policy objective to enrich those people who happen to own property in polluted areas, but in view of the nearly universal enthusiasm for clean air legislation I will take it as given. Then if Grimyville land rents rise by more than $10 million the council has performed admirably. But if rents rise by only, say, $8 million, the council has passed up an opportunity to do better. Instead of passing clean air legislation, they could simply confiscate $9 million a year from Grimyville Steel and give it to the landlords.

This policy would be cheaper for the steel company, better for the landlords, and a matter of indifference to everybody else, who neither gains nor loses from clean air legislation anyway. It would also have the advantages of directness and honesty: Nobody would be able to claim that this special-interest legislation serves the general public or a noble cause. And that would be a real breath of fresh air.

Grimyville landlords capture all the benefits of clean air legislation because their land is the only fixed resource. The fixity of land renders its owners unusually susceptible to changes in the economic environment and gives landowners an unusually strong incentive to lobby for favorable changes.

Throughout the world, farmers have managed to appropriate disproportionate shares of government largesse. In the United States farmers are routinely paid to leave land uncultivated, whereas nobody would think of paying motel operators to leave rooms vacant. That's a riddle: Why the asymmetry? Some say that farmers have successfully capitalized on the romance of the family farm. But is the family farm inherently so much more romantic than the mom-and-pop grocery store? Why do we subsidize the vanishing lifestyle of the small farmer while allowing the corner grocery to fade into the mists of nostalgia?

The Indifference Principle suggests an answer: Motel owners and grocers don't bother mounting the kind of lobbying effort that farmers do because they are well aware that they stand to gain very little from government subsidies. If motels were paid to keep rooms vacant, room rates might rise initially, but new motels would soon appear in response. Before long the motel industry would be no more profitable than it ever was. Motels are not a fixed resource, so nothing can make motels more profitable than, say, gas stations. But if there is a fixed quantity of farmland, then farmers are at least partially exempt from the Indifference Principle. New farms can't arise to take advantage of farm subsidies. Therefore farmers *can* gain from a change in economic conditions, and it is worth their while to work toward the changes they prefer.

My goal is to make an argument with three steps, and I have made two of them. First is the Indifference Principle: When one activity is more attractive than another, people switch to it until it stops being more attractive (or until everyone has switched, if that happens first). Second is its corollary: Only fixed resources generate economic gains. In the absence of fixed resources, the Indifference Principle guarantees that all gains are competed away.

The final step is a corollary to the corollary and the moral of my next fable: *When a fixed resource is not owned by anyone, economic gains are discarded.* If nobody owns the only source of benefit, then there can be no benefit.

FABLE 2: THE SPRINGFIELD AQUARIUM

The town of Springfield is blessed with a magnificent city park where townspeople spend their weekends picnicking, hiking, and playing softball. Although the park is popular—almost the entire population can be found there on a nice Saturday afternoon—it is large and never crowded.

Unfortunately there is not much to do in Springfield, and although people enjoy the park, there's always been talk about the need for some variety. A few years ago the City Council responded to popular demand by authorizing the construction of a municipal aquarium, funded by tax dollars and open to the public free of charge.

The Springfield Aquarium has been open for several months now, and it is truly a first-class establishment. The exhibits are beautiful, entertaining, and informative. The aquarium's only drawback is that it is always crowded.

There is not much diversity in Springfield. Everybody has pretty much the same preferences and the same opportunities in life. So if we want to understand how the aquarium affects Springfield, we can concentrate on how it affects a typical Springfield family.

The Simpsons are a typical Springfield family. On a recent Saturday, Homer Simpson suggested that the aquarium would be a welcome change from the family's usual weekend picnic. His son, Bart, however, was quick to remind Homer that a visit to the aquarium meant a long and unpleasant wait to get in. After some negotiation, the family agreed to drive by the aquarium and see how long the line was. If the waiting time to get in was less than 45 minutes, they would stay at the aquarium; if it was more than 45 minutes, they would go on to the park.

The Simpsons, unschooled in economic theory, failed to reckon on the Indifference Principle. All over Springfield, families just like the Simpsons were willing to wait up to 45 minutes in the aquarium line. Whenever the wait grew slightly shorter, new families entered the line. Whenever it grew slightly longer owing to unexpected bottlenecks at the entranceway, people at the end gave up and went to the park. The line at the aquarium was *always* exactly 45 minutes long. This was the one contingency the Simpsons hadn't planned on. They couldn't decide whether to stay and ended up flipping a coin.

On special occasions the aquarium line is not exactly 45 minutes long. Two Saturdays ago, for example, it rained. On rainy days the park doesn't look so good, and the Simpsons were therefore willing to wait up to 90 minutes to get into the aquarium. When they got there, the line was exactly 90 minutes long. They flipped another coin.

The Springfield Aquarium makes *absolutely no contribution* to the quality of life in Springfield. When the Simpsons wait 45 minutes to visit the aquarium, their entire outing is neither more nor less enjoyable than visiting the park—which is an option that was available long before the aquarium was ever conceived. A choice between what you've already got and an equally attractive alternative is no improvement over what you've already got with no alternative at all.

The Simpsons cannot benefit from the aquarium because they own no relevant fixed resources. The only relevant fixed resource is the aquarium itself, and the aquarium "belongs" to the entire town, which is to say that it belongs to nobody. Nobody, therefore, is exactly whom it benefits.

It cost the people of Springfield $10 million to construct their aquarium. Every penny of that $10 million was pure social waste. If the town had spent $10 million to purchase gold bullion and throw it in the ocean, the residents would be no worse off than they are today.

The mayor of Springfield might well commiserate with his counterpart in the neighboring town of Grimyville; their recent experiences have much in common. Grimyville's Clean Air Act imposes costs on local businesses, whereas Springfield's aquarium imposes costs on local taxpayers. In each case, the offsetting benefit failed to materialize as expected. The legislation in Grimyville was supposed to benefit everyone; instead it benefited only landlords. The Aquarium in Springfield was supposed to benefit all who took advantage of it; instead it benefits nobody at all.

In that sense, Springfield's mistake is far worse than Grimyville's. In Grimyville at least the landlords are happy.

This suggests a way to improve the situation in Springfield: Just as Grimyville landlords are entitled to charge rent for the use of their land, allow someone in Springfield to charge an admission fee for the use of the aquarium.

Suppose, for example, that the town of Springfield decides to give the aquarium to the mayor's cousin, in appreciation for unspecified acts of good citizenship. The cousin immediately sets a $10-per-family admission fee.

How does that admission fee affect the Simpsons? Obviously it makes the aquarium initially less desirable. The maximum time the Simpsons will wait to get in on a normal day falls from 45 minutes to 10 minutes. The same is true of all their neighbors, and consequently the actual waiting time falls to 10 minutes. A visit to the aquarium is now more expensive in terms of dollars and less expensive in terms of waiting time; on net the aquarium must remain neither more nor less attractive than the park. The Simpsons value the aquarium as much—which is to say, as little—as they ever did.

After allowing for the improvement in waiting time, *the admission fee costs the Simpsons nothing*. Nor does it cost their neighbors. The *only* way the admission fee affects anybody's well-being is that it enriches the mayor's cousin. If the choice is between maintaining the aquarium as a free but valueless municipal operation and allowing the mayor's cousin to operate it for his own benefit, it would be churlish to deny him.

Of course, there is nothing special about the mayor's cousin; any owner collecting admission fees could benefit at no expense to anyone. Perhaps the City Council would prefer to start charging its own admission fee, using the proceeds to improve city services or to lower taxes. This would yield a benefit to everyone in Springfield with no offsetting cost. Here is a rare occurrence of the most sought-after and frequently elusive goal in economic policy: a genuine free lunch.

Alternatively the city could auction off the aquarium to the highest bidder. Once again the lunch is free. The proceeds of the auction can be used to do good, while the new owner's profit-maximizing behavior is of no consequence to anybody but himself.

*   *   *

Fixed resources—land in a particular location, a unique aquarium, an unusual skill, or an unusual preference—yield economic gains to those who own them. If there are no owners, there are no gains. The Indifference Principle ensures that all gains are either transferred to a fixed-resource owner or effectively discarded. Economists tend to feel that it is better for *someone* to reap the benefits of a resource than for *no one* to reap them, and therefore tend to think that the institution of property is a good thing.

Economists love fables. A fable need not be true or even realistic to have an important moral. No tortoise ever really raced against a hare, yet "Slow but steady wins the race" remains an insightful lesson. Grimyville and Springfield are figments of the imagination, stripped of complications that would make any real-world analysis vastly more intricate. But when complications are stripped away, simple and important truths can be exposed. In any specific application, the Indifference Principle might require a host of qualifications—just as in specific circumstances, fast but erratic might vanquish slow but steady. Still, it provides a starting point. We begin by expecting people to be indifferent among activities. When we are right, we are able to derive remarkable consequences. When we are wrong, we are led to ask, "In what essential way does this situation differ from life in Grimyville or Springfield?," and the search for answers is enlightening. A good fable has a good moral, and a good moral is instructive whether or not it is always true to the last detail.

CHAPTER 5

THE COMPUTER GAME OF LIFE
Learning What It's All About

There is an idea going around that if you want students to learn anything these days you'd better put it in some kind of electronic game. Acting as CEOs or railroad tycoons or Hollywood moguls, students can compete in the virtual marketplace, funding their businesses with the sale of stocks or bonds, purchasing inputs, creating value, and serving customers.

None of these games is terribly realistic, but then neither is anything else we teach. The absence of realistic detail is rarely a problem; more often it's a virtue. We strip away the less important aspects of reality to concentrate on what matters. I want my students to have a grasp of how the price of cars affects the price of steel; I don't care if they know that the steel plants in Gary, Indiana are 252 miles from the auto plants in Detroit.

The real problem with the games lies in their scoring systems, which typically reward profit to the exclusion of everything else. This is no harmless abstraction; it's in direct opposition to everything we know about what human beings strive for.

If I were designing a Game of Economic Life, I'd want to measure success the same way economists measure success in the Game of Life itself: not by asset holdings or productivity, but by the amount of fun you have along the way.

Let the computer reward profitable trades by printing coupons that players can exchange for consumption goods of real value: movie tickets, pizza, a kiss from the graduate student of their choice. You can spend coupons as they arrive, or save them for the future, or borrow them from other students who are willing to lend. Eventually there comes a randomly selected day when a text message informs you that your character has died; your savings are transferred to a designated heir, and your own consumption opportunities have come to an end.

That's it. You receive no grade for playing this game. There is no instructor looking over your shoulder. Nobody ever tells you that you did well or did poorly. You live and you die, and if you play well you collect rewards. If you decide it's not worth the trouble to play well, that's fine too.*

Students would learn a lot from this game. They would learn that your success in life is measured not by comparison with others' accomplishments but by your private satisfaction with your own. They would learn that in the Game of Life there can be many winners, and one player's triumphs need not diminish anybody else's. They would learn that hard work has its rewards, but that it also takes time away from other activities, and that different people will make different judgments about what to strive for. Most important, they would learn that consumption and leisure, not accumulation and hard work, are what Life is really all about.

I had a friend in college whose parents were concerned that his life lacked direction. Once his father came to visit him for a heart-to-heart talk and asked, "Mitch, do you have any vision at all of what you want to *be* in ten years?" Slowly and with deliberation, Mitch replied, "I want to be—a *consumer*. I want to consume as much as I can of as many different things as I can for as long as I

---

* Second Life, with over 20 million players, is an online game with no preset objectives where players create businesses, hire labor, buy and sell goods in the marketplace, and are never told whether they've won or lost.

can." I think Mitch would have been an enthusiastic player of my computer game.

I want to create another version of the game, in which students produce consumption goods for one another. In one class, students bake brownies; in another they do each other's laundry. Halfway through the semester, I would lower trade barriers and allow students from one class to exchange services with those in the other.

This "international" version of the game would convey two valuable lessons. One is that trade expands opportunities. The second, and more important, is that trade is beneficial not because you get to export but because you get to import. The export business is the *down*side of international trade. You don't enjoy doing the other class's laundry but you do enjoy eating their brownies.

Politicians on both sides of the aisle have a tendency to miss this point. When the Bush administration relaxed import restrictions on Japanese pickup trucks, former president Bill Clinton griped that the United States had gotten absolutely nothing in return. President Bush responded that his action had helped open Japanese markets to American goods. Apparently both failed to notice that what Americans gain when they buy Japanese pickup trucks is: Japanese pickup trucks. Selling is a painful necessity; buying is what makes it all worthwhile.

Do not imagine that I am an outwardly crusty but inwardly mellow economist acknowledging that there is more to life than economic models admit. On the contrary, my electronic Game of Life is a loud affirmation of the values that matter to economists. All mainstream economic models assume that people strive to consume more and to work less. All mainstream models judge an economic policy to be successful only when it helps people to accomplish at least one of those goals. By the standards of economics, a policy that does nothing but encourage people to work harder and die wealthy is a bad policy.

We live in an age of "policy wonks" who judge programs by their effect on productivity, or output, or work effort. Wonkian analysis uses the jargon of economics while ignoring its content. Economists view the wonks' fixation on output as a bizarre and unhealthy obsession. Wonks want Americans to die rich; economists want Americans to die happy.

The industrialist politician Ross Perot was infected with an extreme form of wonkism when he called on Americans to produce computer chips, not potato chips. Even if we grant the false premise that computer chips are invariably more profitable than potato chips (ask the people who founded Frito-Lay!), the prescription overlooks the fact that producing potato chips might be *less work* and therefore more desirable.* If our goal is to maximize profits without regard to the effort involved, then most Americans should probably be in forced labor camps. The fact that camps strike most people as a bad idea should give pause to those who are quick to judge policies by productivity measures alone.

In 2011, after five years of contentious debate, the U.S. Congress approved free trade agreements with Colombia, Panama, and South Korea. Throughout those five years, opponents warned that the agreements would reduce American wages and employment. Defenders, for the most part, played on their opponents' turf by disputing those warnings. A much better response would have pointed to the agreements' potential for reducing the prices of consumer goods and expanding the array of goods available. If a free trade agreement leads Americans to work less and consume more, then Americans win.

As a teaching tool, my game has another nice feature: There are no development costs. All we have to do is point out to our students that they, like you, are already playing it. I hope you're doing well.

---

* The work involved in *learning* to produce computer chips should be counted as part of the work of producing them.

II

Good and Evil

CHAPTER 6

TELLING RIGHT FROM WRONG
The Pitfalls of Democracy

My dinner companion was passionate in her conviction that the rich pay less than their fair share of taxes. I didn't understand what she meant by "fair," so I asked a clarifying question: Suppose that Jack and Jill draw equal amounts of water from a community well. Jack's income is $10,000, of which he is taxed 10 percent, or $1,000, to support the well. Jill's income is $100,000, of which she is taxed 5 percent, or $5,000, to support the well. In which direction is that tax policy unfair?

My companion's straightforward response was that she had never thought about the issue in those terms before and was unsure of her answer. I have no problem with that; I *have* thought about the issue in those terms quite a bit and am still unsure of my own answer. That's why I hesitate to pronounce judgment on the fairness of tax policies. If I can't tell what's fair in a world with two people and one well, how can I tell what's fair in a country with 300 million people and tens of thousands of government services?

With never a thought to what "fairness" might consist of in the abstract, my companion was prepared to pass judgment on specific instances, confident that if she couldn't define it, she could at least recognize it when she saw it. But if she could really recognize fairness when she saw it, she'd have been able to recognize it in the world of Jack and Jill.

What she lacked was a moral philosophy. There are many moral philosophies to choose among, and I believe that economic reasoning is the most powerful tool we have for evaluating their merits. The initial proving ground for any moral philosophy is the artificial world of the economic model—a world where everything is specified in the explicit detail that is never available in reality.

That is why, if I could ask one question of every presidential candidate, it would probably be something along these lines:

> *Which is better: A world where everyone earns $40,000 a year, or a world where three-fourths of the population earns $100,000 a year while the rest earn $25,000?*

I'm not sure how I'd answer this myself, and I wouldn't disqualify a candidate for coming down on either side of it. But I *would* like to see some evidence that he found such questions interesting.

Those reporters who actually get access to the candidates seem to lean more toward questions about health care delivery systems or industrial policy, probing for mastery of detail instead of broad philosophical insights, exploring the intellectual territory that would have invigorated Herbert Hoover and glazed the eyes of Thomas Jefferson. The candidate knows what questions to expect and is prepared to answer them. He describes his health care plan and touts its benefits. But if you allow me to ask the follow-up question, it will be this:

> *Why do you believe that your health care plan is a good thing?*

Thinking perhaps that I must have dozed off during his recitation of his program's virtues, the candidate patiently reviews the high points of his argument. In other words, he ignores my question completely.

One of the first rules of policy analysis is that you can never prove that a policy is desirable by listing its benefits. (Nor can you prove a policy is undesirable by listing its costs.) It goes without saying that nearly any policy anybody can dream up has some advantages. If you want to defend a policy, your task is not to demonstrate that it does some good, but that it does more good than harm.

And if you are going to argue that a program does more good than harm, you must at least implicitly take a stand on a fundamental philosophical issue. Put most succinctly, the issue is: What does *more* mean?

Suppose it can be demonstrated that the candidate's health care plan would deliver additional health care worth $1 billion to the nation's poorest families. At the same time, middle-class and wealthy taxpayers would see their taxes increase by a total of $1.5 billion. Does this program do more good than harm? It all depends on what you mean by *more*. What is the right standard for weighing one kind of cost against another kind of benefit?

In the real world, any meaningful policy proposal must entail a huge number of trade-offs involving innumerable gains and losses to innumerable people. Anybody with something substantive to say about how we should compare those gains and losses must surely have something substantive to say about a fictitious simple proposal that does nothing but enrich the poor by $1 billion and impoverish the rich by $1.5 billion. Anybody who has given reasoned consideration to the underlying issues must have some thoughts that bear on the ideal income distribution in an imaginary world.

Policymakers need a dose of abstraction to keep their heads out of the clouds. It's easy to get carried away making long lists of pros and cons, all the while forgetting that sooner or later we must decide how many cons it takes to outweigh a particular pro. We can commission experts to estimate costs and benefits, but when the costs are measured in apples and the benefits in oranges, mere arithmetic can't illuminate the path to righteousness. When all the facts are in, we still need a moral philosophy to guide our decisions. If we can't address a simple, abstract question about a mythical income distribution, how can we possibly have principles that are sufficiently well developed to guide our preferences about health care delivery?

Health care is not the only issue on which politicians pontificate with less moral foundation than is appropriate to a pontiff. During his years in the White House, President George Bush occasionally wished out loud for lower interest rates to ease the burden on young home buyers. For heaven's sake, everybody already knows that lower interest rates ease the burden on home buyers. Everybody also knows that lower interest rates can devastate people who are saving for their retirement. To call attention to one side of the cost-benefit ledger while ignoring the other is plain dishonest. If a politician wants to argue legitimately for lower interest rates, he needs to explain not why it is good to help borrowers, but why it is good to *simultaneously* help borrowers and hurt lenders. In other words, he needs to defend the view that one income distribution is better than another. If he has no general thoughts about what constitutes a "better" income distribution, then he has no business having an opinion about which way the interest rate should move.

Unlike my dinner companion and various former presidents, I do not yet know what justice is. But I do believe that economics illuminates the issues.

One approach to justice is the extreme democratic view that the majority should always rule. I doubt that anyone in human history has ever subscribed to quite so stark a majoritarian principle. I do not know anyone, or expect to know anyone, or want to know anyone who believes that the majority should prevail when 51 percent of the populace vote to gouge out the eyes of the other 49 percent for their idle entertainment. Typically majoritarians temper their views with some concept of individual rights that are either inalienable or alienable only under special circumstances. This is roughly the approach of the U.S. Constitution, which institutionalizes a variation on majority rule while enumerating certain rights that are not to be abridged.

A problem with majority rule is that it provides no guidance on what to do about multiple options, none of which garners a majority. Few would want to choose a national economic policy on the grounds that it received 4 percent of the vote while its 32 opponents received 3 percent each.

Any voting procedure must include rules for what to do when there are many options. If several policies, or several candidates for office, are up for consideration, should we hold a preliminary election followed by a runoff among the two or three top vote getters? Should we hold a round-robin, pitting two candidates against each other and then a third against the winner and so on until only one is left standing? Should we let people vote not just for their first choice but for their first two or three or ten and see whether a clear majority winner might emerge?

To choose randomly among these alternatives would be at best unsatisfying. To choose on the basis of a vague aesthetic preference would not be much better. A more systematic approach is to list some characteristics that would be undesirable in a voting procedure, then narrow the list to those that avoid these shortcomings.

First, it seems uncontroversial to require that if everybody unanimously prefers Tinker to Chance, then Chance should not be able to win an election in which Tinker is a candidate. Any procedure that allowed Chance to defeat Tinker through some quirk in the rules ought not to be acceptable. This rules out silly procedures like "whoever gets the most last-place votes wins."

Second, the outcome of a vote ought not depend on arbitrary choices about the order in which things are carried out. This rules out the round-robin, where a candidate with the bad luck to be scheduled in an early round has more chances to be disqualified than opponents who enter later in the game.

Third, a third-party candidate with no chance of winning should not be able to affect the outcome of a two-way race. This rules out the simple "plurality wins" rule. With plurality rule, a candidate's prospects can improve when a third-party candidate draws votes from his opponent.

In the early 1950s the economist Kenneth Arrow (subsequently a Nobel prize winner) wrote down a list of reasonable requirements for a democratic voting procedure. They all have the flavor of the three I've just listed. Then Arrow set out to find all of those voting procedures that meet the requirements. It turns out that there aren't many. Arrow was able to prove—with the inexorable force of pure mathematics—that the *only* way to satisfy all of the requirements is to select one voter and give him all the votes. The only "democratic" procedure that meets the minimal requirements for democracy is to anoint a dictator!

Arrow's discovery must give at least a moment of pause to anybody who imagines it is possible to conduct an ideal democratic voting system. But it seems to me that there is a far more fundamental reason to be skeptical of democracy, or even of democracy coupled with a charter of inalienable rights. The reason is that we have absolutely no justification for the expectation that democracy leads to good outcomes. How can we, when we have continued to skirt the issue of what "good" means?

Is it good for a majority's mild preference to overcome a large minority's passionate opposition? Most people think not and prefer a system that can avoid such outcomes. It is often asserted that our system of republican government works well in this regard, because the passionate minority can organize to exert more pressure on their representatives than the sluggish majority can muster. This assertion has the ring of plausibility, but a ring of plausibility is not a proof. What would it take to prove that republican government leads to good outcomes? First, you would need a positive theory of politics, politicians, and pressure groups. (By a *positive* theory I mean one that makes predictions about outcomes without judging their desirability.) Your theory would specify assumptions about how politicians behave; for example, "Politicians act to maximize their reelection prospects" or "Politicians act to maximize their power while in office" or "Politicians act to enrich their friends" or some combination of these. Economic theory could guide you from your assumptions to their logical consequences, enabling you to predict what kinds of legislation would be enacted under various circumstances. Presumably you would want to test your theory against real-world observations before putting too much confidence in it.

Second, you would need to state quite precisely which outcomes you consider desirable. Just how large or passionate must a minority be before it ought to be allowed to block the desires of the majority? Answers such as "reasonably large and fairly passionate" will not do; your specifications must be stated with mathematical precision. Such specifications constitute a *normative* theory as opposed to a positive theory; they describe what is desirable, not what will necessarily occur.

Finally, you can compare your positive theory's predictions about actual outcomes with your normative theory's carefully stated criteria for desirable outcomes, and try to prove something about the frequency with which they coincide. Once again you will need a lot of theory, probably in a reasonably mathematical form.

The positive theory of pressure groups is in its relative infancy. In the past 30 years or so, several papers have appeared that attempt to deal with the problem; many are interesting, but none is definitive. Even if we had the (presently unthinkable) luxury of a fully developed and well-tested positive theory, we would still need a separate normative theory to tell us whether our system is desirable. We keep returning to the same point: It takes a moral philosophy to distinguish right from wrong.

Now a simple preference for democracy, or for limited democracy, or for some variation on democracy, already *is* a moral philosophy, at least a rudimentary one, and it is quite enough philosophy for some tastes. It is not, however, a *consequentialist* philosophy; it judges the political system by an arbitrary standard of intrinsic merit ("Democracy is good") rather than by its consequences for human happiness. The research program I've just outlined can be summarized as follows: Determine the consequences of democracy, and then decide whether those consequences (as opposed to the idea of democracy itself) are desirable.

Much of the philosophy that finds its way into common political discourse is nonconsequentialist. Any assertion of "rights" appeals to our preferences for specific rules as opposed to the consequences of those rules. Both sides in the abortion debate—whether lobbying for the "right to life" or the "right to choose"—appeal to something that goes beyond consequentialism.

Economics offers no objection to a philosophy of rights. But consequences matter also, and it pays to consider them in a systematic way. Because the consequences we care about concern human happiness, it is convenient to believe that happiness is measurable at least in principle, so that, for example, we know what it means to say that Jack is happier than Jill. Many economists scoff at such comparisons, contending that Jack's happiness and Jill's happiness are entirely different commodities incapable of being weighed against each other. But for the sake of advancing the discussion, let's suspend our disbelief.

If happiness is measurable, then it is easy to list a menu of consequentialist moral philosophies (or in economic jargon, normative criteria). One is: Pursue the greatest good for the unhappiest person. If happiness can be equated with income, this means that a world of middle-income earners is better than a world where some are rich and some are poor. But it also means that inequality is tolerable provided that it benefits even those at the very bottom. A society with a wide range of incomes where even the poorest have enough to eat is preferable to one in which we all starve equally.

A different normative criterion is: Maximize the sum of human happiness. Our philosophical baggage gets a little heavier now, because we are required not just to compare Jack's happiness with Jill's but to assign each of them a number. A system that gives Jack 4 units of happiness and Jill 10 (for a total of 14) is better than one that gives Jack 6 and Jill 7 (for a total of 13).

Once you've accepted the possibility of numerical measurements, there is nothing special about maximizing the *sum*. An alternative normative criterion is to maximize the *product* of human happiness. This reverses some judgments. Now a system that gives Jack 4 units of happiness and Jill 10 (for a product of 40) is *inferior* to one that gives Jack 6 and Jill 7 (for a product of 42).

Whatever their merits, each of these criteria takes an unambiguous moral stand, as opposed, for example, to the oft-repeated but utterly meaningless "Seek the greatest good for the greatest number." (When you compare an income distribution of $40,000 for all with one of $100,000 for three-fourths and $25,000 for the rest, which constitutes "the greatest good for the greatest number"? Your guess is as good as mine.) They are also thoroughly abstract and strictly applicable only in highly stylized artificial examples. But as I've said before, if we can't understand highly stylized artificial examples, we have no hope of understanding the world.

The problem with all these criteria is that the choice among them seems entirely arbitrary. Who is to say whether it is better to maximize the sum of happiness or the product? I am aware of two approaches to overcoming this difficulty.

One approach is to begin by writing down some reasonable requirements that a normative criterion ought to satisfy. For example, we might require that whenever there is an opportunity to make everybody better off, our normative criterion ought to approve it; this rules out criteria like "Always try to make the unhappiest person as unhappy as possible" or "Minimize the sum of human happiness." We might require that our normative criterion treat everyone symmetrically; we should not be allowed to care more about the welfare of whites or of women than about that of blacks or of men.

Once we've agreed on a few such requirements, it becomes an exercise in pure mathematics to list all of the normative criteria that qualify for the job. Unfortunately, even for short lists of uncontroversial requirements, the most frequent result is that *no* normative criterion satisfies them all at once. This shifts the focus of the debate to: Which of your reasonable requirements are you most willing to abandon? Do we care more or less about interpersonal symmetry than we do about approving every opportunity to make everybody better off? The mathematics guides our understanding of the trade-offs; it tells us that *if* we want a criterion with certain properties, then we must be willing to abandon certain others.

Although this approach does not settle the issue, it moves the argument to higher ground. We have no obvious basis for preferring a sum-of-happiness approach to a product-of-happiness approach, but we seem to have deep visceral preferences for requirements like symmetry. A clear vision of those preferences, plus some pure theory, dictates the normative criterion we are forced to choose.

There is a second approach to the problem, first introduced by the economist John Harsanyi but associated primarily with the name of the philosopher John Rawls, who made it the basis for his monumental work on the theory of justice. In Rawls's or Harsanyi's vision, we must imagine ourselves behind a *veil of ignorance* where even our own identities are concealed from us. Behind the veil, we know that we are destined to lead *someone's* life, but all earthly lives are equally probable. According to Rawls, the just society is the one we would choose to be born into if forced to choose from behind the veil.

Rawlsians argue that if we were stripped of all knowledge of individual circumstances, we would all agree on how the world should be. Observations of actual behavior can even help us guess what we would agree to. We know that when people can insure at fair odds against catastrophic diseases, they typically do so. It is reasonable to infer that if we could insure against being born untalented or handicapped or otherwise unlucky, we would do that as well. Behind the veil, such insurance would be available: we could all agree that those born smart and healthy would share their incomes with the rest. Because we all would want to sign such a contract behind the veil, Rawlsians argue that it should be enforced in real life. It seems to me that there's a lot of merit to that argument.

But Rawls himself went further. He believed that after agreeing on certain fundamental liberties, we would concentrate our efforts on improving the welfare of the least happy person. In its extreme form, this means that we would prefer a world in which everyone barely subsists to a world of billionaires where one unfortunate soul starves to death.

Rawls and other Rawlsians have generated a lot of verbiage to justify their guesses about what we'd have agreed on behind the veil.

Economists, by contrast, have taken a more quantitative approach. Returning to the question earlier in this chapter, would you rather be born into a world where everyone earns $40,000 a year or one where three-fourths of the people earn $100,000 while the remaining fourth earn $25,000? That's a lot like asking: Would you rather earn $40,000 a year, or determine your salary by reaching into an urn with three balls labeled $100,000 and one labeled $25,000? Instead of speculating idly about the answer, we can look for real-world situations where people have faced analogous choices. Then, instead of guessing, we can *observe* their preferences.

There are quite a few real-world situations that are like that. People choose between careers with predictable salaries on the one hand and risky entrepreneurial ventures on the other. They decide how much insurance to buy. They decide whether to invest their retirement funds in bonds with fairly predictable returns or stocks that combine upside potential with downside risk. By observing the choices people make in a variety of circumstances, we can estimate the amount of risk they're comfortable with—and so we can estimate the choices they'd make from behind the veil.

To carry out this exercise in detail is considerably more complex than I've made it sound—especially if you want to do actual policy analysis, as opposed to pure philosophy. To compare the merits of two potential tax codes, you first have to estimate how each tax code, with all of its first-, second-, and third-order incentive effects, is likely to affect the income distribution. Only then can you begin to ask which tax code is preferable. Research in this direction has been the stuff of Nobel prizes.

While the veil criterion has much to recommend it, it does seem inadequate for dealing with some critical moral issues, because it fails to specify who exactly is behind the veil. The usual answer is "everybody," but there are circumstances in which "everybody" is more ambiguous than it sounds. Should people be allowed to slaughter seals to make coats? I might give one answer if I knew that I was going to be born a random person, and quite another if I thought I might be born a seal. Should abortion be legal? My answer behind the veil might well depend on whether "aborted fetus" was one of the identities I thought I might be assigned. To decide whether fetuses stand behind the veil with the rest of us is to ask whether we consider them fully human; this seems to bring us full circle back to the question we were trying to solve.

I believe that arguments from basic properties or from behind the veil can be enormously helpful in clarifying our thinking and warning us about hidden inconsistencies. I suspect, though, that the choice of a normative criterion is ultimately a matter of taste. And that very fact is the source of an intriguing paradox.

Let me illustrate the paradox in a case so extreme that it seems almost frivolous. Suppose that we agree to make policy based on a normative criterion that calls on us to maximize the welfare of the world's least happy person. Following a massive search, we locate that unfortunate soul and ask what we can do to make him happier. His reply is that he would prefer to live in a world where the normative criterion did not involve the welfare of the least happy person.

Given this preference, it is literally impossible to apply our normative criterion consistently. The only way to apply it is to abandon it.

Alternatively suppose that we have agreed to maximize the sum of human happiness and discover that we can increase that sum by agreeing *not* to maximize the sum of human happiness. Our goal is again self-contradictory.

Under various circumstances, we can prove mathematically that almost all normative criteria must become entangled in paradoxes of this sort.* If we discard these paradoxical candidates, the choice among normative criteria is automatically narrowed to a manageable number long before we start philosophizing.

This might be the most delicious paradox of all. It is sometimes maintained that moral behavior is so much a matter of personal taste that pure theory can contribute very little to the discussion. In fact it is precisely *because* moral behavior is a matter of personal taste that pure theory is able to uncover paradoxes that rule out a host of normative criteria as literally impossible to enforce.

If you took a poll of economists, you would probably find a clear preference for a normative criterion that I have not yet mentioned. The criterion goes by the deceptively callous-sounding name of *economic efficiency* or *cost-benefit analysis*. I think it deserves a chapter to itself.

---

* You can read more about this in my paper "On the Methodology of Normative Economics," *Journal of Public Economics* (2007).

CHAPTER 7

WHY TAXES ARE BAD

The Logic of Efficiency

What's wrong with taxes? The obvious answer is that it's no fun to pay them. But the obvious response is that it's *great* fun to collect them. Since every dollar paid is a dollar collected, you could argue that the good and the bad wash out.

If the tax collector takes a dollar from you and gives it to my mother as part of her Social Security payment, you might legitimately grumble. But I (who care more about my mother than I care about you) will view things rather more positively. Nothing in the science of economics can reveal whether you are more or less deserving than my mother, so to a disinterested observer, the transfer is on balance neither good nor bad.

The real problem with taxes is not that we have to *pay* them, but that we strive to avoid them. Avoidance is costly and it comes with no offsetting benefit to anyone.

Consider, for example, my sandals. I found them on the Internet for $40, though I'd have happily paid $50. There's a very real sense in which buying these sandals made me $10 richer. Better yet, my gain came at nobody's expense, so it made *the world as a whole* $10 richer. That $10 gain—the difference between what I was willing to pay and what I actually paid—is what economists call *consumer surplus*.

Now, if a sales tax had added, say, $6 to the price of those sandals, I'd still have bought them. I'd be $6 poorer than I am today, but someone else would be $6 richer. So far so good. But if a larger sales tax had added, say, $12 to the price of those sandals, I'd have avoided the tax by not buying the sandals. I would lose my $10 consumer surplus and nobody would win. That's unambiguously bad.

Even a small sales tax will probably discourage at least a few people from buying the sandals. Their lost consumer surplus is what economists call a *deadweight loss* because it comes with no offsetting benefit to anyone.

Taxes nearly always do more harm than good. To collect a dollar, you need to take someone's dollar; almost invariably, in the process, you discourage someone else from buying a pair of sandals, or building a house, or working overtime. When a policy does more harm than good—that is, when it creates deadweight losses—we call it *inefficient* and tend to deplore it.

The only sort of tax that avoids deadweight losses completely is a *head tax*, according to which everybody pays an amount that is determined without reference to income, assets, purchases, or anything else over which the taxpayer has any control. In theory, economists love head taxes; in practice, we recognize that they represent a rather extreme solution to the problem of inefficiency.

So if we're going to have any sort of government at all, and if we're not willing to go to the extreme of financing it through head taxes, then we're going to have to accept some amount of deadweight loss. But the deadweight loss from one tax policy might be much larger than from another. When a policy creates particularly large deadweight losses, economists start looking for alternatives.

*   *   *

The key to the analysis is to weigh individual gains and losses. What's the impact of, say, a tariff on imported cars? Policy analysts not trained in economics might approach this question by estimating the effects on employment in the auto industry, the balance sheet at General Motors, and even the government's trade and budget deficits. That's a start, but by itself this kind of analysis largely misses the point. It provides no criterion for weighing the good against the bad. (Is a 4 percent increase in unemployment among auto workers worth it for a 3 percent decrease in the price of cars? What about a $1 billion decrease in the trade deficit?) It doesn't even provide a criterion for deciding what goes on the positive or negative side of the ledger. (Is an increase in domestic car production—with its attendant consumption of valuable resources—a good or a bad thing?)

Economists address these issues by staying focused on how policies affect *individuals*. (Of course, individuals are affected by auto industry profits and government deficits, so we might still have to consider such things—but only as intermediate steps.) For each individual in the economy, we ask: Does this person gain or lose as a result of this tariff, and by how much? Gains and losses include changes in consumer surplus, changes in producers' profits, transfer payments that are made out of the tariff revenue, and anything else that any individual values. We add up the gains to the winners and the losses to the losers. If the winners gain more than the losers lose, we tend to view the policy as desirable. If the losers lose more than the winners win, we declare the difference a deadweight loss, pronounce the policy inefficient, and take the size of the deadweight loss as a measure of its unattractiveness.

It's important not to make the traditional noneconomist's error of overemphasizing that which is purely material. We mean it when we say we count everything people value.

Suppose the Exxon Corporation acquires oil drilling rights in a remote area where it's generally agreed that drilling will cause only negligible environmental damage in the traditional sense. Nevertheless a group of militant mineral rights activists, contending that their personal serenity is threatened by the knowledge that oil is being removed from its natural resting place in the ground, files a lawsuit to prevent Exxon from proceeding. By the logic of cold-blooded economic efficiency, which side should prevail?

By the logic of cold-blooded economic efficiency, we don't yet have enough information to answer. If Exxon proceeds, the winners will be some combination of Exxon's stockholders, employees, suppliers, and customers. The losers will be the mineral rights activists. The efficiency criterion dictates that we measure all gains and losses in terms of *willingness-to-pay* and measure one total against the other.*

A stockholder who stands to gain $50 from the project would presumably be willing to pay up to $50 to secure a ruling in Exxon's favor. That counts as 50 votes on the pro-drilling side. A determined opponent might be willing to pay up to $3,000 to prevent that ruling. That counts as 3,000 votes against.

One of the local unemployed, who expects to earn $30,000 working for Exxon if the deal goes through, also casts votes in favor, but fewer than 30,000 of them. He'd be willing to pay something to get that job, but he surely wouldn't be willing to give up all his expected wages in exchange for the privilege of reporting to work each morning. Let's say he'd be willing to pay up to $10,000 to get the job (which is the same thing as saying he'd be willing to work for as little as $20,000 but no less). Count another 10,000 votes in favor of drilling.

---

* You might quite reasonably object that willingness-to-pay is not the only measure of how much someone cares about the outcome. I promise to come back and address this objection just a few paragraphs down the line.

In principle, everyone with an interest in the outcome gets to cast a number of votes proportional to his willingness to pay for the outcome he wants. The efficient decision is, by definition, the one that gets the most votes.

The battle between Exxon and its detractors gets to the heart of why economists deplore inefficiency. An inefficient decision *always* entails a missed opportunity to make *everyone* happier. Suppose the total willingness-to-pay of the pro-drillers is $10 million, and the total willingness-to-pay of the anti-drillers is $5 million, but the judge rules (inefficiently) against drilling. Then here is an alternative ruling that *both sides* would have preferred: Allow drilling, but make the pro-drillers collectively pay the anti-drillers $7.5 million to assuage their disappointment.

Under the alternative ruling, the pro-drillers get $10 million worth of benefits for a bargain price of $7.5 million, while the anti-drillers get $7.5 million to compensate them for a $5 million loss. In fact the collections and payments can (at least in principle) be orchestrated so that each individual pro-driller pays exactly 75 percent of his drilling-related gains, and each anti-driller receives exactly 150 percent of his drilling-related losses. If a referendum were held, with this and the judge's actual ruling as the only alternatives, the vote to overturn the judge would be unanimous.

Any proposal that manages to garner zero votes in a two-way election must be regarded as seriously flawed. And any proposal that is economically inefficient will always garner zero votes in a two-way election against an appropriately designed alternative.

An argument that inefficiency is always bad is not quite the same thing as an argument that efficiency is always good. But because efficiency is the only alternative to inefficiency, economists tend to favor it.

Notice that this argument would fail if we'd allocated voting rights according to something other than willingness-to-pay. Let's try it: Suppose that if drilling is allowed, pro-drillers stand to gain 10 million "units of happiness" (whatever that means) and the anti-drillers stand to lose 5 million. Nevertheless the judge rules against drilling. I could attempt to argue that this is a bad ruling because I can imagine an alternative ruling that would have made *everybody* happier. But that argument would fail. After all, what is that alternative ruling? To allow drilling and transfer 7.5 million units of happiness from the pro-drillers to the anti-drillers? I can make no sense of that proposal, because I have no idea how to transfer a unit of happiness. That's why the argument fails.

I *can*, however, understand what it means to transfer a dollar. The argument for efficiency works only when the definition of efficiency is couched in terms of dollars.*

There are (at least) two obvious objections to this line of reasoning, of which one is entirely beside the point and the other is substantial. The first is that a judge endowed with anything short of omnipotence is in no position to guess what a laborer would be willing to pay for his job, let alone what a mineral rights activist would be willing to pay to maintain a pool of oil in its natural habitat. This is partly true but wholly irrelevant.† Judges, being human, are doomed sometimes to miss their targets. This does not relieve them from the responsibility to choose their targets appropriately. The question is not "Should policies always be efficient?" but rather

---

* This does not prove that it's impossible to employ a criterion based on units of happiness, but it does prove that this particular argument cannot be used to defend such a criterion.

† It is only partly true because economists have devised some ingenious mechanisms for eliciting true responses from people who are being questioned about their willingness to pay. See, for example, the discussion at the end of chapter 3 on how my wife and I discover each other's willingness to pay for the right to choose a movie.

"Should we in general strive to devise efficient policies, doing the best we can with the information at our disposal?"

The more important objection is that it is not necessarily a fatal flaw for a candidate to lose an election—even unanimously—to a candidate who isn't even in the race. In my example, the judge must either allow drilling or forbid it. To allow drilling and simultaneously order a complicated system of side payments might not be an option. Should the anti-drilling position be eliminated just because it's inferior to a plan that's not even under consideration? And if this eliminates the argument *against* inefficiency, what argument *for* efficiency remains?

Many economists find these questions troubling. That's one reason most of us are reluctant to embrace pure efficiency as our only vision of the ultimate good. Yet I think it's a fair statement that most economists generally agree that efficiency should play a significant role in formulating social policy.

The logic of efficiency dictates that economists see common issues from an uncommon perspective. Take, for example, the chronic debate about military manpower. It's been 40 years since the last American was conscripted into service, but there's always someone looking to revive the draft. As recently as 2010 the U.S. Congress considered a bill that would have conscripted every adult American into some form of military or nonmilitary national service.

Commentators frequently opine that the draft, despite its disadvantages, is at least cheaper than a volunteer army. Those commentators are wrong. The wages paid to volunteer soldiers come out of the pockets of taxpayers' jeans and business suits and go into the pockets of military uniforms. Those wages aren't lost; they're simply transferred from one segment of society to another. By the economist's reckoning, those transfers are not net costs.

The cost of maintaining an army is equal to the value of the opportunities that young people forgo when they become soldiers. The value of those opportunities is measured by what the soldiers would be willing to pay to retrieve them. When a mechanic or a student or a beach bum joins the army, he loses the opportunity to repair cars, or to pursue his studies, or to catch the big wave. Those opportunities really do vanish; the world becomes a place with fewer working cars, or fewer trained scholars, or less fun.* Vanished opportunities are costs in any reckoning. In the economist's reckoning, they are the *only* costs.

Imagine a young woman who would require $30,000 as an inducement to volunteer. If she is drafted and paid nothing, then she's lost $30,000 worth of freedom. If she is drafted and paid $18,000, then she's lost $12,000 and the taxpayers who pay her wage have lost $18,000; the total cost to society is still $30,000. If we hire the same young woman into a volunteer army and pay her $30,000, then she breaks even, while the taxpayers have to fork over $30,000. The total cost to society is still $30,000. Raising or lowering the wage rate can shift that burden, but the size of the burden is unchanged.

The best way to see the absurdity of the allegation that a draft is cheaper is to imagine taxing *the young woman herself* $30,000 and then offering it back to her as a wage for joining the army. Surely that proposal does not differ in any meaningful way from drafting this young woman and paying her a wage of zero. If your accounting system tells you that paying soldiers is always more expensive than drafting them, then this example should convince you that you need a new accounting system.

The same principles apply to another recurring controversy: congressional pay raises. A raise has two effects. First, it redistributes

---

* A new mechanic might arise to take the old one's place, but then the world loses whatever it is the new mechanic might have been producing instead.

income by enriching sitting congressmen at taxpayers' expense, and second, it attracts a better class of candidates in the future.* The usual noneconomist's view is that the first effect is bad and the second is good. But if we take efficiency seriously, we must conclude that the first effect is neutral and the second might well be bad.

As to the first effect, the logic of efficiency requires that we be neutral regarding pure transfers of income, even when the recipient is a congressman. As to the second, keep in mind that our new, improved congressman must come from the ranks of some other profession, so that if we attract a better class of officeholders, we must also have a poorer class of judges or lawyers or doctors or economists. The true cost of a good congressman is not his salary but the forgone opportunity to bring his excellence to bear in other fields. Is the cost worth the benefit? I have no idea.

The logic of efficiency drives the economist's distaste for inflation. Inflation is costly for those who receive fixed nominal incomes, but it is beneficial—and to exactly the same degree—for those who *pay* those fixed nominal incomes. An unexpected inflation can be a boon to the borrower who repays his loan with inflated dollars, but it's simultaneously a curse—and of exactly the same magnitude— to the lender who receives those dollars. Those effects, which are so often cited as the primary economic consequences of inflation, cancel each other out and have exactly zero effect on efficiency.

The true economic cost of inflation, like the true economic cost of a tax, is that people take costly actions to avoid it, and these actions

---

* Actually, this second effect is far from certain. Higher salaries guarantee that future contests will be more hard-fought. The costs of participating in tougher campaigns might completely erase the benefits of higher salaries. On balance, it could become either easier or harder to attract high-quality candidates. But for the sake of argument, I will assume that higher salaries really do draw forth better candidates.

benefit nobody. In times of inflation, people carry less cash, because cash loses value just by sitting in their pockets. They carry smaller checking account balances for the same reason. This can make it more difficult to buy a hot dog on a whim, to hail a cab in an unexpected rainstorm, or to get through the day without a trip to the ATM. Retail stores keep less cash in the till and run out of change more often. Large firms keep less cash on hand to meet unexpected emergencies and have to deal with those emergencies via expensive financial transactions. These losses are all deadweight losses—they come with no offsetting gains. They might sound unimportant in the grand scheme of things, but the deadweight losses due to a year of 3 percent inflation in the United States are estimated to be roughly $18 billion per year, or $60 per American—hardly devastating, but hardly trivial either.

In times of very high inflation, the deadweight losses can become enormous. In the Hungarian hyperinflation that followed World War II, prices multiplied by a factor of roughly 100 every month. This means that a cup of coffee that sold for 10 cents on January 1 sold for $10 on February 1, $1,000 on March 1, $100,000 on April 1, $10 million on May 1, $1 billion on June 1, $100 billion on July 1, and $10 trillion on August 1. Workers were paid three times a day and their spouses were employed full time running back and forth between the workplace and the bank, trying to deposit paychecks before they became worthless. All that sacrifice of time and energy, which benefits nobody, is a classic example of a deadweight loss.

During the German hyperinflation that followed World War I, John Maynard Keynes reported that tavern goers frequently ordered several beers early in the evening—before the price went up. Drinking warm beer can be a hidden cost of inflation.

Hollywood screenwriters and denizens of the college lecture circuit periodically rediscover the dramatic potential of a burning dollar bill. Typically the torching is accompanied by impassioned commentary—issuing from a sympathetic character on the movie screen or an aging cultural icon in the college gym—about how a dollar bill is nothing more than a piece of paper. You can't eat it, you can't drink it, and you can't make love to it. And the world is no worse off for its disappearance.

Sophisticated audiences tend to be uncomfortable with this kind of reasoning; they sense that it is somehow dreadfully wrong but are unable to pinpoint the fatal flaw. In reality, it is their own discomfort that is gravely in error. The speaker is right. When you spend an evening burning money, the world as a whole remains just as wealthy as it ever was.

Let me suggest a probable source for the audience's false feeling that something is amiss. The audience recognizes—correctly—that by the end of the evening the money burner is poorer than he was at the beginning. If *he* is poorer, and he is part of the world, must not the world as a whole be poorer too?

The answer is surely no. The world is not poorer because nothing of value has been destroyed. So if the money burner is a dollar poorer, somebody else must be a dollar richer. All we have to do is figure out who that somebody else is.

The key to the mystery is the observation that the supply of money determines the general level of prices. When the money supply increases, prices rise, and when it decreases, prices fall. When a dollar bill turns to ashes, the money supply falls ever so slightly, and prices throughout the economy fall. If only one dollar bill is burned, prices fall only imperceptibly, but they do fall. The beneficiaries of that event are *those people who are holding money at the moment when the dollar bill is burned.* As prices fall, the money in their pockets gains value.

An imperceptibly small reduction in prices creates an imperceptibly small increase in wealth for each of the many millions who have money in their pockets at the time of the change. Many millions of imperceptibly small increases in wealth can add up to something perceptible. In this case they add up to exactly one dollar. After all, we know that the total value of real goods in the world is unchanged, and we know also that the speaker has lost a dollar; we are therefore entitled to conclude that exactly one dollar has been gained somewhere else.

Every now and then some eccentric altruist gathers up his assets and donates them to the U.S. Treasury. As a result our current or future tax bills must fall.* The beneficiaries are the many millions of U.S. taxpayers, each of whom experiences a tiny reduction in his tax burden. But we do not all benefit equally. Those of us in the highest tax brackets—by and large, the richest Americans—collect disproportionate shares of the gift.

An alternative strategy for the altruist would be to convert his assets to cash and, instead of giving them to the Treasury, hold a bonfire. The result is essentially the same. Tiny benefits accrue to millions of Americans (this time in the form of falling prices rather than falling tax bills), and the total of all those benefits is equal to the altruist's sacrifice. In the bonfire scenario, your share of the benefits is proportional not to your tax bill but to the quantity of cash you happen to be holding at the moment of the bonfire. This still tends to favor the rich, but probably less dramatically. So if you are thinking of remembering the Treasury in your will, and if you are something of an egalitarian, consider a bonfire instead.†

---

* The most plausible scenario is that the Treasury reduces its current borrowing, so that its future obligations and the future tax burden are reduced. Under *any* scenario, unless the gift causes the government to revise its spending plans, a gift to the Treasury must lower taxes one way or another.

† It might be worth noting, however, that when you make a gift to money holders, the biggest winners of all are likely to come from that class of people who frequently travel with suitcases containing several million dollars.

*   *   *

On a windy day in New Orleans, the dollar bill I was holding got away from me. As it headed for a sewer and oblivion, I started to grab for it. David Friedman—my companion, my fellow economist, and for that moment the guardian of my soul—stayed my hand. I had just been arguing that economic efficiency is a good guide not just to public policy but to personal conduct. By that standard David's interference saved me from thoughtlessly committing an immoral act.

If I kiss the dollar good-bye, the cost-benefit accounting looks like this: I lose a dollar, the rest of the world gains a dollar through falling prices, and the world as a whole is neither richer nor poorer than before. The consequences for economic efficiency: none.

But if I grab the dollar, I exert approximately 3 cents' worth of effort. (That is, 3 cents is about what I'd have been willing to pay David to retrieve the dollar for me instead of running after it myself.) The cost-benefit accounting: I lose 3 cents, the rest of the world neither gains nor loses, and the world as a whole (including me) is 3 cents poorer. The consequence for economic efficiency: a 3-cent deadweight loss.* The logic of efficiency compels me to let it go.

Or does it? Let me distinguish between two quite different propositions. One is that economic efficiency should be an important consideration in resolving issues of *public policy*. The other is that economic efficiency should be an important consideration in resolving issues of *personal conduct*. It is only the first of these propositions that economists frequently defend. Like most people,

---

* Notice that if it had been my iPod heading for the sewer, the logic of efficiency would argue for retrieving it. If I can exert 3 cents' worth of effort to rescue a $200 iPod, that's all to the good. That's because the iPod is worth $200 not just to me, but to the world as a whole (including me). By contrast, $200 in cash is worth exactly zero to the world. If I let *that* go, I'm $200 poorer and everyone else is $200 richer.

economists are vocal when they criticize governments but coy when they criticize each other.

The efficiency criterion treats everybody equally. A cost is a cost, no matter who bears it. In the realm of public policy, this is an appealing feature. But in our private affairs, it seems odd to insist that we should behave as if our own concerns carry no more weight than those of distant strangers.

There are times—as on that day in New Orleans—when I think that efficiency fails entirely as a guide to how I should behave. But there are other times when it serves me pretty well. When my lawn gets shaggier than the neighbors would prefer, I have to ask myself whether I am morally obliged to take action. In the process, I think about what it would cost me to get the lawn mowed, and how unhappy I think the neighbors really are. If it seems likely to cost me $30 worth of effort to save the neighbors from $20 worth of grief, I pour myself a lemonade and stop worrying. If I believe that with $30 worth of effort I could save the neighbors from $50 worth of grief, then I feel like a jerk until I mow the lawn.

That's an efficiency calculation, and it leads me to conclusions that feel right. I'm not entirely consistent about this. When I decide whether to operate an internal combustion engine or an aerosol can, I *do* care about the harm that I might do to others by damaging the air quality. I emphatically do *not* care about the psychic harm that I might do to others who are morally offended by the very idea of my operating an internal combustion engine or an aerosol can. I think that this distinction would be very hard to justify philosophically. If my driving makes you unhappy, then I have made the world a less happy place in a way that's independent of *why* my driving makes you unhappy. The strict logic of efficiency would say that if I am prepared to stay home rather than cause $10 worth of damage to your lungs, then I should also be prepared to stay home rather than cause $10 worth of damage to your moral sensibilities.

I infer that my moral philosophy is incomplete, but efficiency considerations play a major role. But a recent trip to Boston shook my faith a bit.

My wife and I flew from Denver, and our round-trip tickets totaled just under $2,500. I offered alternatives to the publisher who was footing the bill, but he insisted that we come anyway. Still, I'm sure that if I'd been paying my own way I would have canceled the trip.

This led me to formulate the following moral dilemma: Suppose that getting to Boston and back is worth $300 to you. It costs the airline $200 to provide that transportation. But because of some extraordinary degree of monopoly power, the airline charges $1,000 for the ticket. Should you fly?

If you care only about efficiency, then you certainly should. If you fly, you are worse off by $700 (the difference between what you pay and the value of the trip), while the owners of the airline are better off by $800 (the difference between what they collect and the cost of flying you). There is a net gain of $100, and the efficiency criterion pronounces the trip a Good Thing.

Yet I am sure that I would not buy the ticket, and I am equally sure that I would lose no sleep over it. I am sure that I would reach the same conclusion no matter how much the airline owners stood to gain, or how little I stood to lose. So while I still believe that efficiency is usually the right general guide to government policy, and often the right general guide to personal behavior, I now think that we need a much subtler criterion before we can really know what it means to be good. I believe that there are times when I ought to try to behave efficiently and other times when I need not. I just haven't figured out the rules for knowing which times are which.

I did retrieve that dollar, without a moment's concern for its effect on the general price level. I feel no guilt, though I'm not sure why.

CHAPTER 8

WHY PRICES ARE GOOD

Smith versus Darwin

I once attended a party where a learned man, a prominent physicist, held forth. His topic was the analogy between Darwinian evolution, advancing the species biologically by allowing only the fittest to survive, and the Invisible Hand of the marketplace, advancing our species economically by eliminating all but the most efficient producers.

I suspect that he didn't know much about biology. I'm sure that he didn't know much about economics. And his analogy, though familiar, was profoundly wrong.

In biology there is no equivalent of the Invisible Hand. Survival of the fittest is a different thing altogether. Nothing in evolutionary theory either promises or delivers the spectacular efficiency of the competitive marketplace.

Male birds of paradise have ridiculously long tails. Evolution has cursed them with tails far too long for any practical purpose, and in fact long enough to be a substantial hindrance in locomotion. Their bodies expend precious resources to grow and maintain these tails, increasing the birds' food requirements while simultaneously rendering them more susceptible to predators.

How could such a handicap have survived natural selection? In fact Darwinism requires us to ask something far more perplexing: How could such a handicap have been a *consequence* of natural selection?

Remarkably, the biologists have answers. Male birds compete for female birds, who want mates capable of fathering healthy offspring. By growing a tail slightly longer than his rivals', the male demonstrates that he is robust, that he eats well, and perhaps that he is sufficiently athletic to survive even when burdened with an absurd encumbrance. These are just the qualities that the female wants in her sons, and so she seeks a mate who evidently has them. Long tails are a reproductive advantage, and are therefore rewarded by natural selection.

Now let's be fanciful: The male birds of paradise, concerned about escalating competition, have called a peace conference. Some of the more scrawny-tailed birds have made a radical proposal: universal "disentailment," by which all will agree to immediately and permanently discard all unnecessary plumage. Their literature emphasizes advantages in the area of fox avoidance but underplays the possibility of a redistribution of females.

The bird now occupying the podium is the bearer of a particularly magnificent specimen (he needed three assistants to carry it as he ascended the stage). He rejects the radicals' proposal out of hand but offers a grand compromise: "Let each and every one of us cut the length of his tail by half. To this there can be no objection. The tails that are now the longest will remain the longest. Those who are now most attractive to females will remain most attractive to females. At the same time, each of us will benefit from reduced maintenance costs, improved aerodynamics, and decreased visibility to our friends the foxes."

What's remarkable about this proposal is not just that it benefits the birds as a *species*; it actually benefits each and every individual bird. The scrawny-tailed birds like it less than their own proposal, but that one never had a chance of adoption anyway. The compromise is a game in which every player wins. Only the foxes might object.

For birds of paradise, it is an unfortunate truth that such a compromise can never be enforced. By the time the proposal has been moved, seconded, and adopted, unscrupulous males (and what male is not unscrupulous in such matters?) will be scheming to avoid the shears. Any bird who suspects widespread cheating must cheat in order not to be outdone by his rivals. Any bird who does *not* suspect widespread cheating is *still* likely to cheat, hoping to gain an unfair advantage over his more honest fellows.

An economist would describe this outcome as *inefficient*, because of the lost opportunity to make a change that is unanimously agreed to be desirable. The outcomes of biological processes are often inefficient, for the simple reason that there is no reason they shouldn't be. The outcomes of economic processes can be inefficient also, but they are efficient remarkably often, and thereby hangs our tale.

The best way to appreciate the spectacular efficiency of the competitive marketplace is to see some examples of outcomes that are inefficient. For one such example, let's make the pessimistic hypothesis that students learn nothing of any value in college. Nevertheless employers prefer to hire college graduates, because grads are smarter, on average, than nongrads. Going to college did not make them smart; rather being smart enabled them to survive college. Still, if employers have no other way to distinguish between the smart and the not-so-smart, then they will be willing to pay higher salaries to those with more education.

In this example, students are like male birds of paradise, employers are like female birds, and getting a college education is like growing a long tail: It is an expensive way to acquire something useless that nonetheless signals your inner qualities. Suppose that students could all agree to attend only half as much college as presently: Those who now graduate from four-year schools will attend two-year schools instead; those who now spend eight years getting a PhD will spend four years and get a bachelor's degree. With this plan in effect, the employers' ranking of the students would not change, and each student would save half his tuition costs (as well as being able to enter the workforce earlier). Every student would benefit and nobody would lose.

But college students, like male birds of paradise, are notorious cheaters, and the agreement breaks down as each decides to violate its provisions and gain an advantage over his fellows. The result is an inefficient return to the status quo.

Examples abound, both in the animal kingdom and in human affairs. Consider a population of cattle that graze in a restricted area. If they all agree to eat a little less this year, the grass will replenish itself faster and all will have more to eat in the future. Perhaps every cow and bull can agree that this trade-off would be worthwhile. Yet each animal cheats, eating a bit more than his allotment this year, secure in the knowledge that his own extra portion will have only a negligible effect on next year's crop. Alas, the herd is large and these negligible effects add up. Next year everyone is hungry.

Rational behavior is no vaccine against inefficiency. In each of our examples, every individual acts rationally—the male bird who grows his tail long, the college student who extends his years of schooling, the cow who eats a little more than she promised to. If rationality cannot save us, what can?

Remarkably—incredibly—miraculously—there is an answer. Under quite general conditions, when goods are produced and exchanged in competitive free markets in which people trade at market prices, economic activity leads to efficient outcomes. This fact is what economists have in mind when they talk about the Invisible Hand.

In the 18th century Adam Smith described the economic actor who "intends only his own gain" but is nevertheless led "by an invisible hand to promote an end which was no part of his intention," that end being the welfare of society, which economists call efficiency. The metaphor endures, having survived countless misinterpretations. It has been said that Smith was expressing a religious sentiment, a faith that Providence oversees our affairs. It has been said more often, most recently by my physicist friend, that Smith meant something like this: Individual rationality, coupled with the ruthless pressure of natural selection (in the marketplace as in the biosphere), must necessarily serve the social good and the ultimate advancement of the species.

But if Smith had meant that, he would have been wrong. Any bird of paradise could tell you so. What he did mean was something far more subtle and far more remarkable: Individual rationality, coupled with competition *and prices,* leads to efficient outcomes; that is, outcomes in which there remain no unexploited opportunities to improve everybody's welfare. This is so even though individual rationality and competition *without* prices rarely leads to such desirable outcomes.

The Invisible Hand Theorem is not at all obvious, but it is true. In the 1950s the economists Gerard Debreu and Lionel McKenzie, working separately, successfully translated the Theorem into a statement of pure mathematics and rigorously proved that statement. Their accomplishment is one of the triumphs that ushered in the modern age of economics.

Along with its modern formulation, the Invisible Hand Theorem has acquired a modern name. It is now called the First Fundamental Theorem of Welfare Economics, and it can be stated succinctly: Competitive markets allocate resources efficiently. There is also a Second Fundamental Theorem of Welfare Economics, which deals with the fact that there are many different ways to allocate resources efficiently. The Second Fundamental Theorem says this: No matter which of the many efficient allocations you want to achieve, you can always achieve it by first redistributing income in an appropriate way, and then letting competitive markets function freely.

The critical feature in the formulations and proofs of these theorems is the existence of market prices. Without prices, there is no reason to expect efficient outcomes. I see no analogue of prices in the origin of species, and conclude that evolutionary biology bears only the most superficial resemblance to the economics of the marketplace.

I cannot hope to explain completely why the Invisible Hand Theorem must be true. But I do think that I can give enough of its flavor to clarify the crucial role of prices. The next few paragraphs will be just slightly rougher going than the rest of this chapter, but with a little close attention I think you'll find them understandable. Your reward will be a glimpse of one of the great intellectual achievements of humankind.

Suppose that I appoint you the czar of American agriculture. It has been determined that 1,000 bushels of wheat will be produced in America this year, and your job is to ensure that it is produced as cheaply as possible. How do you manage this?

What you want to avoid is having one farmer spend $10 producing a bushel of wheat that some other farmer could have produced for, say, $4. That would make the national wheat supply $6 more expensive than it needs to be.

So you start by investigating the cost of wheat production on each individual farm. That's more complicated than it sounds, because even within one farm, the cost varies from bushel to bushel. My friend Miranda owns a farm, and she finds that coaxing her land to yield two bushels of wheat costs more than twice as much as coaxing it it to yield one. So the information you need includes not just the total cost of producing, say, 100 bushels of wheat on

Miranda's farm, but the cost of producing the first of those bushels, the cost of producing the second, the cost of producing the third, and so on. And you'll also want to know the projected cost of producing bushels 101, 102, and 103, even if they're not currently being produced.*

Okay, suppose you've somehow managed to gather all that information. How do you use it?

Well, suppose Miranda produces 100 bushels of wheat, and you've determined that the cost of her 100th bushel is $10. At the same time, her neighbor Nathan produces 100 bushels of wheat, and you're aware that he could produce a 101st at a cost of, say, $4. Now here's where you earn your keep: You order Miranda to produce one fewer bushel, order Nathan to produce one more, and thereby reduce the cost of the national wheat supply by $6.

Well, since that worked so well, maybe you should try it again. But now the numbers are different. Miranda is producing 99 bushels, not 100, so you'll need to know the cost of her 99th bushel. Say it's $9. Then if Nathan can produce yet another bushel at a cost of, say, $5, you can repeat your trick and save the world another $4.

Eventually you reach a point where the cost of an additional bushel is the same on both farms; now your trick won't work anymore. But that doesn't mean your job is finished. It only means you should start over with another pair of farmers. Your work isn't done until the cost of an additional bushel is the same on every farm.

That bears repeating: To produce wheat at the lowest possible cost, you must ensure that *the cost of an additional bushel is the same on every farm.*†

---

* As a general rule, these numbers tend to increase, at least beyond a certain point, so the 103rd bushel is more expensive than the 102nd, which is more expensive than the 101st.

† In case you like jargon, the cost of growing an additional bushel on a given farm is what economists call the *marginal cost* of growing wheat on that farm.

In principle, that's all there is to it. In practice, you might be more successful passing camels through eyes of needles. Not only do you need to know the cost of producing each individual bushel of wheat on each individual farm; you need to update your information every time there's a change in a weather forecast or a fuel price; every time a tractor breaks down or a farmhand calls in sick; every time there's a bit of extra space available on a delivery truck (because the cost of delivering wheat is part of the cost of producing it).

Here, though, is a better plan: Announce a price of wheat. (You are the czar, after all.) If you announce a $6 price, then every farmer will produce every bushel that costs her less than $6—and will choose *not* to produce any bushel that costs her more than that. If Miranda's 100th bushel costs her $10 and Nathan's costs him $4, you won't *have* to tell Miranda to produce one fewer and Nathan to produce one more. Thanks to the profit motive, they'll do this of their own accord. They and other farmers continue to make adjustments until the cost of one additional bushel is just about $6 on every farm. The cost of an additional bushel is the same on every farm! That's exactly what it takes to minimize the total cost of the national wheat supply.

Let it be emphasized that no farmer cares about minimizing the total cost of the national wheat supply—it is "an end which was no part of his intention." Yet she or he is led to this end as if by an Invisible Hand.

Note the key role in all this of a *single* market price. If different farmers face different prices, the whole thing falls apart. If Miranda can sell her wheat for $12 a bushel while Nathan is forced to sell for $2, then Miranda will produce the bushel that costs her $10 and Nathan will fail to produce the bushel that costs him $4. For us as a society, that's a forgone opportunity to save $6.

In a well-functioning price system, everyone faces the same

price, which is why the price system, when it works smoothly, minimizes the cost of wheat production. But it does far more than that.
For reasons similar in flavor to what you've just seen, it also guarantees that we get the right *quantity* of wheat: neither too much (in
the sense that we'd have been better off diverting resources to some
other activity) nor too little (in the sense that we'd have been better
off with more wheat and less of something else).

Even more is true. An economy consists of far more than just a
wheat market, and economic activity consists of far more than just production. Here is the gist of the two Fundamental Theorems of Welfare
Economics: Even when we consider a complete economy, with many
goods and many activities, all of which interact with one another in
complicated ways, the existence of competitive markets and market
prices is exactly what is required to guarantee efficient outcomes.*

The world abounds with inefficiency, and to the untrained eye
much of it seems to be the result of "cutthroat competition" or
"markets run amok." But the Invisible Hand Theorem tells us that
if we seek the source of inefficiency, we should look for markets that
are *missing*, not for markets that exist. We should look for goods
that are not priced, which often means that we should look for
goods that are not owned.

Consider pollution. A factory emits noxious smoke, causing discomfort to its neighbors. This might or might not be inefficient.
The factory benefits some (its owners, people who buy its products, perhaps others who interact with it more indirectly) while
hurting others (the neighbors). In principle, we can measure all

---

* Some other conditions must be satisfied as well. For example, when different groups
of people have access to significantly different information, the Invisible Hand Theorem
may fail. This is essentially what went wrong in the earlier example with the college students, who know more about their own abilities than employers do.

of the gains and losses in dollar terms (for example, by asking the neighbors, How much would you be willing to pay to get rid of the factory? or How much money would the factory have to give you before you were glad it was there?). The factory might, on balance, do more good than harm, in which case it is efficient for it to be there, pollution and all. But it is equally possible that it does more harm than good. If so, its existence is inefficient.

What is the ultimate source of this inefficiency? Some might say it is the consequence of too much market capitalism and the unenlightened pursuit of profits. Actually it is the consequence of too *little* market capitalism: There is no market for air.

Suppose that somebody owned the air around the factory and could charge for its use. The factory would have to pay for the right to pollute, while the residents would have to pay for the right to breathe freely. This creates a powerful disincentive for the factory to continue polluting. Even if the air belonged to the owner of the factory, there would be the same powerful disincentive, because by polluting he forgoes the opportunity to sell clean air to the neighbors! Regardless of who owns the air—the factory owner, some of the neighbors, or an absentee "airlord"—the factory is likely to stop polluting. In fact it is not hard to show that the factory will continue to pollute if and only if that is the efficient outcome.

None of this is meant to imply that it would be easy to organize and maintain a market for air, or that this is a practical way to deal with the problem of pollution. What it is meant to illustrate is this: Inefficiencies arise from missing markets. Wherever there is an inefficiency, it is a good bet that a missing market is lurking (or, more precisely, failing to lurk) in the background.

African elephants are hunted for their ivory at far too great a rate, and these magnificent animals may be headed for extinction. While this problem may have no simple solution, it *does* have a simple cause: Nobody owns the elephants. An owner—any owner—would want to be sure that enough elephants survive to keep him in business. The demand for beef is far greater than the demand for ivory, but cattle are not threatened with extinction. The key to the difference is that cattle are owned.

Similarly paper companies have every incentive to replenish the forests they own, and these forests are in no danger of disappearing. Concerned environmentalists advocate recycling paper so that fewer trees are harvested. Ironically, the companies respond to the reduced demand for trees by maintaining smaller forests. A world where paper is recycled is a world with fewer trees.*

Roy Romer, the former governor of Colorado (and the father of a prominent economist), once told a story about going for a walk on an autumn day and watching each Denver homeowner blow his leaves into the next homeowner's yard. He concluded that the problem consists of too *many* markets; we'd all be better off if nobody bought a leaf blower. Perhaps his son could have told him that there are also too *few* markets: If there were a way to charge the neighbor for using your yard as a trash can, the problem would vanish.

The governor was onto something, though: Two missing markets can be better than one. We know from Adam Smith that it would be best if there were markets for everything. But *given* the fact that there is no market for yards-as-trash-cans, it *can* be better to eliminate the market for leaf blowers as well.

On the other hand, the governor's description does not ring true to me. In my neighborhood you don't blow leaves onto your

---

* The North Carolina Forestry Association, in its FAQ on recycling, raises the question, "Does cutting down trees for papermaking lead to deforestation?" and answers, "No . . . Forest products companies not only allow trees to grow back but actually encourage new growth by replanting and caring for trees and by creating forest lands in areas where they previously did not exist."

neighbor's lawn. Or if you do, then you don't count on him for favors, like taking in your mail when you're away. In fact there is something very like a market, with a going price to be paid for violating unspoken rules. Even without any formal organization, markets tend to develop precisely because they are such powerful tools for improving everyone's welfare.

Today we are everywhere enjoined to respect the delicate ecological balance of nature, in which each creature is so miraculously designed to fill its special niche, and in which each part interacts in glorious intricacy with the whole. Let us save some respect too for the equally delicate structure of the marketplace, which routinely accomplishes feats that even nature dares not attempt.

CHAPTER 9

OF MEDICINE AND CANDY, TRAINS AND SPARKS

Economics in the Courtroom

Frederick Horatio Bridgman was a prominent citizen of Victorian London—by royal appointment, confectioner to Her Majesty the Queen. Among his other perks, Bridgman worked from home, where he operated two giant mortars and pestles producing delicate sweets for the royal family and slightly less delicate sweets for sale to the general public. He got along well with his neighbors, including the distinguished Dr. Octavius Sturges, a member of the Royal College of Physicians.

In 1879 Dr. Sturges built a new consulting room at the end of his garden, adjacent to Bridgman's kitchen. Only after the construction was complete did he discover that, thanks to Bridgman's machinery, it was pretty noisy back there. How noisy? Noisy enough, according to Dr. Sturges, to completely drown out the beating of his patients' hearts when he tried to examine them with his stethoscope.

As long as Bridgman ran his mortars and pestles, Dr. Sturges's consulting room was unusable. Eventually Sturges brought suit in an attempt to shut Bridgman down.

The judges who heard the case believed their decision would matter not just to Bridgman and Sturges, but to the community at large. If they ruled for Sturges, the neighborhood would have one more medical office and one less candy maker. A ruling for Bridgman meant the opposite.

But the judges were wrong. They were in fact powerless to affect the allocation of resources between candy and medical care. In a case like this, no matter how the judges rule, the enterprise that survives is the one that's worth more to its owner.

Take an example: Suppose Bridgman values his candy business at $200 and Sturges values his medical practice at $100. If the judges favor Bridgman, allowing him to operate his machinery at will, then of course Bridgman goes on quite merrily making candy. If, on the other hand, the judges favor Sturges, allowing him to shut Bridgman down, then—well, you might suppose that of course Sturges shuts Bridgman down. But that's not at all what happens. Instead Bridgman somewhat less merrily trots around the corner, knocks on Sturges's door, and offers him, say, $150 to throw away the judges' order and let him go on making candy. *Either way*, Bridgman stays in business.*

Or take a different example: Suppose Bridgman values his candy business at $100 and Sturges values his medical practice at $200. If the judges rule for Sturges, allowing him to shut Bridgman down, then he surely shuts Bridgman down and resumes his medical practice. If, on the other hand, the judges rule for Bridgman, allowing him to make noise freely, then Sturges offers Bridgman, say, $150 to shut off the damned machines—and, once again, resumes his medical practice.

What the two examples have in common is this: In neither case does the court's decision have any effect on whether Sturges practices medicine or whether Bridgman makes candy. Economists are fond of summarizing this observation by saying that the court's decision "does not matter."

---

* Depending on their bargaining skills, Bridgman might get away with offering only $101, or Sturges might hold out for $199.

Bridgman and Sturges might not approve this wording, because as far as they're concerned, the decision matters very much indeed. It's definitely more fun to have a court rule in your favor than to shell out $150 to get your way. So a more precise statement is that while the judges' decision matters to Bridgman and Sturges, it doesn't matter to anyone else. The decision does not change the allocation of resources; it has no effect on what gets produced or how. Economists are usually far more concerned about the allocation of resources than about transfers of income between individuals; we reveal our priorities when we say that judicial opinions "don't matter."

The conflict between Sturges and Bridgman is ultimately a conflict over control of a resource, that resource being the air around Sturges's office, which Sturges wants to use as a contemplative atmosphere and Bridgman wants to use as a dumping ground for noise. The law can grant control of this resource to either party, and the court can protect that grant in a variety of ways. It can give Sturges the power to shut Bridgman down, in which case an economist would say that Sturges is protected by a *property right* to the air, or it can require Bridgman to compensate Sturges for any damage to his medical practice, in which case we say Sturges is protected by a *liability rule*. There are similar options if the court wants to favor Bridgman.

But whoever controls the resource, and however his control is protected, he'll find it to his private advantage to direct that resource to its most profitable use, regardless of whether that use is by him or by his neighbor. The court can't control the profitability of either enterprise, and therefore it can't control how the resource is employed.*

---

* Perhaps the best way to see this is to note that there's one set of arrangements that maximizes the joint profits of the candy and medical businesses. Surely both parties can agree to institute those arrangements, and then split the profits. No matter how much you and I may squabble about the best way to split a pie, the one thing we'll agree on is that the pie should be as big as possible.

This startling observation about the impotence of judges might be obvious once stated, but it was once very far from obvious to the world's best economists. The first economist to think hard about this issue, and the first to get it wrong, was Arthur C. Pigou nearly a century ago, in his pioneering study of the economics of *externalities*. (An externality is a cost imposed on others, like Bridgman's noise.) Pigou argued that polluters (including noise polluters like Bridgman) always behave very differently when the law restrains them, and somehow, for decades, all economists believed him. It took a law professor named Ronald Coase to set them straight.

One day about fifty years ago, Professor Coase, then teaching at Virginia, requested permission to visit the University of Chicago, the world center of research on the interaction between law and economics, and explain exactly how Pigou (along with every other economist then living) had gotten this wrong. This was even gutsier than it sounds. A Chicago economics seminar can be notoriously similar in tone to a gladiatorial event. I've witnessed this on several occasions, including one where a prominent full professor from an Ivy League university was reduced literally to tears as his research was being shredded in a Chicago seminar room.

Coase's seminar has become legendary among economists. It drew the most brilliant and intellectually relentless audience imaginable. George Stigler, one of the four future Nobel laureates in the room, recalled the audience as a "simply superb" collection of theorists and the occasion as one of the intellectual highlights of his life. Before the talk, a vote was taken. There were 20 votes for Arthur Pigou and one for Ronald Coase. Stigler later commented, "If Ronald had not been allowed to vote it would have been even more one-sided."

Stigler's recollection continues: "As usual, Milton [Friedman] did much of the talking. . . . My recollection is that Ronald didn't persuade us. But he refused to yield to all our erroneous arguments.

Milton would hit him from one side, then from another. Then, to our horror, Milton missed him and hit us. At the end of the evening the vote had changed. There were 21 votes for Ronald and no votes for Pigou." Soon the entire profession had been won over, and eventually Coase was awarded a well-deserved Nobel prize for ushering in a new era in the economic analysis of law.

In Coase's honor, his observation about the impotence of judges has come to be called the *Coase Theorem*. It applies whenever the parties to a dispute can negotiate, strike bargains, and know that their bargains are enforceable.

But there are clearly many circumstances where the Coase Theorem doesn't apply, because negotiation is either impossible or prohibitively expensive. This can happen, for example, if the number of parties to a dispute is very large.

For example, railroads sometimes run tracks through farmland. The trains throw off sparks, which occasionally ignite the surrounding crops. Farmers suffer damage, for which they demand compensation from the railroad. What are the consequences of rulings for or against the farmers? How would various rulings affect the number of trains that are run, or the quantity of crops brought to market, or the amount of land devoted to farming?

If there's only one farmer involved, and if there are no impediments to negotiation, then the Coase Theorem answers "None" and "Not at all." If the court grants the farmer the right to order the trains off his land, the railroad can always buy back the right-of-way. If the court rules that the trains can run but the farmer must be compensated, the railroad can either stop running trains, or run fewer, or install spark-control equipment, or go ahead and pay the damages, or eliminate the damage by offering the farmer a flat fee to remove his crops. If the court denies the farmer any legal recourse, he can pay the railroad to stop running trains, or to run fewer, or to install spark-control equipment, or he can go ahead and live with the damage, or he can remove his crops. Just as in the case of *Sturges v. Bridgman*, the Coase Theorem tells us that any solution that is instituted following a ruling for the railroad will also be instituted following a ruling for the farmer, and vice versa.* The only thing the court can really decide is who pays whom.

But when many farmers are affected, as opposed to just one, the situation becomes more complicated. Arranging a negotiation among a hundred individuals leads to obvious logistical problems. And more subtle difficulties crop up. Even when a contract is reached that benefits everyone, any single farmer can threaten to hold out and refuse to sign unless he is given a share of everyone else's gains. If several farmers adopt this tactic, there can be a hopeless impasse.

So in a case like this, the court's decision *does* matter. Whatever the court orders is unlikely to be undone by subsequent negotiations. If the railroad is made liable for crop damage, it might run fewer trains or install spark-control equipment, but it is unlikely to be able to strike deals with all of the farmers to remove their crops. If the railroad is freed of liability, the farmers might remove their crops but are unlikely to form a coalition to buy spark-control equipment for the railroad.

Which liability rule yields the more efficient outcome? Prior to that legendary Chicago seminar, economists would unanimously have answered "Make the railroad liable." The argument is this: The railroad creates sparks, the sparks create damage, and therefore the railroad should be forced to account for that damage each time it decides to run another train. If running a train brings the railroad

---

* Once again, the key is to note that there is one set of arrangements that maximizes the joint profits of the farm and the railroad, and that's the set of arrangements the parties will ultimately agree on.

$100 worth of profit while inflicting $200 worth of crop damage, then it is economically inefficient for the train to run. How do we convince the railroad not to run such trains? Make them pay the $200 cost.

Coase analyzed this argument and pronounced it wrong. It goes wrong exactly where it says that "the sparks create damage." In fact what creates damage is the simultaneous presence of sparks and crops in the same place. In view of this, it makes no more sense to say that "the sparks create damage" than it does to say that "the crops create damage." If either sparks or crops are removed, the problem goes away.

It's true that each additional train causes more burned crops, but it's equally true that each additional crop planted near the tracks causes more burned crops. It's true, as Pigou would have observed, that if you free the railroads from liability, they have no incentive to run fewer trains or install spark-control equipment. That's bad. But if you make the railroads liable, so the farmers are fully reimbursed for all fire damage, then *they* have no incentive to remove their crops or install a firebreak. That's also bad, if removing the crops or installing a firebreak is a cheap and easy solution to the problem. *Is* it cheap and easy? Economic theory can't tell you that.

And so we come to the flip side of the Coase Theorem and the second of the two great intellectual bombshells Professor Coase dropped on those Chicago economists: When circumstances prevent negotiations, entitlements—liability rules, property rights, and so forth—*do* matter. Moreover the traditional economist's prescription for efficiency—making each individual fully responsible for the costs he imposes on others—is meaningless. It is meaningless because any conflict between two activities is exactly that: a conflict between two activities. It therefore makes no sense to ascribe all the harm to one activity or another.

Pigou's great insight was that things tend to go badly when people can escape the costs of their own behavior. Factories pollute too much because someone other than the factory owner has to breathe the polluted air. Railroads run too many crop-destroying trains because the crops belong to someone else. Farmers keep too many unfenced rabbits when they don't care about the lettuce farmer next door. The solution, he said, was to make sure that people *do* feel the costs of their actions, via taxes, fines, or liability rules. Do a dollar's worth of damage, and you're charged a dollar.

Coase's great insight was that Pigou's analysis runs in both directions. If my factory pollutes your air, I've imposed a cost on you, but if you try to restrain my behavior, then *you've* imposed a cost on *me*. After all, if you lived someplace else, you wouldn't be complaining about my smoke and I wouldn't have all these taxes and fines to pay. If my railroad sets your crops on fire, I've imposed a cost on you, but if you insist on planting crops near my railroad tracks (and then suing me for the damage), then *you've* imposed a cost on *me*.

And as for that rabbit farmer—the one who lets his rabbits run wild on the lettuce farm next door—where Pigou would have insisted that the rabbit farmer cover the damages, Coase is more even-handed. There are a lot of ways for the rabbit farmer to solve this problem: Put the rabbits in cages, or file down their teeth, or raise a different breed of rabbit, or switch to keeping geckos. There are also a lot of ways for the lettuce farmer to solve this problem: Fence the lettuce, or spray it with rabbit repellent, or move away, or switch to growing barley. If the rabbit farmer is immune from lawsuits, he'll have no incentive to implement his solutions. But if the lettuce farmer is routinely reimbursed for lost lettuce, then *he'll* have no incentive to implement *his* solutions. Which outcome is worse? That depends on whose solutions are better. Pure theory can't tell you.

For three months in 2010 oil gushed uncontrollably into the Gulf of Mexico. By the end almost 5 million barrels of oil had escaped, and the Gulf's fishing and tourism industries were devastated. In response to apparent pressure from the White House, BP (the oil company formerly known as British Petroleum) set up a $20 billion fund to compensate the victims.

Journalists and bloggers were quick to explain that economic theory recommends such compensation so that BP and others will have an incentive to be more careful in the future. This would have been accurate if economic theory hadn't advanced at all in the past 50 years. The conclusion—that BP should be held liable for damage—might be correct, but we now understand that it also might not be. And the resolution lies not in theory but in facts.

The journalists have learned the lesson of Arthur Pigou: We get better outcomes when decision makers feel the consequences of their actions. But they have ignored the lesson of Ronald Coase: Pigou's observation cuts both ways. Thousands of shrimp boats were idled partly because BP drilled for oil in the Gulf, but also partly because the shrimpers chose to operate in the vicinity of an oil rig. Compensation makes BP feel the consequences of its actions, but only at the cost of shielding the shrimpers from the consequences of theirs.

Economic theory does not weigh in on the question of whether it's more important to get the incentives right for BP or for the shrimpers. That depends on the value of the oil, the value of the shrimp, the cost to BP of modifying its drilling methods, and the cost to the shrimpers of either trawling elsewhere or finding a different occupation.

What, then, is a court supposed to do? Much depends on what the judges are trying to accomplish. If their goal is something other than economic efficiency—if their primary concerns involve justice, or fairness, or some abstract legal criterion—then economic analysis has relatively little to contribute. But if the goal is economic efficiency, then there is much to be learned from Coase's analysis and the body of knowledge that has grown from it. Judges often express explicit interest in the economic consequences of their actions, and economists believe that such considerations have played a major role in the evolution of the common law. For now, I will imagine a judge who shares these concerns, and ask what advice we can give him.

First, we can offer a note of reassurance: If the opposing parties can negotiate and enforce contracts, then your decision does not matter and you cannot be wrong. Subsequent negotiations will lead to an efficient allocation of resources that is entirely independent of what you decide.

Second, a note of caution: Don't try to decide a case by deciding who's at fault. Even if you think that you can make sense of this notion, there is no reason why it should lead to an efficient decision. The costs of damage should be borne by the party who can prevent the damage more cheaply, not necessarily by the one who would be labeled the "perpetrator" by misguided common sense.

Third, a note of condolence: It's often not easy to determine who can prevent the damage more cheaply. Suppose you announce in court that the trains will be liable for spark damage *unless* farmers can prevent the damage at low cost, in which case the trains bear no liability. Do you then expect the farmers to reveal that they can prevent the damage at low cost? Of course they won't, and unless you are an expert in both farming and railroading, you are unlikely to know where to place the burden.

Fourth, a suggestion: Try to make it easier for the parties to negotiate. If they can, then we are back in the situation where you can't go wrong.

Let me expand a little on this suggestion by way of an example. The example does not pretend to take account of everything that might be important in the real world; it is stripped down to illustrate a point.

Coal miners suffer a lot of work-related injuries. The number and severity of these injuries can be reduced if owners install safety equipment. According to the Coase Theorem, the decision about whether to install such equipment is independent of whether owners are liable for injuries to miners.

If a machine can be installed for $5,000 that prevents $8,000 worth of medical costs, an owner who is required to pay those medical costs will install it. If the owner is *not* required to pay medical costs, then he will *still* install the machine, because his employees will offer him some amount like $7,000 to do so. (In practice, the form of this payment is likely to be an acceptance of lower wages.)*

Therefore, from the point of view of getting the right amount of safety equipment installed, the judge cannot go wrong no matter how he rules.

However, there is another way to prevent accidents: Miners can behave more cautiously while underground. If they are liable for their own medical costs, they have an incentive to be cautious. But what if the owner, rather than the miners, is liable for those medical costs?

On the one hand, you might think that if the owner covers all their medical costs, the miners will be less cautious. On the other hand, you might remember the Coase Theorem: The owner can offer to raise the miners' wages in exchange for their cautious behavior. The resulting level of care is exactly the same as when the miners themselves are liable.

That's exactly right if the pay-for-caution contract is enforceable. But let's add another twist: The owner offers each miner an

---

* Conversely, if the same machine prevents only $4,000 worth of injuries, then it will *not* be installed, regardless of whether the owner is liable.

additional $10 per day in exchange for exercising extra caution in the mine. The miners accept the money, descend into the dark earth where the owner never goes, and continue to engage in horseplay just as if there had been no bargain. The owner is never the wiser.

In this case, the unenforceability of the contract, brought on by the unobservability of the miners' behavior, renders the Coase Theorem inapplicable. Miners *do* behave differently—and more recklessly—when somebody else is paying their medical bills.

Now let's put ourselves in the judge's position. He has no idea whether the safety equipment is cost-justified because he has no experience in mining and no good way to estimate how many accidents it will prevent. He does not know whether cautious behavior by the miners is cost-justified for the same reason (and also because he has no way of estimating the monetary equivalent of the cost to a miner of being always on his guard).

But he does know this: If the miners bear their own medical costs, all things are possible. They will voluntarily choose caution if caution is efficient, and they will pay the owner to install safety equipment if the equipment is efficient. However, if the costs fall on the owner, only half of all things are possible. It is still true that there will be safety equipment if safety equipment is efficient. But there cannot be caution, because caution requires an enforceable contract, which requires that the owner observe the miners' behavior, which is impossible.

The moral in this simple example is to let the miners bear the costs of accidents so that *every* cost-justified means of preventing accidents can be adopted. The greater moral is that judges should assign liability in such a way as to maximize the opportunities for post-trial negotiations. Because judges are not omniscient, they should make rulings that can be easily reversed through bargaining among the participants. It is the participants, after all, who know the most about the costs and benefits of their own actions.

The suggestion here, then, is that the court shouldn't even attempt to estimate costs and benefits that are best revealed through private negotiations. The right question for the court to consider is: Which liability rule is least likely to interfere with those negotiations? We might not always know the right answer, but finding the right question is progress of a sort.

III

How to Read the News

CHAPTER 10

CHOOSING SIDES
IN THE DRUG WAR

How the Atlantic Monthly *Got It Wrong*

Richard J. Dennis is the former chief adviser to the Drug Policy Foundation in Washington, DC. He is also a hypersuccessful commodities trader, having once turned $1,600 into a reported $200 million over a period of 10 years. He's a former part owner of the Chicago White Sox, has been a member of several foundation boards, and the author of a serious contender for the most poorly executed cost-benefit analysis ever to appear in print.

I learned some of this from Wikipedia and most of it from the *Atlantic Monthly*, which once had the poor judgment to publish an article by Mr. Dennis entitled "The Economics of Legalizing Drugs." His affiliations and career are advertised in the "Contributors" section at the front of the magazine. His championship exhibition of economic illiteracy is on display in the article itself.

Mr. Dennis concludes that the benefits of legalization would exceed the costs, and I have no doubt that his conclusion is correct. But he reaches that conclusion only by counting costs as benefits, counting benefits as costs, omitting a variety of important factors on each side of the ledger, and double counting some of those that he remembers to include.

A fiasco of this magnitude merits wider recognition. We learn from the mistakes of others, so it is a stroke of fortune to find so many mistakes gathered in a single place. There are more recent examples of bad cost-benefit analyses, but none that manages quite so thoroughly to commit every conceivable error. What better way to master the principles of cost-benefit analysis than to analyze a single study that violates them all?

For example:

Principle 1: *Tax revenues are not a net benefit, and a reduction in tax revenues is not a net cost.* Mr. Dennis estimates that if drugs were legalized and taxed, governments could earn at least $12.5 billion in revenue every year, and he counts that revenue as a benefit of legalization. But tax revenues are just money out of one person's pocket and into another's. From the viewpoint of the entire society—the viewpoint on which cost-benefit analysis insists—they are neither gains nor losses. There is no point in computing them, and they should neither be added nor subtracted on either side of the ledger.

If tax revenue represented a net gain to society, then it would follow that the road to riches is for government to tax every activity at the highest possible level. After the revenue was redistributed, it could be taxed again to create still more wealth. Nobody who has ever paid taxes will have difficulty finding the flaw in this scheme: Whatever the tax collector gains, the taxpayer loses.

If the government ordered everybody with an even-numbered address to pay a dollar to somebody with an odd-numbered address, nobody would argue that there had been a net increase in society's resources. If the government imposed a tax of $1 on each of the 150 million Americans who live at even-numbered addresses and distributed the proceeds to people at odd-numbered addresses, government revenue would increase by $150 million without any net benefit to society.

Of course, this assumes that the government *does* redistribute the income, either directly (say, through Social Security payments) or indirectly (say, by building a post office or maintaining a national park). If instead the government chose to spend its $150 million in newfound revenue on some wasteful project rather than distributing it, then society would be made poorer. But this impoverishment should be attributed to the wasteful project itself, not to the taxation that financed it. The tax revenue per se is neither a net benefit nor a net cost.

Mr. Dennis rests a lot of his case on the observation that if drugs were legal we could tax them. But if the goal is to raise taxes, there is no need to legalize drugs; there are plenty of other activities available to tax. If there is a social benefit to legalization, it must lie elsewhere.

Principle 2: *A cost is a cost, no matter who bears it.* At this point Mr. Dennis has counted $12.5 billion in nonexistent benefits of drug legalization. To this he adds another $28 billion per year that could be saved in government expenditures on the arrest, prosecution, and imprisonment of drug law violators. Having grossly overestimated the benefits of tax revenue (which, correctly measured, are $0, not $12.5 billion), he now veers off in the other direction by grossly underestimating the cost of law enforcement.

Mr. Dennis's $28 billion consists of direct cash outlays by the government. But he has forgotten to add those costs of imprisonment that are borne by the prisoners themselves. Several hundred thousand of them are deprived of opportunities to hold jobs, care for their families, or walk on the beach. Legalization would restore those opportunities. That benefit is at least of the same order of magnitude as what Mr. Dennis thinks law enforcement agencies could save.

Now some or all of these benefits might accrue to some pretty unsavory characters or to characters whom one or another of us might judge to be undeserving. But they are benefits nonetheless, and must be counted as such. Cost-benefit analysis makes no moral distinctions; it simply totals all of the good that arises from an action and contrasts it with the bad. If a drug dealer is unhappy or unproductive when he is in jail, his losses in that dimension are as much social costs as the jailer's salary and the cost of prison construction. The prospect of abolishing those costs is a legitimate benefit of legalization.

How are we to place a monetary value on the prisoner's potential freedom? In principle, the right number to use is determined by the prisoner's willingness-to-pay: It is the dollar amount that he would be willing to sacrifice to avoid a prison term. In practice, we can approximate this number by the income that the prisoner could earn by virtue of his freedom. (This may be a poor approximation but the best one available.) That income, added over all drug-related prisoners, is certain to run into many billions of dollars. To this we should add the costs that drug users incur in their attempts to avoid detection, prosecution, and conviction, which Mr. Dennis also overlooks.

Principle 3: *A good is a good, no matter who owns it.* Mr. Dennis believes that drug use causes crime and in particular is responsible for $6 billion per year in theft. He views this theft as a $6 billion cost of prohibition. But stolen property does not cease to exist. When a television set is moved from one house to another, it remains as reliable a source of entertainment as it ever was. This is true even when the new recipient of those services is a thief or a dealer in stolen property.

Theft does have social costs. One is the value of the thief's time and energy, which might otherwise have been employed in some productive capacity. (If I spend an afternoon plotting to steal your bicycle, we end up with one bicycle between us; if I spend the same afternoon building a bicycle, we end up with two.) But this cost is probably far less than the value of the property stolen.

The least efficient thief in America must expend about $100 worth of effort every time he steals $100. If his costs were below $100, others even less efficient than he would find thievery profitable; those others would enter the profession, and he would no longer be the least efficient thief in America. If his costs were more than $100, he wouldn't remain a thief for long.

But that describes only the *least* efficient thief. Because other thieves are more efficient, they must each be able to steal $100 worth of property with *less* than $100 in effort. Consequently the value of stolen property almost always overstates the cost of stealing it.

On the other hand, we have not yet accounted for all of the social costs of theft. Other costs arise from victims' efforts to protect themselves by purchasing burglar alarms, hiring police and security guards, and avoiding walks in risky neighborhoods. When these are accounted for, the social cost of crime could be either more or less than the value of the stolen property. Therefore Dennis's $6 billion could either underestimate or overestimate the benefit of reducing crime via drug legalization; my own guess is that it is a substantial overestimate. In any event, the number $6 billion is totally irrelevant to the correct calculation.

To summarize the case so far, Mr. Dennis counts the following as annual benefits of drug legalization: $12.5 billion in tax revenue (a $12.5 billion overestimate), $28 billion in savings in law enforcement costs (a gross underestimate, because it ignores the value to prisoners of being free), and $6 billion in theft prevention (a completely random estimate that measures the value of stolen property but has nothing to do with the true cost of theft). To this he adds $3.75 billion saved on military expenditures to fight Colombian drug lords, for a total annual benefit of $50.25 billion.

Having completed his survey of the benefit side, Mr. Dennis turns his analytical powers to the calculation of costs. Here he starts right off by violating the most important principle of all:

Principle 4: *Voluntary consumption is a good thing.* Mr. Dennis recognizes that legalization would lead to lower drug prices and an increase in drug use. He counts this as a *cost* of legalization.

But consumers who can increase their consumption as the result of lower prices are reaping a benefit, not bearing a cost.

Of course, this assumes that people know what's best for themselves, and one might argue that in the case of drugs, this isn't always true. But all of the theoretical machinery that has been set up to justify cost-benefit calculations relies crucially on this assumption; consequently cost-benefit analysis is impossible without it. Either we accept the assumption, or we are forced to evaluate policies on something other than a cost-benefit basis.

Because Mr. Dennis wants to do cost-benefit calculations, let us accept the required assumption and estimate the benefit of legalization.

When you are hungry enough to pay $15 for a pizza and are able to buy one at the market price of $10, economists say that you have earned $5 worth of *consumer's surplus*. You earn some consumer's surplus on almost everything you buy; the maximum you are prepared to pay almost always exceeds the amount you actually do pay in the marketplace. In a competitive economy in the long run, all of the benefits created by markets tend to show up in the form of consumer's surplus. In almost any cost-benefit analysis, consumer's surplus is one of the major sources of benefit.

When the price of pizza falls from $10 to $8, your consumer's surplus increases, for two reasons. First, you earn an additional $2 worth of consumer's surplus on each pizza that you buy, just because the price is lower. Second, you probably buy more pizzas and therefore have more opportunities to earn surplus. (Some people might even start eating pizzas for the first time, earning surplus where before they earned none.)

The first of these—the advantage of a lower price—is not a real social benefit. Paying $8 instead of $10 for a pizza is nice for the consumer, but the pizza maker probably has a different view of the matter. Whatever the consumer gains from lower prices is offset by an equivalent loss to the producer. The lower price in and of itself does not affect the balance of costs and benefits when the interests of both consumers and producers are accounted for.

However, the *second* source of increased surplus—the fact that people eat and enjoy more pizza than before—is a genuine social gain and must be counted as a benefit. If a change in government policy caused the price of pizza to fall by $2, one of the critical tasks in analyzing that policy would be to estimate the increase in consumer's surplus from increased pizza consumption.

Likewise with drugs. For the sake of argument, let us accept the numbers in Mr. Dennis's article: 30 million cocaine users at the time of his writing, spending a total of $100 billion annually, and an additional 7.5 million users after legalization causes the price to drop to one-eighth of its current level.* A little arithmetic shows that those new users would spend a total of about $3 billion on drugs at the new low price. It is also reasonable to infer from these numbers that the total *value* of those drugs—the amount the new users would be willing to pay if necessary—is about $10 billion.†

Therefore legalization would create a net benefit for new cocaine users of over $7 billion per year. Even that estimate does not include gains to existing users who would increase their own consumption.

Instead of the $7 billion benefit that his own numbers imply, Mr. Dennis counts increased drug use as a $25 billion *cost*. Why $25 billion? That is his estimate of private health costs and lost personal income due to drug use by new users. (It is at least heartening to see that at this late juncture, Mr. Dennis has at last decided to

---

* These numbers, like all the numbers in this chapter, were current when Mr. Dennis's article was published. Today the numbers might have changed, but the correct mode of analysis is eternal.

† This number can be calculated from the numbers in this paragraph, a little economic theory, and an additional technical assumption. For econogeeks who are curious about the technical assumption, either a straight-line or a constant-elasticity demand curve will do.

start caring about lost personal income. Back when personal income was being *taxed* away, it didn't seem to bother him.)

In any event, the $7 billion increase in consumer's surplus is already net of health costs and lost income. Any such losses would have been reflected in people's willingness to pay for drugs and so would have been implicitly accounted for in the original calculation. Mr. Dennis, however, would have us list these personal expenses in a separate category, thereby violating yet another principle:

Principle 5: *Don't double count.*

"The Economics of Legalizing Drugs" is one of the worst cost-benefit studies ever done. Its author (presumably in common with the editors of the *Atlantic*) has failed to master two simple super-principles from which all of the other principles follow:

Only Individuals Matter

and

All Individuals Matter Equally

These are the rules of the cost-benefit game. You don't have to follow them, but if you don't, you're playing some other game.

If Mr. Dennis had remembered that only individuals matter, he would not have made the elementary error of counting government revenue as a good thing. The government is not an individual, so the government doesn't count. Government revenue *distributed to individuals* is a good thing, but is offset by the collection of taxes *from* individuals, which is a bad thing of equal magnitude. You can count both (in which case they cancel each other) or, more simply, you can count neither.

Despite what you may have heard, economists are entirely indifferent to what's "good for the country," "good for the economy," or "good for General Electric." If General Electric's profits increase by $100 million, economists will be pleased because the individual owners of General Electric are $100 million richer. If General Electric shuts down while the owners devote themselves to meditation, achieving a state of transcendent peace that they collectively value at $100 million, economists will be equally pleased.

Should Americans work harder and invest more to increase industrial production? The economist's answer is: Only if it makes them happier. Newscasters report economic growth as if it were a benefit with no offsetting cost. Growth does benefit individuals, because it allows them to increase their consumption in the future. The conditions that create growth impose costs on individuals, who must work harder and consume less in the present. Is the trade-off worth it? The answer depends solely on the preferences of the individuals themselves. What's "good for the economy" is not one of the economist's considerations.

If Richard J. Dennis had cared more about individuals than abstract entities like economies or governments, he would not have made the error of counting only *government* expenses when it came to law enforcement costs. (Government expenses *are* real costs, but *only* because the bills are ultimately paid by individual taxpayers.) He would not have overlooked the costs of individuals who spend time in jail, individuals who spend resources to shield themselves from crime, and individual drug offenders who spend resources to avoid being caught.

Because all individuals matter, and because different individuals can have opposing interests, we need a rule for weighing one person's preferences against another's. If we are called upon to decide whether to expand the logging industry, and if Jack values newspapers while Jill values woodlands, we need a way to compare Jack's potential gains with Jill's potential losses. There are many philosophically defensible stands here, and the logic of cost-benefit analysis (which is another name for what I have elsewhere called "the logic of efficiency") chooses unambiguously among them.* Its position is enunciated in our second superprinciple: All individuals matter equally, with the strength of their preferences measured by their willingness-to-pay. If Jack values a tree in the sawmill at $100 and Jill values a tree standing in the forest at $200, then we declare the benefit of logging to be $100 and the cost to be $200. We don't inquire into the moral worthiness of Jack or Jill.

In principle, if we envision a change in policy (say, from drug prohibition to drug tolerance), we can imagine the following experiment: Line up all of the people who support the status quo and ask each of them, "How much would you be willing to pay to prevent this policy from being changed?" Add the responses, and you have measured the total cost of the policy change. Now line up all of the people who support the change and ask each of them, "How much would you be willing to pay to see this policy changed?" The sum of their responses is the total benefit.

Our insistence on counting all individuals equally has some striking implications. One implication is that a change in price is never either good or bad. Whatever buyers gain, sellers lose. Price changes often result from changes in technology or in the legal environment, which can *simultaneously* affect production costs or consumption levels in ways that can be good or bad. But a price change *in and of itself* is neither a good nor a bad thing.

Following a substantial fall in interest rates back in 1992, the *New York Times* ran a feature article on what a fine development this was: Borrowers now found it easier to finance cars, homes, and capital equipment. As a minor caveat, the article acknowledged that the

---

* There are people who seem to believe that cost-benefit analysis should be purely objective in the sense of incorporating no moral preconceptions, as if that were possible.

picture was not so rosy for lenders; it referred to this problem as an unfortunate "secondary effect."

But an interest rate is like a price. For every borrower there is a lender, and every dollar borrowed is a dollar lent. *All* of the advantages of a low interest rate are exactly offset by its disadvantages. Borrowers and lenders matter equally.

When we set out to do a cost-benefit analysis, we commit ourselves to treat everybody equally. Buyers are on a par with sellers, borrowers are on a par with lenders, and drug dealers, thieves, and addicts are on a par with police officers, commodities brokers, part owners of the Chicago White Sox, and saints.

If Mr. Dennis had remembered that all individuals matter equally, he would have treated jail time for pushers as a cost and increased consumption for willing users as a benefit. He would have realized that shifting income around through taxes or through theft does not create or destroy any wealth; it only transfers wealth among individuals, all of whose preferences are equally important.

Perhaps Mr. Dennis does not fully approve of every philosophical or political implication of treating all individuals equally. No economist would deny his right to such a position, and many—quite possibly most—economists will have much sympathy for it. If that is his position, however, it commits him to evaluating policies on something other than a cost-benefit basis. Furthermore it is incumbent on him to tell us just what that alternative basis *is*. Enumerating a list of things that he is willing to consider costs and another list of things that he is willing to consider benefits is not terribly enlightening to the reader who wants to know whether the author's philosophical preconceptions match his own. Any policy analyst ought to reveal up front what his moral criteria are—and then present an evaluation that is demonstrably consistent with those criteria.

Many economists, much of the time, adopt the cost-benefit criterion as a general guide to policy.* Sometimes its implications make us uneasy. Confronted with a policy that would enrich an Internet gazillionaire by $1,000 at the cost of $900 to a struggling single parent, the cost-benefit criterion recommends acceptance. The same is true if the gazillionaire is replaced with a murderous organized crime chieftain. In such cases, I feel sure that almost every economist would want to depart from the strict application of the cost-benefit criterion.

Nevertheless when an economist is confronted with a policy decision, one of his first instincts is to analyze costs and benefits in accordance with the two superprinciples. There are at least two reasons for this instinct.

First, if the cost-benefit criterion is applied consistently, then most people will probably gain more than they lose over the course of many policy decisions. This is so even though any *particular* application of the criterion can hurt good people in unfair ways. When we ban logging to confer a $200 benefit on Jill at the cost of a $100 loss to Jack, Jack can at least take comfort in knowing that we will side with him in future controversies where his potential benefits are large. We who are guided by the cost-benefit criterion will be against you when you have a little to lose and for you when you have a lot to gain; on balance we will probably do you more good than harm.

Second, economists are fond of the cost-benefit criterion because they are skilled at applying it. Economic theory allows us to deduce what outcomes the criterion supports without having to do specific calculations. For example, we know on theoretical grounds that when property rights are well defined and markets are competitive, market prices maximize the excess of benefits over costs. In

---

* The cost-benefit criterion is equivalent to what I have called the "efficiency criterion" in other chapters.

these circumstances, we can confidently predict that a price control must be a bad thing relative to a market outcome, even without calculating any costs or benefits explicitly.

We like the cost-benefit criterion first because we think its application makes almost everybody better off over the long haul, and second because it is easy to apply. In other words, the benefits are high and the costs are low. The reasoning may be slightly circular, but the cost-benefit criterion recommends itself highly.

CHAPTER 11

THE MYTHOLOGY OF DEFICITS

At the rate of $1 per second, it would take over 400,000 years to pay off the national debt. Such facts titillate, but they do not enlighten. Unfortunately they've come to pervade public discourse and to crowd out the public's understanding of debt and deficits.* In place of that understanding is a collection of unsubstantiated beliefs—myths, if you will—that are routinely and uncritically repeated in the halls of Congress, the pages of the mainstream media, and the comments section of every blog on the Internet. These myths have become almost as widespread as they are indefensible.

The myths about the deficit underlie (at least) three grand misconceptions. One is that the numbers that are officially reported and widely analyzed actually reflect anything approaching economic reality. Another is that certain identifiable groups (individual taxpayers, "future generations," private industry in general) are clearly and unambiguously hurt when the government runs a deficit. A third is that government deficits affect interest rates via simplistic mechanisms that people think they understand.

---

* The government's *deficit* is the amount it borrows in a given year. The government's *debt* is the amount it owes altogether. A $100 billion deficit adds $100 billion to the debt.

The myths themselves bear individual dissection. But first, a parable to clarify the key ideas.

A PARABLE

Suppose you hire a professional shopper—let's call him Sam—to do your clothes shopping for you. Sam goes to the store, decides how much to spend and what to buy, and then decides how to pay for it.

To focus on that last decision, let's suppose that Sam has already decided, wisely or unwisely, to buy you a certain $100 suit. Now he has to decide how to pay for it. He's got three choices: Plan A is to withdraw $100 from your bank account and pay up front. Plan B is to use your credit card and pay off the debt a year from now, incurring a $10 interest charge along the way. (We'll assume an annual interest rate of 10 percent.) Plan C is to use your credit card and *never* pay off the debt, in which case you'll be billed for $10 interest every year, forever.

To calculate the effects of those options, let's assume you've got $1,000 in a bank account that earns the prevailing 10 percent interest rate.* In the absence of any clothes purchases, your balance next year would be $1,100. Anything Sam does will deplete that balance; let's calculate how much.

Plan A removes $100 from your bank account today, reducing it from $1,000 to $900. A year from now that $900 will have earned $90 interest, and your balance will be $990 instead of the $1,100 you'd have had if you'd bought no clothes. Where did the $110 difference go? Answer: Sam paid $100 up front; the other $10 is interest forgone *because* he paid up front.

---

* You might reasonably object that no bank account pays the same interest rate that you pay on your credit card. But bear with me; I promise this example will be instructive.

Under Plan B, there are no payments until next year, when your bank balance will be $1,100. From this, Sam will withdraw $110 to pay the credit card bill ($100 principal plus $10 interest), leaving you with a balance of exactly $990—the same as Plan A.

Which do you prefer, Plan A or Plan B? There's really no reason to care. Plan A costs you $100 for the clothes plus $10 in forgone interest; Plan B costs you $100 for the clothes plus $10 in interest paid. Same difference.

Then there's Plan C: Charge the purchases and never pay down the principal—a policy of "eternal debt." After a year on this plan, you've got $1,100 in the bank, from which Sam deducts $10 to make the first interest payment. That leaves you with $1,090. But it also leaves you with a commitment to pay $10 a year forever, which forces you to set aside a fund from which to make these payments. How big a fund do you need? Answer: $100, which is just what it takes to generate $10 a year in interest.

So your bank balance is $1,090, but of this there is $100 that you dare not withdraw. This leaves you with usable assets of $990— exactly the same as you would have under Plan A or B.

Questions of finance, then, can safely be left to Sam; it makes no difference what he decides. If he plunges you into debt, you will incur interest charges, but you'll earn just enough more on your savings to exactly cover those charges. The whole thing is a wash.

That's not to say you might not be very unhappy (or very happy) with Sam for some other reason. If you think he has a habit of spending too much or too little, or if you think his taste in clothes hasn't changed since 1983, maybe you'll want to fire him. (Or if he's got a knack for finding bargains, you might want to renew his contract.)

Likewise, you might be very unhappy with a government that you think spends too much or too little or unwisely. But once the level of spending has been set and the spending projects have been chosen, there are only three ways to pay for them: Your government can tax you today; it can borrow money and pay off the debt (with interest) at some future date, taxing you on that date to get the needed funds; or it can borrow money and keep rolling the debt over forever, periodically taxing you enough to meet the interest payments. The analogy between your Uncle Sam and Sam the Shopper suggests that it doesn't make a bit of difference to you which method is selected.

In fact—and this is important—the parable becomes more realistic when we replace Sam the Shopper with Sam the Government. We have been assuming that your savings account's interest rate is the same as your credit card's. That (as I said in the footnote on page 129) is almost surely false. But when the government acts as your shopper, it borrows at the Treasury bill rate, which you surely *can* earn, simply by investing your savings in Treasury bills.

Now there's a lot left out of this parable. If you expect to die in six months, and if you don't care about the size of your bequest, then you can come out ahead by running up huge debts due a year from now. That undermines the moral that says you won't care whether Sam pays with cash or credit. (On the other hand, if you view your heirs' well-being as an extension of your own, the moral is restored.) Also, individuals might have preferences between being taxed now and being taxed later if they expect to be in different tax brackets at different times.

Another thing left out is that taxes, unlike bank withdrawals, have unpleasant disincentive effects, and there are good arguments for spreading those disincentive effects equally over time, rather than letting them pile up and pummel us all at once. That's an argument for trying to keep current and future tax rates roughly equal, which is the same thing as not letting the debt get too large (or too small!).

But the analogy is still a powerful one, which suggests that if deficits do "matter," then they do so for rather subtle reasons. It demonstrates that deficits, in and of themselves, are no better or worse than taxation and makes it plausible that our primary concern should be with the level and composition of government spending, rather than with how that spending is financed.

Now to the myths.

MYTHS ABOUT WHAT THE NUMBERS MEAN

The official measurements of government spending (and consequently of government deficits) arise from a hodgepodge of numbers that are arbitrarily added together with no theoretical justification. These figures include actual consumption of resources by the government (e.g., spending for education or the military), transfer payments (like Social Security), and interest on past debt. The result of adding together these apples, pears, and oranges (and then subtracting tax revenues to compute a deficit) has no economic significance, although it appears to be a powerful totem in our society. Government agencies attempt to estimate it, newspapers solemnly report it, and bloggers agonize over it. None of them ever seems to ask what the number signifies. Here are some of the myths underlying the widespread acceptance of this meaningless calculation.

Myth 1: *Interest on past debt is a burden.* Interest payments on past debt are counted as expenditures in the calculation of the deficit, which creates the impression that these payments are a net burden to the taxpayer. They're not.

Suppose the government borrows $5 in order to avoid raising your taxes this year. True, this adds $5 to your debt burden—but it also adds $5 to your savings account. A year from now, your debt burden has grown to (say) $6—and so has that extra $5 in your savings account.

In other words, the interest on past debt pays for itself. The burden of that interest is canceled by the anti-burden of the interest you earn on your savings, leaving you on balance with no burden at all. Therefore interest on past debt should not be included in any meaningful measure of government spending or government deficits. But it always *is* included, which means that all reports of the size of the deficit are, at least on this account, grossly over-estimated. (Later we'll see some reasons why it might be grossly *under*estimated.)

Ironically, politicians frequently depict interest on the national debt as the *most* burdensome component of the deficit—the exact opposite of the truth!

Myth 2: *A dollar spent is a dollar spent.* According to this myth, a dollar spent in erecting a government office building (which consumes real resources, like steel and labor, that might otherwise have been employed elsewhere) is the equivalent of a dollar paid out by Social Security (which makes one person richer and another poorer without consuming anything). But clearly the first is a burden in a sense that the second is not, and any number that results from pretending they are equivalent must be highly suspect.

No private business would make this error. When General Electric spends a dollar to refurbish a factory or buy art for the corporate lobby, that's an expense. But when General Electric mails money to its shareholders, that's not an expense—it's a dividend. When the U.S. government spends a dollar to build a tank or hire a forest ranger, that's an expense. But when the U.S. government mails money to a Social Security recipient, that's very like a dividend. If we count the Social Security recipient among "the taxpayers"—and why shouldn't we?—then the payment doesn't cost the taxpayers a dime. It merely moves money around from one taxpayer to another. (Contrast this with a dollar spent buying a missile or maintaining a national park, where the payee is required to do an honest day's work or supply actual goods, thereby forgoing alternative income opportunities.)

That's not to say you can't have strong opinions about those transfer programs. Unlike GE, which is required to treat all shareholders equally when it mails out dividends, the government sometimes favors one group over another when it mails out transfer payments. If you're a member of the unfavored group, you might have a legitimate gripe. But that gripe has nothing to do with the deficit.

Myth 3: *Inflation doesn't count.* Inflation is a boon to any debtor, including the government. If the government owes $15 trillion, then a 5 percent annual inflation rate reduces the real value of that debt by $750 billion every year. That $750 billion is government revenue, just as surely as $750 billion raised in taxes is government revenue, and it ought to be counted as such. It isn't.

Myth 4: *Promises don't count.* Suppose a new president promises to increase spending on highways or education or military preparedness. Even before the program gets under way, that promise is a debt (just as my promise to send you a $100 check next week is a debt). It should therefore probably be counted in calculating the current deficit. It isn't.

The problem gets trickier if there is legitimate uncertainty about whether the president will actually deliver on his promise. If I promise to send you a $100 check next week and neither of us is sure how serious I am, is that a debt? There's no clear answer.

As of this writing, official statistics peg the national debt at somewhere between $14 and $15 trillion. But that doesn't count the government's promises to maintain Social Security and Medicare.

When you make a payment to the Social Security system, it's called a tax; when you collect a benefit, it's called a transfer payment. That's how the current accounting system works. But a different and equally legitimate accounting system might count payments into the system as loans to the government, and count benefits as repayments of those loans. That simple change in labeling would add another $8 trillion or so to the national debt. Do the same for Medicare and you've added almost $40 trillion more.

So why is the government debt reported as roughly $15 trillion instead of somewhere north of $60 trillion? Only because somewhere back in the mists of time, some accountant performed the equivalent of a coin flip. How much economic significance can underlie a number whose value depends on a perfectly arbitrary choice among equally legitimate accounting methods?

MYTHS ABOUT THE BURDEN OF THE DEBT

Next we come to myths about the burden of the debt. Since it's not clear that the debt *is* in any sense a burden, it might seem superfluous to examine these too closely. But these myths are particularly seductive, and I think it's worth fully exposing their flawed foundations.

Myth 5: *There's nothing I can do to escape the burden of the debt.* Sure there is. You can pay off your share. Any time you like, in fact.

Let's say your share of the national debt is $50,000, on which the government makes an annual $1,500 interest payment. That money has to come from somewhere, so every year your tax bill is $1,500 higher than it would be in a government-debt-free world. That $1,500 a year is, presumably, the burden you claim you can't escape.

What you seem to be wishing, then, is that the government would pay off its debt once and for all and relieve you of that annual $1,500 obligation. That's tantamount to wishing that the government would, once and for all, take $50,000 from you, pay off your share of the debt, and lower your taxes by $1,500 a year forever. The government, however, stubbornly refuses to do this.

No problem. Here's what you do: Take $50,000, put it into a savings vehicle that pays the same interest rate the government is paying,* and pretend that your $50,000 is gone forever. Every year you'll earn $1,500 in interest, which you can arrange for your bank to send directly to the government for credit toward your tax bill. And every April 15 you can subtract $1,500 from what you owe the government.

That strategy is exactly equivalent to paying off your share of the debt and escaping your burden forever. Feel free to use it.†

Myth 6: *Tax revenue for the government is like income for a household.* Suppose that year after year, you spend more than you earn. You are worried that you've become fiscally irresponsible. Which of the following could be paths back to fiscal sanity for your household?

(a) Spend less.
(b) Earn more.
(c) Stop at the ATM so you'll have more money in your pocket.

I hope it's crystal clear that (c) is a really bad answer. Now let's try another one.

Suppose that year after year, your government spends more than it collects in taxes. You are worried that it's become fiscally irresponsible. Which of the following could be a path back to fiscal sanity for your government?

(a) Spend less.
(b) Collect more tax revenue.

The myth is that collecting more tax revenue for the government is analogous to earning more income for the household. But a much

---

* For example, you could put it all into government bonds.

† Of course if you prefer *not* to use it, it's probably because you think you have something better to do with that $50,000. So why are you asking the government to tax it away?

closer analogy is that collecting more tax revenue is like visiting the ATM. In most circumstances, this makes (b) a really bad answer.

The government's debt *is* the taxpayers' debt. If we pay down the debt through higher taxes, we will, to a large extent, pay those taxes by drawing down our savings. Drawing down your savings to pay for an ill-advised government program is no more "fiscally responsible" than drawing down your savings to pay for a $500 haircut.

When it comes to that haircut, you're unlikely to placate an angry spouse by saying, "Don't worry dear; I got the money from our retirement account." If you consider some government programs unwise and extravagant, you shouldn't be placated by a tax increase that induces you to withdraw funds from that same account.

Here's another way to say essentially the same thing: The government's chief asset—in fact, pretty much its only asset—is its ability to tax people, now and in the future. The taxpayers are the government's ATM. Make a withdrawal today, and there's less available tomorrow.

Now, the ability to tax is a pretty huge asset and the U.S. government has never come close to depleting it. (In some other countries, the situation is grimmer.) But no matter how much you've got in the bank, a policy of ever-increasing withdrawals can't make you richer.

The moral is that "deficit reduction" in and of itself makes no sense as a policy goal. Spending programs are sometimes wise and sometimes unwise, but for the most part they deserve to be evaluated on their merits, not on how they're financed. Which brings us to the next myth:

Myth 7: *A tax increase is the economic equivalent of a spending cut.* When a woman gives birth to twins and then murders her husband, the best headline for the story is *not* "Population Increases by One."

Likewise when government spending increases by $50 billion and tax revenue increases by $40 billion, the big story is not that the budget deficit increased by $10 billion. Instead there are two big stories, one about taxes and one about spending. Like birth and death, these are of independent interest.

Myth 8: *Our debts will make our grandchildren poorer.* The only way to make your grandchildren poorer is to spend their inheritance. You can do this yourself, or your government can do it for you. But debt-financed spending hurts your grandchildren no more (and no less) than pay-as-you-go spending. Spend a dollar today, put it on the national credit card, and your grandchildren will owe two dollars tomorrow. Spend a dollar today out of your interest-bearing savings account, and you'll reduce their inheritance by that same two dollars.

Once the money's spent, our grandchildren are hosed no matter what. We can't undo the damage. If we tax ourselves to make a one-dollar debt payment today, we can certainly free our grandchildren from a two-dollar debt burden tomorrow, but only at a cost that undoes the favor: We pay the tax out of our interest-bearing savings accounts (or, if we don't have savings accounts, we borrow to pay the tax), and there goes two dollars out of their inheritance.

Myth 9: *The Myth of Crowding Out.* It is argued that government borrowing uses resources that could be better employed in the private sector. This is wrong because government borrowing does not use any resources. What consumes resources is government *spending.* If the government buys a million tons of steel, then a million tons of steel become unavailable to the private sector. This is equally true whether that steel is bought with tax revenues or with borrowed funds.

MYTHS ABOUT INTEREST RATES

Once upon a time, it was an article of faith among journalists and politicians that the public debt and the interest rate are like a kite and its tail: When one goes up, the other must follow. Economists were more skeptical.

Ever since the financial crisis of 2008 ushered in an era of soaring public debt and historically low interest rates, those same journalists and politicians have quietly abandoned their theories, though few have had the grace to acknowledge that maybe the economists knew something all along.

But old fallacies never die, and I predict with confidence that every time the interest rate blips upward, these will be disinterred. There are already those who argue that the post-2008 years somehow don't count.

Perhaps they're right. I don't claim to know whether or how government debt affects the interest rate. What I do claim is that the usual arguments—the ones you'll see on the blogs and the editorial pages—make no sense. They rest on the next two myths.

Myth 10: *The Goliath Myth.* According to this notion, the country is populated by little "Davids" competing against the "Goliath" of the federal government for a limited supply of money. This competition drives up interest rates to the point where poor David can't even afford to finance a slingshot.

What this overlooks is that borrowed money doesn't disappear. The government borrows a dollar, uses it to buy a paper clip, and that dollar is immediately available for David or anyone else to borrow all over again.

Myth 11: *The Myth of Competition.* Here the fallacy runs like this: "If the government wants to borrow more, it's got to convince more people to lend to it. This means it's got to offer higher interest rates. Then everyone else must offer higher interest rates to stay competitive."

The mistake is believing that the only way to get people to lend more is to pay a higher interest rate. In fact a different way to get people to lend more is to put more money in their pockets, say by keeping their taxes down—which is exactly what happens when we run a deficit.

Here's another way to think of this: The government spends a dollar this year on your behalf. Instead of collecting that dollar today, they run a deficit and promise to collect the dollar (with interest) sometime in the future. That's exactly like taking your dollar and then lending it right back to you. Every dollar of deficit spending is automatically accompanied with an implicit one-dollar loan to the taxpayers.

There is no limit to how much you can borrow as long as you simultaneously lend the same amount. If you don't believe me, try this experiment: Find a friend, and simultaneously lend $10 trillion to each other. The next morning, pick up a copy of the *Wall Street Journal* and see how much effect you've had on the market interest rate.

Not every false argument reaches a false conclusion. It's perfectly possible that government debt affects interest rates. But if it does, it's for reasons substantially subtler—and substantially less certain—than the usual myths suggest.

The only way to drive up an interest rate is to get people to spend more. Government debt puts more money in people's pockets, which might indeed make them spend more. But at the same time, it might make them expect higher future tax bills and shake their faith in Social Security and Medicare; if so, they're likely to save more, and therefore spend less. Depending on how accurately people perceive the future, the net effect could be either more or less spending, and hence either higher or lower interest rates.

Or maybe debt leads people to spend more because it puts money in their pockets today, and they expect to be in their graves before the repayments come due. In other words, they buy more stuff because they expect their grandchildren to pay the bills—effectively reducing the value of their bequests, possibly below zero. This is possible, but not terribly consistent with all the rhetoric about how we're all so concerned with saving for our grandchildren. People who have prioritized saving for their grandchildren rarely seek to leave negative bequests.

(Ironically, "deficit hawks" frequently argue that the more we care about our grandchildren, the more important it is to pay down the government's debt. Arguably the exact opposite is true. A deficit holds down your taxes at your grandchildren's expense. The more you care about your grandchildren, the more likely you are to add those tax savings to their inheritance. Therefore the more we care about our grandchildren, the less the deficit can hurt them.)

The magnitude (and direction) of these effects is an empirical question, and, because of the many confounding factors that also affect interest rates, not an easy one to settle.

Those who would engage the public's attention find it useful to have an instinct for the sensational. So it's not surprising that those myths about the deficit that have found their way into public circulation all tend to exaggerate either its size or its importance or both. It's important to deflate such myths and to defuse the near-hysteria they engender. But it's also important not to be lulled into a false sense of security.

Every argument in this chapter assumes a fixed level of government spending. There is no question that excessive spending can be detrimental, in precisely the ways that excessive deficits are often claimed to be.

Indeed the most harmful effect of deficits might very well be that they distract attention from our most urgent economic priority, which is to get spending under control. If we fail to meet this challenge, our obsession with balanced budgets can't save us from the consequences.

CHAPTER 12

UNSOUND AND FURIOUS

Spurious Wisdom from the Media

My Uncle Morris collected meat, which he stored in the freezers that lined his basement. When you went to visit him, he'd take you on a proud tour of his collection, pointing out a roast from 1975 and a prime rib that he'd picked up on his honeymoon.

Me, I collect bad economic reasoning. I scan the Internet for snippets of extraordinary ignorance, and I keep them in a file that I've labeled "Sound and Fury," partly because people who are flat-out wrong are often simultaneously flat-out angry, and partly because, while not all these tales are told by idiots, they are at least told by people who (as happens to all of us on occasion) have succumbed to a moment of idiocy.

Unlike some of my other hobbies, this one occasionally pays off, in the form of a choice exam question that begins with the words "Prove you are smarter than the editor of the *New York Times* (or *Forbes*, or the *Wall Street Journal*) by identifying the irredeemable error in the following article."

Let me give you a brief tour of my collection.

From the front page of the *New York Times* (June 7, 2010):

New York Nannies May Get a Workers' Bill of Rights

New York may soon become the first state to offer employment protection for nannies.

The state Senate passed a bill of rights for domestic workers this week, a measure that would require employers to offer New York's approximately 200,000 household workers paid holidays, overtime pay and sick days.

Supporters say the step will provide needed relief to thousands of women—and some men—who are helping to raise the children of wealthier New Yorkers without any legal workplace rights beyond the federal minimum wage.

Now a reporter with the opposite bias might just as well have written:

New York Nannies May Suffer from New Employment Restrictions

New York state may soon become the first state to restrict employment opportunities for nannies.

The state Senate passed a bill this week that would prohibit New York's approximately 200,000 household workers from accepting any position that does not include paid holidays, overtime pay and sick days.

Opponents say the step will bring unnecessary hardship to thousands of women—and some men—who have found employment because of labor markets that operate freely, except for constraints imposed by the federal minimum wage.

A more neutral observer might have noted that this bill, if passed, will be good for some nannies who retain their jobs, bad for the many nannies who will be driven out of the business, bad for those nannies who would prefer to take less vacation in exchange for higher pay, and extremely good for people like Ai-jen Poo, director of the National Domestic Workers Alliance, who will represent the winners and can conveniently ignore the losers. Instead Ms. Poo is quoted, without apparent irony, as calling the measure "a huge step forward in reversing the long history of exclusion that domestic workers face."

The mistake here is to confuse the legislation's *stated purpose* with its *likely effects*. If you make workers less valuable to their employers, then employers will hire fewer workers. Then, as workers compete for a smaller number of jobs, wages are likely to fall.

Sometimes people find this hard to believe, because they know too many people who would never give up their nannies over an issue of overtime pay. Here's what that overlooks: First, it's not always safe to generalize from the people you happen to know. Second, and more fundamentally, there always *must* be people who are on the verge of firing their nannies. If there were no such people, then competition for nannies would intensify, raising nannies' wages and pushing people to that verge. (This is one of the key insights of labor economics.) And third, it doesn't take very many laid-off nannies to have an effect that cascades through the whole profession.

My collection contains a whole subgenre of stories that declare some piece of workplace legislation a "victory" for precisely the group that has the most to lose from it. Family leave legislation requiring employers to provide lengthy maternity leaves is hailed as a victory for female workers, but it seems odd to label as "victors" those whom the legislation comes closest to rendering unemployable. Job applicants aren't even allowed to opt out of the program in a voluntary bid to rise to the top of the applicant pool, or in exchange for a higher wage. Therefore the natural advantage that the legislation confers on male workers (who are also eligible for family leave benefits, but are much less likely to claim them) is really cemented in. In my "Irony" subfolder, I have a transcript of an old presidential debate where Al Gore hammered away at the first Bush administration on the issue of family leave ("Did you make it *mandatory?* Why didn't you make it *mandatory?*")—immediately after extolling the virtues of *choice* in the abortion segment of the program.

Likewise when a court ruling made it easier for surrogate mothers to renege on contracts and keep the babies they had carried, a spate of editorials were quick to hail a victory for potential surrogate mothers—but it was a "victory" that for several years rendered surrogacy contracts all but obsolete. (Since then the legal situation has evolved differently in different states.) If the court had ruled that henceforth all mortgage payments are voluntary, would the same editorialists have hailed a victory for home buyers, or would they have realized that the court had made it nearly impossible to buy a home?

In the same genre, the *New York Times* reported on the plight of Harriet Ternipsede, an airline ticket agent whose employer monitored her every keystroke, so that her supervisor was alerted instantly if she so much as stopped to stretch her muscles.

The *Times* took it for granted that Ms. Ternipsede would have been better off without a supervisor breathing down her neck at every moment. But strict supervision doesn't just allow the employer to observe low productivity; it also allows him to observe high productivity—and to reward it. An employer who can observe, reward, and thereby elicit high productivity is an employer willing to pay higher wages.

If you doubt that, consider the opposite extreme. Imagine a world where your employer had *zero* information about your work performance, to the point of not even being able to tell whether you've been showing up every day. Unless you are an extraordinarily motivated employee, you won't put much effort into that job. Your employer, recognizing that fact, won't be willing to pay you very much. Clearly employees are better off with *some* monitoring. If some monitoring is good, then it's an empirical question how much monitoring is optimal.

March 2011 marked the 100th anniversary of the fire at the Triangle Shirtwaist Factory, the worst industrial disaster in New York's history. A hundred forty-six workers died in that fire, most of them young women. The great tragedy was that escape routes were cut off by doors that had been locked to prevent employee pilfering. In the aftermath of the fire, the New York state legislature passed over two dozen new occupational health and safety laws. Henceforth all workplaces were required to have well-marked (and unlocked!) fire escapes.

Both the newspapers of 1911 and the newspapers of 2011, in their coverage of the centennial, declared the new safety legislation a victory for workers. Perhaps it was. But also, perhaps, it wasn't. I can find no evidence that any journalist, then or now, has deigned to investigate that question before passing judgment.

For a garment worker in 1911, open doors mean greater safety, and safety is valuable. That's a good thing. But open doors also mean more pilfering, which makes workers less valuable and leads to lower wages. That's a bad thing. The interesting question is: How would a well-informed garment worker in 1911 have felt about that trade-off?

I don't know the answer, but here's some relevant information: First, the labor market in the garment industry was highly competitive on both sides. There were hundreds of garment factories in New York, some of them in the same building as the Triangle Factory. (The fire was confined to Triangle's three floors.) They drew their workers from the teeming tenements of the Lower East Side, both as direct employees and as independent contractors.

Second, in a competitive labor market, the forces of supply and demand ensure that workers are paid their marginal product. (For this there is ample theory and evidence that no economist disputes.) What this means is that a seamstress who adds $6 a week to the company's revenue can expect to be paid $6 a week (a historically accurate wage rate).

Now I turn to the back of my envelope. Suppose the typical employee pilfers two blouses a week, with a wholesale value of 60 cents apiece. (Sixty cents is a guesstimate based on a retail value of a little over a dollar, which I found by perusing an old Sears catalogue. Two blouses a week is a number I pulled out of thin air. Feel free to adjust my assumptions, and the subsequent calculations, in whatever direction you think makes them more realistic.) That employee's marginal product falls by $1.20, so competitive pressures force her wage to fall by $1.20 also. That's a 20 percent wage cut, though it's partly offset by having a full clothes closet, an infinite supply of rags, and presumably a profitable little sideline selling shirts at half price. Call it the equivalent of a 10 percent cut.*

And so the question becomes: Would our typical employee have considered it a victory to gain a fire escape and lose 10 percent of her income? Again, I don't know the answer. I don't believe that I would trade 10 percent of my income for a fire escape, but that proves almost nothing because I don't work in a wooden building filled with fabric and tissue paper. At the same time, I'm a lot fur-

---

* These calculations are for the average worker. The average *honest* worker feels the full 20 percent wage cut.

ther from starvation than a garment worker in 1911. So introspection tells me little about what the worker would have chosen.

What other evidence could we look to?

On the one hand, there seems to be no pre-fire record of workers offering to take wage cuts in exchange for better fire safety, or of firms anticipating that they could cut their wage bills by putting in fire doors. There was plenty of labor unrest, but as far as I am aware it was all about wages and hours, not safety. The most straightforward reading is that workers preferred higher wages to more safety, but of course an alternative reading is that workers were blissfully unaware of the extent of the fire risk.

On the other hand, there is an extensive post-fire record of workers applauding those same safety regulations, despite the fact that the regulations must have depressed wages. The most straightforward reading is that workers preferred more safety to higher wages, but of course an alternative reading is that workers were blissfully unaware of how the law affected their wages. Another alternative reading is that pilfering was never such a big problem in the first place, so the effect on wages was minimal. (It's hard to measure the effect directly because wages change for so many other reasons as well.)

Sorting all this out would be a major project for an economic historian; it might be a great topic for a PhD thesis. I certainly don't expect a newspaper article to be the equivalent of a PhD thesis, but it would be nice if the authors at least admitted that these issues exist rather than jumping to the naive conclusion that workplace safety laws—even in the extremely unsafe environment of the Lower East Side in the early 20th century—are always, on balance, a boon for workers.

In May 2010 a Boston water main broke, rendering tap water undrinkable (unless it was boiled) for several days. This inspired the news department at Boston station WHDH to produce some highly emotional footage about two tragic side effects—side effects that, as far as the folks at WHDH could tell, appeared to be entirely unrelated.

The first report, on price gouging, featured a woman weeping—weeping!—because her son had been charged $1 a bottle for water instead of the recent sale price of $3.99 for a case of 24. The clear implication was that store owners who raised prices were making a bad situation worse.

The second report featured frustrated customers who had visited up to five stores and/or waited in long lines to buy bottled water. Apparently nobody at WHDH thought to ask how much longer those lines might have been if prices hadn't risen.

In fact the whole *point* of prices is that they adjust quickly to market conditions, and that's a *good* thing. Even a purely altruistic convenience store owner who refuses to profit from a crisis would be well advised to raise the price of water and donate the proceeds to charity, rather than allowing all the water to be snapped up by whoever happens to arrive first or manages to elbow everybody else out of the way.

The underappreciation of prices is a substantial genre in my Sound and Fury file. It infects, for example, almost all coverage of the locavore movement, the branch of environmentalism that promotes locally grown food, often with an eye toward minimizing the energy costs of transport.

Andrew Martin of the *New York Times* reported recently on a series of challenges to locavorian orthodoxy from a team of researchers at the University of California, Davis. What if shipping fruit by the truckload from California to Chicago uses less fuel than delivering it by pickup to individual farmers' markets? What if the energy cost of shipping a tomato from California to New York is less than the energy cost of growing that same tomato in a heated greenhouse on the Hudson? What about the energy cost of packaging, or the energy spent by consumers making multiple trips to local markets instead of one weekly trip to the grocery store?

So off we go on a merry chase through what Mr. Martin calls a dizzying ethical maze. The implicit recommendation seems to be that when you choose a tomato, you should ideally care about *all* the energy costs.

And so you should. You should also care about the myriad *other* costs your food habits impose: the grapes that were sacrificed by growing a California tomato where there might have been a vineyard, the morning commutes that are lengthened because the New York greenhouse displaces a conveniently located housing development, the cab rides and teaching services and bartending and art projects that California or New York workers might have provided if they hadn't been growing tomatoes, the sacrificed alternative uses of the fertilizers and the farming equipment—or better yet, the resources that went into producing those fertilizers and farming equipment—in each location.

Traditional locavores ignore 99 percent of what's important. Mr. Martin and the Davis researchers improve on that by ignoring only 98.5 percent. The problem with both groups is that they're insensitive to the quality of our environment. They've forgotten that our homes, schools, and work and leisure opportunities are also part of our environment, so that a calculation focused exclusively on carbon footprints must be ludicrously incomplete.

Unfortunately it would be impossibly difficult to list all the relevant costs of eating a New York or California tomato. Fortunately it's not necessary. There is a single, easily observable number that reflects *all* of those trade-offs. That number is called the *price* of the tomato.

When additional New York land is needed for a housing development or a theater complex, the price of New York land rises and the price of New York tomatoes follows. When California workers are needed to build an aquarium or put out a forest fire, the price of California labor goes up and the price of a California tomato follows suit.

Markets aren't perfect, so the price of a tomato does not, with 100 percent accuracy, reflect the social cost of acquiring that tomato. But in most circumstances it comes tolerably close, and in virtually all circumstances it comes a lot closer than the kind of crabbed accounting you might find in the *New York Times*.*

Now a dedicated locavore might quite reasonably respond that there are important costs *not* reflected in the price, for example the environmental costs associated with carbon emissions from heating a greenhouse. The way to account for those costs, though, is not to ignore all the costs that *are* reflected in the price. It's to start with the price, and make some adjustments that usually turn out to be relatively minor.†

The other quite marvelous thing about the price is that it not only reflects most costs, but it also gives you a reason to care about them. Not directly, of course—few tomato consumers stop to think about the grapes that were sacrificed for their pleasure—but indirectly, and that's just as good. The more valuable those grapes, the more you'll

---

* The *Times* is not infallibly fallible. It also published a piece by the historian and self-described "liberal curmudgeon" Stephen Budiansky that starts off down Mr. Martin's road to confusion but makes a midcourse correction toward sanity, concluding that the best way to make use of precious resources like land, favorable climate, and human labor is to grow food wherever it can be grown most efficiently and then pay the relatively tiny energy cost to get it to market. To an economist, the phrase "most efficiently" automatically means "accounting for all the relevant forgone alternatives." I am 95 percent sure Mr. Budiansky meant the same.

† Of course, once you start making adjustments, there's no reason to restrict yourself to carbon emissions. You might equally observe that taxes are relatively high in California, so the price of California tomatoes overstates the social cost of producing them. (Unlike, say, the cost of land that's needed for an aquarium, taxes don't represent social costs, because somebody gets to collect them.) Once you start correcting for imperfections in prices, there are a lot of corrections to make, and there's no particular reason to think that on balance they'd point you toward the local tomato.

pay for your tomato, and the more likely you are to pause and ask yourself whether this particular tomato is really necessary.

Mr. Martin, then, earns two spots in the Sound and Fury file: one for the error of focusing on energy costs to the exclusion of everything else we value, and one for failing to recognize how much socially valuable information is reliably packed into a price.

In a March 2010 *New Yorker* essay, Elizabeth Kolbert takes at face value the widely reported statistic that "the average level of self-reported happiness, or subjective well-being, appears to have been flat going all the way back to the nineteen-fifties, when real per-capita income was less than half what it is today." Starting with the assumption that these self-reports tell us something about actual happiness, Kolbert proceeds to muse on the policy implications, quoting former Harvard president Derek Bok with approval:

> If rising incomes have failed to make Americans happier over
> the last fifty years, what is the point of working such long
> hours and risking environmental disaster in order to keep on
> doubling and redoubling our Gross Domestic Product?

Wait a minute now. Self-reported happiness has been flat for 50 years despite rising incomes. Self-reported happiness has also been flat for 50 years despite dramatic increases in leisure and environmental quality. (Since 1965 the average American has gained about six hours a week of leisure, the equivalent of seven vacation weeks a year.) So why aren't Bok and Kolbert asking why we bother to come home from the office, take vacations, and clean our air and water?

Either you take this happiness research seriously or you don't. If you do, you can't just pick and choose the policy implications you happen to like. If these numbers imply that we have nothing to gain from earning more, then they also imply that we have nothing to gain from working less.

It would be discouraging indeed to learn that none of the advances of the past 50 years—the nearly 10-year increase in life expectancy, the nearly 75 percent drop in infant mortality, those six extra leisure weeks a year, the improvements in air and water quality, instant access to information and entertainment, the ease of communication—have done nothing whatsoever to make Americans happier.

Fortunately there are plenty of reasons to be skeptical that self-reported happiness numbers tell us much of anything about actual happiness. For example, the city of Somerville, Massachusetts, circulates an annual questionnaire asking residents, on a scale of 1 to 10, "How happy do you feel right now?" The problem with such surveys is that when people are asked "How happy are you?," the question they actually answer is liable to be something like "Are you happier than normal?" or "Are you happier than your friends?" Regardless of the ambient level of happiness, about half of us will always answer "no."

The average American man is about two inches taller than men 100 years ago, but you might never learn that from a survey that asks people "Are you tall?" That's because a 5'9" man would probably have answered "yes" 100 years ago and "no" today. Likewise people might be far happier today than people 100 years ago, but you might never learn that from a survey that asks "Are you happy?" or "How happy are you?"

Nigerians, with a per capita annual income of $1,400, rate themselves as happy as the Japanese, who are 25 times as rich. Kolbert, channeling the public policy professor Carol Graham, entertains several possible explanations (maybe Nigerians have "happy DNA"; maybe the Japanese strive harder because they are malcontents; maybe people learn to adjust to living on a few dollars a day), but never manages to stumble on the most obvious explanation of all: Maybe poor Nigerians, with their $1,400 incomes, their 48-year life expectancies, and their near-world-champion infant mortality rate, say they're happy because *they've never seen how happy it's possible to be.* Perhaps raising their incomes could help with that.

The journalist Elizabeth Lesley Stevens reports on Charles Kendrick, eccentric heir to the $84 million Schlage lock fortune, who apparently does pretty much nothing but park and repark his four cars around San Francisco all day, sometimes pushing them up and down the city streets from one parking spot to another.* It would be a good thing, suggests Ms. Stevens, if wealthy heirs like Mr. Kendrick were heavily taxed to support worthy government programs. After all, she seems to imply, a man who does nothing but push cars around will hardly miss the money. Why not take some of that $84 million and use it to construct, say, a classroom building in Berkeley?

The problem here is that classroom buildings are not made out of money; they're made out of glass and steel. They require land and they require labor. In other words, they require resources. And you can't get any substantial resources from Mr. Kendrick, because (at least if he really does nothing but push cars around) he's neither hoarding nor consuming any substantial resources to begin with.

Whether or not the building project is wise, it's sure to be expensive, and if it's expensive, somebody's got to bear the burden of that expense. The burden is borne by people who consume fewer resources so that Berkeley can have more. Who, exactly, are those people?

That depends on how Mr. Kendrick is storing his wealth at the point when you tax some of it away. If he's got it in a bank account, from which he makes a withdrawal to pay his taxes, then the bank-

---

* "The Idle Rich Should Give Something Back: Taxes," *New York Times*, April 16, 2011.

ing system can make fewer loans, interest rates rise, and those rising rates cause someone, somewhere, to abandon a building project or put off buying a new car. That frees up the resources that allow Berkeley to have its new classroom building.

Alternatively, if Mr. Kendrick has been storing his wealth in a mattress stuffed with green pieces of paper, and if he uses some of those pieces of paper to pay his taxes, then he's effectively increased the money supply. (Money stuffed in mattresses doesn't circulate and therefore doesn't count.) The increased money supply leads to a general rise in prices. Because prices are higher, somebody somewhere abandons a building project or a car purchase and off we go again.

There are many other possible scenarios, but in none of them does the burden actually fall on Mr. Kendrick. If he doesn't feel the burden, then someone else must.

The key lesson here is that if you want to track the burden of a tax you must *follow the goods, not the money.* The same is true if you want to track the burden of a charitable contribution. Suppose Bill Gates or Warren Buffett contributes $84 million to the construction of that classroom building, and suppose that Bill or Warren is sufficiently comfortable that this contribution has no effect on his lifestyle, and therefore no effect on his resource consumption. Then once again the resources for the classroom building have to come from someone, and that someone is not Bill or Warren. If Bill takes $84 million out of his bank account, he'll drive up the interest rate until someone *else* bears the burden of his contribution. If Warren takes $84 million out of his mattress, he'll do the same thing via the price level instead of the interest rate.

That doesn't mean that taxation or charity is a bad thing. That classroom building might very well be worth forcing someone else to go without a roller rink. But we should not deny the existence of that someone else. And above all, we should not lose track of the fact that what matters is not money, but the stuff we buy with it.

*   *   *

On December 10, 2010, Senator Bernie Sanders of Vermont earned a place of honor in my Sound and Fury file when he complained on the Senate floor that General Electric had paid absolutely no tax on $26 billion of earnings over the past five years.

Where to begin? First of all, General Electric is an abstract entity, so in that sense it *can't* pay taxes. It can only serve as an intermediary in collecting them. All taxes come, ultimately, from the pockets of real live people.

So perhaps the senator wanted to say that the *shareholders* of General Electric collectively earned $26 billion on which they paid no taxes. That averages out to maybe a couple of hundred dollars per shareholder.*

I suppose that Senator Sanders cited the total of $26 billion (as opposed to saying something like "$200 apiece") to create the impression that GE shareholders are very rich. But one could equally well point out that over the same five-year period, American janitors collectively earned over $250 billion, most of which was not subject to federal income tax (because most janitors are in the zero tax bracket). The reason that number is so big is not that janitors are rich; it's that there are a lot of janitors.

In any event, Senator Sanders is factually incorrect when he says that GE's income is never taxed. Nearly every penny of it is taxed when it's paid out as dividends or realized as capital gains.

But more interestingly, nearly every penny of that income was *taxed in advance*, before it was even earned. Let me explain.

Suppose you earn $1, use it to buy a share of GE stock, and earn a dividend of 6 cents a year for the rest of your life. Wait, let's go

---

* It's hard to be more accurate than this because I don't know how many people own GE stock through various mutual funds.

back and make that more realistic: Suppose you earn $1, pay half of it to the government in the form of payroll and income taxes, use the remaining half-dollar to buy a half-share of GE stock, and earn a dividend of 3 cents a year for the rest of your life.*

As you can see, your one-time up-front tax payment has cut your dividend stream in half forever. In that sense, your one-time up-front tax payment is equivalent to a 50 percent tax on dividends. At the same time, the government, which has your other half-dollar, is free to invest that half-dollar in GE and collect the other half of your dividend stream.

So by taxing away half your wages, the government has also, in effect, taxed away half your dividends (and/or capital gains). If the remaining dividends are also subject to tax (as they are), then they're effectively taxed twice. Senator Sanders's complaint is that they're not taxed a third time.

There's nothing unreasonable about believing that certain people should pay higher taxes. If that's the senator's goal, there are multiple ways to fulfill it. One is by collecting more taxes at the corporate level; another is by raising the tax on dividends and capital gains. Those are pretty much equivalent policies, though the senator seems oddly fixated on the former.

But whatever your goal may be, there's little excuse for misstating the facts. Even if it avoids the corporate income tax entirely, GE's income is taxed (at least) twice, not zero times, as Senator Sanders claims.

Michael Kinsley, a journalist I much admire (and who hired me years ago to write for *Slate* magazine, for which I will be forever grateful), has a very persistent bee in his bonnet about capital gains, which he

---

* I am assuming a 50 percent tax rate for simplicity. Any other tax rate would illustrate exactly the same point.

believes should be taxed at the same rate as wage income. The Kinsley argument, which he has repeated in countless (well, I at least have lost count) magazine and newspaper columns, runs like this:

(a) Economic theory tells us that everything should be taxed at the same rate.
(b) Q.E.D.

Step (a) is correct. Economic theory *does* tell us that we generally get better outcomes when everything is taxed at the same rate. If apples were taxed at 10 percent and oranges at 30 percent, some orange lovers would switch to eating apples just to save a buck. Better to tax both at 20 percent and encourage people to eat the fruits they prefer.

It's in the transition from step (a) to step (b) that Kinsley loses his intellectual footing. He goes wrong because he misinterprets the word "everything." The argument applies to apples and oranges, it applies to Coke and Pepsi, and it applies to red sneakers and blue sneakers. It also applies to apples consumed today and apples consumed tomorrow. If apples are taxed at 10 percent today and 30 percent tomorrow, some people will eat more apples today and fewer tomorrow just to save a buck. Better to tax all apples at 20 percent and encourage people to time their meals as they prefer.

But unlike apples and oranges or red sneakers and blue sneakers, "wage income" and "capital gains income" are not consumption goods that people choose between. Therefore the argument doesn't apply to them.

But it's worse than that. It turns out that if you take the Kinsley principle seriously—if, that is, you are determined to tax both current and future apples at the same rate—then you must be committed to taxing all capital income (including interest, dividends, and capital gains) at a rate of zero.

To understand why, it helps to have an imaginary friend.

My imaginary friend Alice earns $1 a day. Alice can use that dollar either to buy an apple or to invest in an interest-bearing account, wait for it to double, and then buy two apples.*

If we tax Alice's wages at, say, 50 pecent, then her take-home pay falls to 50 cents a day. She can use that 50 cents either to buy half an apple or to invest in an interest-bearing account, wait for it to double, and then buy one apple. Either way, her buying power is cut in half. Instead of taxing her wages, we might as well have imposed a sales tax that doubles the price of apples, both now and in the future.

In other words, *taxing Alice's wages is just like taxing both her current and future apple purchases—and taxing both at the same rate.*

Now along comes Michael Kinsley to complain that Alice pays no tax on her interest earnings. We therefore amend the tax code to include a 50 percent tax on interest.

Alice still pays the wage tax, so her take-home pay is still 50 cents a day. She can use that 50 cents either to buy half an apple or to invest in an interest-bearing account, wait for it to double, pay 25 cents tax on the interest she's earned, and use the remaining 75 cents to buy three-fourths of an apple.

Under the Kinsley tax plan (including both the wage tax and the capital gains tax), Alice's purchasing power today is cut by half (from one apple to half an apple), but her purchasing power tomorrow is cut by by more than half (from two apples to three-fourths of an apple). It's exactly as if we'd imposed a sales tax on today's apples and a *higher* sales tax on tomorrow's apples.

In other words, *taxing both wages and interest is just like taxing current apple purchases at one rate and future apple purchases at another.*

---

* Alice happens to live in an neighborhood where apples cost exactly $1.

In still other words, the Kinsley Tax Plan stands in direct contradiction to the Kinsley Prescription to tax everything equally. By taxing future apples at a higher rate than current apples, the Tax Plan encourages Alice to eat more apples now and fewer later, even when she'd prefer to space out her consumption more evenly.

If it took you a little while to digest that example, don't feel bad; it took the economics profession a long time to digest it too. (And on a personal note, I remember absolutely disbelieving this argument when I first heard about it, and needing it explained to me multiple times before I got it—though my hope is that I'm explaining it to you more clearly than it was explained to me.) The details of the argument were worked out in the 1980s by Christophe Chamley (then at Harvard) and Ken Judd (at Stanford); the Chamley-Judd result is now considered a central pillar of the theory of public finance.

So the argument that Michael Kinsley offers in favor of a *higher* tax on capital gains is in fact, when properly understood, an argument in favor of a *zero* tax not just on capital gains but on dividends and interest as well.

That's not a *proof* that we should never tax capital income; it's *one argument* against taxing capital income, which might or might not be trumped by other arguments in the opposite direction. But surely there's no point in making arguments in the first place if we don't take the trouble to understand them. One reason I've always admired Michael Kinsley (since long before I met him) is that he usually insists on logical clarity. On this issue, his best instincts have failed him.

Gerald Seib, the Pulitzer prize–winning Washington Bureau chief of the *Wall Street Journal*, worries that the interest we pay on our national debt is "a cancer eating away at the budget from within, one

that steadily drains American wealth and sends much of it overseas."*
Here's his explanation:

> When the government pays for health care for its poor and
> elderly, a valuable social benefit is delivered. When Americans
> get a Social Security check, the money by and large stays in
> circulation in the American economy.
>
> The same can't be said for interest payments, which take
> money out of the private economy, sending much of it to for-
> eign investors who hold American Treasury bonds and pro-
> vide no services in return.

It's mind-boggling to learn that there is an educated American
who believes that we receive *no services* from people who are willing
to lend us money. I wonder whether Mr. Seib has ever bought a
house, and whether he thought that his mortgage lender was providing him "no services."

It's true, as Mr. Seib says, that Social Security payments are
mailed to Americans, whereas interest on the debt is often mailed
abroad. But that tells us very little about who *benefits* from those
interest payments. In fact every single dollar that the federal government pays in interest ultimately comes back to an *American*
taxpayer, no less than a dollar paid by Social Security.

That's because every dollar paid in debt service allows the U.S.
government to delay the inevitable tax increase necessitated by its
current spending. That delay allows American taxpayers—*American* taxpayers!—to keep money in their savings accounts and earn
additional interest. So a dollar paid in debt service means an extra
dollar in American pockets. That's equally true whether the government mails its interest payments to America, to China, or to Mars.

---

* "As Budget Battle Rages On, a Quiet Cancer Grows," *Wall Street Journal*, March 8, 2008.

Mr. Seib thinks it's important to curb those interest payments. The only way to do that is to raise taxes, depleting the savings accounts of American taxpayers. For every dollar we avoid sending abroad, there's an American who earns a dollar less.*

None of this is to say that government debt has no important economic consequences. It *is* to say that the consequences are *nothing at all* as Gerald Seib (along with so many others) describes them.

Mr. Seib seems to believe that foreigners are draining our wealth by lending to our government. But if they didn't lend to the government, they'd lend their assets elsewhere—quite probably to American taxpayers struggling to get through the period of high taxes that Mr. Seib implicitly prescribes.

When I find a pair of pants I like, I buy a lot of them. Really a lot. Perhaps there's something genetic here; I collect pants like my Uncle Morris collected meat. I do this because pants wear out.

Is this part of a plot by the clothing manufacturers to keep us buying more? Some people think so. In my Sound and Fury file, I find an old (September 20, 1982) Ann Landers column about pantyhose manufacturers who deliberately create products that self-destruct after a week instead of a year because "the no-run nylons, which they know how to make, would put a serious crimp in their sales." Ann concludes that she and her readers are "at the mercy of a conspiracy of self-interest."

One wonders whose self-interest Ann has in mind. Surely it's not the manufacturers'. If there were a cost-justified way to do it, any self-interested manufacturer would switch from selling one-week nylons at $1 to selling one-year nylons at $52. That pleases

---

* There might be Americans who choose not to save their dollars; presumably this is because they have even more valuable uses for those dollars. It still does them no favor to tax away those dollars.

the customers (whose pantyhose budget doesn't change but who make fewer trips to the store), maintains the manufacturer's revenue, and—because he produces about 98 percent fewer nylons—cuts his costs considerably.

A few more from the file are worth sharing.

I have an op-ed piece from the *Chicago Sun-Times* calling for artists to receive royalties when their paintings are resold at a profit. (Such laws are already on the books in California and much of Europe.) The writer ignores the question of how his proposal would affect the price of original artwork. Let me fill in the gap for him. If the original buyer expects to pay a $100 royalty at resale time, then his willingness to pay for the original painting—and hence the price collected by the artist—is reduced by approximately $100.* What artists gain in royalties they lose on the sales of original artwork.

Actually it's worse than that. Some artists have careers that fizzle unexpectedly. Those artists accept depressed prices for their original work but never collect enough royalties to compensate. Other artists do much better than expected; their royalties *more* than compensate for the depressed price of their originals. So the op-ed writer's plan is a prescription for making unsuccessful artists poorer and successful artists richer.[†]

I have a letter to the editor calling for controls on crude oil prices as an indirect way to control the price of gasoline. But when crude oil prices are controlled by law, the price of gasoline at the

---

* "Approximately" because of an adjustment for the fact that $100 today is worth more than $100 in the future.

† Patricia Cohen of the *New York Times* got this exactly right in a November 2011 column: "The law's main beneficiaries are the artists who need it least: those whose work is famous enough to sell again and again. [Meanwhile], resale royalties hurt new artists selling their work for the first time . . . by reducing future resale value."

pump goes *up*, not down. The control at the wholesale level leads refiners to supply less gasoline. The fall in supply leads consumers to bid up the pump price.

A few years ago a Florida frost caused the price of oranges to rise so high that growers earned more income than usual. One commentator earned a place in the Sound and Fury file by suggesting that the enormous price increase reveals the growers' ability to act as a monopoly. In fact it reveals just the opposite: The incident establishes that growers can raise their incomes by killing oranges. If they were able to act in concert, they wouldn't have waited for a frost.

When there is political turmoil in the Middle East, the Sound and Fury file is guaranteed to swell. An interruption in the flow of oil always elicits a burst of letters and editorials explaining how American oil companies, by exercising their monopoly power, can raise prices so high that their profits increase. Ignore the nagging question of how there can be monopoly power in an industry consisting of Exxon Mobil, Royal Dutch Shell, BP, Chevron, ConocoPhillips, and dozens more. Examine instead just the internal logic. If restricting supply can increase profits, a *monopoly* oil industry doesn't wait for political turmoil before it restricts supply. You can claim that the companies profit from political crises, or you can claim that they collude to act as monopolists, but you cannot claim both and be consistent.

Every Thanksgiving I can count on finding editorials exhorting Americans to eat less meat so that what they forgo will be available to the undernourished. The truth, alas, is subtler. When people eat less meat, ranching becomes less profitable, and the ranching industry contracts. Then at least the grain formerly destined for feed troughs becomes available for human consumption, right? Wrong. Farming contracts also.*

---

* The contraction in ranching and farming makes more resources available for other industries, so your decision to consume less does in fact make more stuff available for others. But, particularly in the long run, it's unlikely that most of that stuff will be food.

*   *   *

Shakespeare notwithstanding, it is not exclusively the idiot who dispenses sound and fury. My file bulges with contributions from demonstrably thoughtful individuals whose insight has failed them on at least one very public occasion. An economist might be tempted to remark that such failures are to be expected because they are not severely punished. Most readers turn to the Internet and the op-ed pages for entertainment, not enlightenment, and the writer's incentive is to supply what his readers demand.

CHAPTER 13

HOW STATISTICS LIE

Unemployment Can Be Good for You

Once upon a time, I lived in Washington, DC. The day I moved there, I asked a cab driver where I should shop for groceries. "Magruder's!" he said emphatically. "It's *wonderful*. It seems like every time I go there, something's on sale."

This was my first encounter with the charming naiveté of Washington consumers. (Later that week our baby-sitter offered a breathless endorsement for a children's shoe store where "they *measure* their *feet*!")

To this day I don't believe I've ever entered a grocery store in or out of Washington where there wasn't something on sale. I gravitate to those sale items. When bananas are cheap, I buy bananas. When apples are cheap, I buy apples instead.

Because the sales keep changing, I can almost never hope to walk into a store and buy last week's sale item at the same low price. One week I buy a pound of apples on sale for $1.35; the next week apples are back up to $1.69, so I buy the oranges on sale for $1.25. The next week oranges are up to $1.49, but the apples are back on sale, so I buy the apples.

If I wanted to talk my cab driver out of shopping at Magruder's, I might try an argument like this: "Prices at Magruder's are spiraling out of control. It seems like no matter what I buy, the price goes up." If I really wanted to impress him, I could compute some percentages. "First I bought apples; then apples went up about 25 percent. Then I bought oranges, and then *they* went up 20 percent. That's a 45 percent price increase in two weeks!"

Of course, this little computation conveniently overlooks the fact that I'm still buying apples at the same old sale price of $1.35. That's got something in common with the way the government reports inflation statistics. The Consumer Price Index (the most commonly reported measure of inflation, often abbreviated CPI) reports price changes not for the mix of goods people buy today but for the mix they used to buy. Therefore it puts a lot of weight on goods that were bargains in the past—the very goods that are most likely to have risen in price. That makes reported changes look worse than they really are.

Twenty years ago airfares were cheap and laptop computers were expensive. People did a lot of flying, but few carried laptops. Therefore a CPI-like calculation puts a lot of weight on airline tickets (which have gotten pricier) and almost none on laptop computers (which have become cheap). When you buy an expensive airline ticket, the CPI goes up. When you buy a laptop you could never have afforded in 1992, the CPI largely ignores it.

These measurements matter. Social Security payments, for example, are indexed to changes in the CPI. A person whose income goes up at the same annual rate as the CPI generally experiences an increase in buying power each year, because the CPI always makes inflation look worse than it really is.

That might sound like a criticism of the Bureau of Labor Statistics, which compiles the CPI, but it's not. In a world of many prices that fluctuate independently, there is no way to construct a single meaningful index that is not biased in one way or another. The U.S. government actually reports several different measures of inflation, each with its own built-in biases, and economists try to be careful about selecting the right index for the right purpose. Particularly in times of high inflation, the media tend to focus on the CPI, perhaps because it serves *their* purpose of making things look bleak. Journalism is the dismal art.

Strictly speaking, statistics never lie, but the truths they tell are often misinterpreted. This is particularly the case with economic statistics. Let me share some more examples.

Before and after living in Washington I've lived in Rochester, New York, where for many years Star Market and Wegmans were the two great competing grocery chains. Star Market used to advertise, "Our average shopper would have paid 3 percent more buying the same goods at Wegmans." I believe them. I also believe the average *Wegmans* shopper would have paid about 3 percent more buying the same goods at Star.

Star's computation is biased in the same way as the CPI. On a given day, Star happens to have a big sale on apples, while Wegmans has a big sale on oranges. So Star shoppers buy a lot of apples and Wegmans shoppers buy a lot of oranges. *Of course* the Star shopper would have paid more at Wegmans and the Wegmans shopper would have paid more at Star. As long as prices at both stores are roughly comparable on average, and as long as there are cross-store differences in individual prices, this is exactly what you'd expect.

Journalists like to use the unemployment rate to indicate the overall state of the economy. The surrounding discussion usually overlooks the fact that unemployment is something to which people aspire. The leisure to be idle or to pursue one's fancies is generally thought of as a *good* thing, but when given the name "unemployment," it is suddenly treated as if it were bad.

Of course, unemployment can be *accompanied* by bad things, such as loss of income, and these are the things that reporters have in mind when they suggest that unemployment is bad. But it is worth remembering that the benefits of unemployment help to alleviate the associated costs. When you lose your job as a $50,000-a-year assembly line worker and spend your time earning $0 a year at the beach, you might be considerably worse off, but it is an exaggeration to suggest that you're worse off by $50,000 a year.

We are all grossly underemployed compared with our ancestors of 100 years ago, who toiled in sweatshops 80 hours a week. Few of us would trade places with them. This observation serves as an adequate warning that unemployment rates are no sufficient measure of our economic well-being.

We of the 21st century work less than our grandparents did because we are wealthier than they were. When employment falls it can mean that times are getting better. As incomes rise, families may decide that they can get by with one wage earner instead of two. Workers who cling to undesirable jobs in bad times may quit when times improve, either because of an improvement in their other income sources or because of a justified new optimism that there are better jobs to be found by those who spend time searching for them.

Economywide unemployment can be a sign that times are getting worse or a sign that times are getting better. The same is true at the level of the individual. When Peter chooses to work 80 hours a week and get rich while Paul chooses to work 3 hours a week and get comfortable in other ways, who is to say which choice is the wiser? I can find nothing in economics, morality, or, for that matter, my personal instincts that says we should approve more of one than of the other. Unemployment, or a low level of employment, can be a voluntary choice and a good one.

It is easy for observers to falsely convince themselves that Peter must have been wiser or more fortunate than Paul, because Peter's income is more conspicuous than Paul's leisure. A very naive observer might argue that fairness requires us to remedy the income discrepancy by transferring some of Peter's income to Paul. But the same argument would require us to remedy the leisure discrepancy by transferring some of Paul's leisure to Peter. If fairness dictates taxing Peter to pay Paul, does it also dictate conscripting Paul to mow the lawn for Peter?*

Because they forget that it is the *fruits* of labor rather than labor itself that is desirable, reporters seem eternally doomed to making the hilarious error of suggesting that natural disasters can be welcome developments because they put people to work. When Hurricane Katrina devastated New Orleans in 2005, this suggestion was rampant. According to newscasters, there were mysterious hidden benefits to massive destruction followed by feverish activity to restore the *status quo ante*. I wonder whether they applied this observation to their own lives, say, by periodically gouging holes in their living room walls so that they could employ themselves as plasterers.

It is not a good thing to build a house. It is a good thing to *have* a house. The having can make it worth the building, but the less building you have to do, the better off you are. A community that ends up with the same physical resources it started with after months of unanticipated effort cannot possibly be collectively wealthier than it was before.

When I go to the little ice cream stand in my neighborhood, I usually order chocolate. Sometimes they're out of it and they offer me vanilla instead. This has led me to wonder why they never run out of vanilla.

---

* It would of course be silly to suggest that all differences in income result from voluntary choices. It would be equally silly to suggest that none of them do.

The answer is that they *do* run out of vanilla, just about as often as they run out of chocolate. It's just that when they run out of vanilla, they have no particular reason to tell me about it. Presumably there are a lot of vanilla lovers out there wondering why they never run out of chocolate.

It's easy to be fooled when you observe some things and not others. You and your doctor probably have different opinions about the average size of his waiting room crowd. Perhaps it's because you are just more aware of people when they are coughing on you and there are no empty chairs. More likely it's because you and your doctor are measuring different things.

Your doctor measures the size of the crowd all day long. You measure it only when you are a patient. And when are you a patient? Probably at the most crowded times. How do I know? Because *most* people are there at the most crowded times—that's what makes them crowded. If the doctor tells me that there were 3 people in the waiting room this morning and 25 in the afternoon, and if I have to guess what time *you* were there, I'd say that the odds are 25 to 3 that it was in the afternoon.

There are always plenty of people around to observe a crowd. There is nobody around to observe a vacuum. The doctor knows that he had 28 patients today, or 14 per half-day on average. Of those 28, only 3 believe that the typical crowd size is 3, but 25 believe that it is 25. The average patient's waiting time estimate is guaranteed to be biased upward.

Unemployment statistics can be misleading in exactly the same way. Suppose you want to know the average length of a spell of unemployment. So you gather everyone who's unemployed today and ask them how long they've been out of work. If you average the responses, you'll get an estimate that's biased upward, for essentially the same reason that most patients overestimate the average size of the waiting room crowd.

After all, the long-term unemployed are very likely to be unemployed on the day the pollster arrives. The short-term unemployed, by contrast, are more likely to be back at work by then. In a sample confined to a single day or a single week, you are sure to encounter a deceptively large number of the long-term unemployed. Many a good economist has been tripped up by failing to correct for this.

For three decades in the United States of America, the income gap between the rich and the poor appears to have been widening. If you looked just at a snapshot of the numbers, you might be forced to conclude that while the rich have gotten richer, the poor have done nothing but stagnate. But there are several reasons to take those numbers with at least a grain of salt.

The first, and the simplest, is that income statistics don't account for everything we value. For one thing, we care about the quantity and quality of our leisure time. Here it's by and large the poor who have made great strides, while the rich have largely stagnated. Since 1965, between shorter workweeks and longer vacations, the average American has gained 300 leisure hours per year—but the poorest Americans have gained twice that. Meanwhile the quality of that leisure time has improved considerably since the days when your home entertainment options consisted of three black-and-white TV stations displayed on a nine-inch screen.

Second, income tax rates were cut dramatically in the 1980s and again in the 2000s under Presidents Reagan and Bush. Those tax cuts had important real effects, but they had important illusory effects also. When tax rates fall, people devote less effort to hiding their incomes. For that reason alone, *reported* incomes go up, especially at the high end. Poor people are less likely to hide their incomes in any event, both because they're in low tax brackets and because their income is primarily from highly visible sources like wages. Rich people, by contrast, have more in the way of both motives and opportunities to be devious. But they become less devious when you cut their tax rates, so any tax cut tends to create an exaggerated appearance of a growing income gap.

Third, family breakups create statistical illusions of falling income. When a household has two $50,000 wage earners, it gets counted as one $100,000 household. When the family breaks up, suddenly there are two $50,000 households, even though no individual's income has changed.

This matters a lot. For example, between the years 1996 and 2005, according to U.S. census data, the median household income (after adjusting for inflation) rose only 5.3 percent. But if you correct for changing household sizes, the increase was a far more substantial 24.4 percent.

Fourth, and I think most interesting, increased disparity among *annual* incomes need not be associated with increased disparity in *lifetime* incomes. This is because people tend to move around a lot in the income distribution.

In the United States, if you are over 25 and in the bottom fifth of the income distribution, chances are considerably better than even that you won't be there nine years from today. (If you're under 25, the chances are even better, but that's because you're likely to be a student.) The same is true if you're in the top 1 percent. There's a lot of mobility across income classes, and the degree of mobility has not changed substantially in recent decades.

Even a decrease in low incomes accompanied by a large enough increase in higher incomes can be good for *everybody* if we all move around enough in the income distribution. Suppose that initially we all have incomes of $50,000, with no inequality whatsoever. Now a change in the economic environment causes half of all incomes to fall to $40,000 while the other half rise to $100,000. You might think that half of all households are worse off and the other half are better off. But if we all take turns, so that half of us earn $40,000 in the even-numbered years and $100,000 in the odd-numbered years while the rest of us do the reverse, then we all average $70,000 a year and we all win.

That vision of extreme income mobility is, of course, quite unrealistic. But the usual stereotype of "the rich and the poor" entrenched in their positions for life is quite unrealistic in the opposite direction. Most people have good years and bad years. In any given year people with high current incomes are likely to be having one of the best years of their lives and people with low current incomes are likely to be having one of the worst. The gap between the highest and the lowest annual income is the gap between one family's best year and another family's worst year. But it's hard to see who—other than a journalist hard up for a sensational story—would want to make that comparison. The right comparison is between two family's incomes, each averaged over many years. Nothing in the annual income statistics can shed light on that comparison.

One way to create a false impression of widening income gaps is to point out that a lot of people with high incomes have recently gained and a lot of people with low incomes have recently lost. All this shows is that people have good years and bad years. *Of course* people near the top have recently gained: For the most part they are having unusually good years, and are therefore doing better than last year. They are also probably doing better than *next* year, when things will be closer to normal again.

Imagine a colony of nomads who wander randomly up and down the slope of a mountain. Take a snapshot of this colony. Those nomads who are near the summit at the moment when the snapshot was taken are likely to have traveled upward in the recent past. Those near the bottom have probably been traveling downward recently. From this we may infer absolutely nothing about whether the altitude gap between high and low nomads is increasing over time.

*   *   *

There is a general lesson here, which is that it is a mistake to judge a person's overall well-being on the basis of his current well-being. To argue, for example, that the elderly are worse off than the rest of us, say, because they have more health problems, is to overlook that we each take a turn at being young and a turn at being old.

This makes it fruitless to adopt permanent policies aimed at transferring income from the "fortunate" young to the "unfortunate" old. If such a policy is in place for multiple generations, you lose when you're young, gain when you're old, and break even over your lifetime.* You can always make one-shot transfers from one generation to another in order to redress some perceived inequity, but a clear-eyed observer will keep in mind that no generation starts with an inequitable endowment of youth.

Actually we don't quite all share a life cycle, because accidents and disease intervene to deprive a few of us of our old age. This means that the young are actually underprivileged with respect to the old. Young people have only a probability of living a full life; old people are assured of it. Transfers from the "fortunate" young to the "unfortunate" old tend to *exaggerate* this underlying inequity.†

Similar considerations apply to the laws against mandatory retirement. Before it became illegal, many firms required employees to step down at a specified age (typically 65 or 70). Apparently firms believe this is an efficient practice; if they didn't, there'd be no need to outlaw it. If they are right, then a permanent ban on mandatory retirement lowers average lifetime incomes. (After all, the efficiency

---

* This is an approximation to the truth; if the generation ahead of you is smaller than yours while the generation behind you is bigger, then you can come out ahead.

† My colleague Mark Bils argues that we should subsidize tobacco for fairness's sake, because smokers don't get their fair share of Social Security benefits.

loss must be felt by *someone*; probably it means that the wages of young people fall.)* The ban on mandatory retirement is touted as a boon to old people, but those old people were once young and so are likely to have overpaid for that boon. To be a net beneficiary, you must be old without first being young, like the newborn 67-year-olds I sometimes encounter in the supermarket tabloids.

The gross domestic product, or GDP, is the most frequently reported measure of general economic well-being. As such, it has some obvious deficiencies. It counts the value of all goods and services produced in the economy, but not the value of time spent relaxing on the beach.

It also has some less obvious deficiencies. First, it really *doesn't* count the value of all goods and services produced in the economy. Many goods and services are produced within the household. Whether you wash your own dishes or pay a maid to wash them, the net benefit is a cabinet full of clean dishes. If you pay the maid, the GDP reflects this benefit; if you wash them yourself, it doesn't.

In less liberated times, the standard textbook example to illustrate this point was that of the man who marries his housekeeper. As a housekeeper, she earns $25,000 a year scrubbing floors, washing dishes, and doing laundry. When she becomes a wife, she earns $0 a year doing exactly the same things. Although nothing has changed, the GDP appears to have fallen by $25,000.

This observation is particularly important when GDP is compared across countries. In less developed countries there is usually more household production and consequently a greater discrep-

---

* Only one group shares in the gains but not in the losses: those who are already old at the time when the ban goes into effect.

ancy between reported GDP and actual output. When you read that per capita GDP in the United States is over 100 times as great as it is in Liberia, remember that people in Liberia grow their own food and make their own clothes and get no credit for it in the national income accounts. They are much poorer than we are but not as much poorer as the statistics seem to indicate.

Another deficiency is that increased output of goods and services can be either a good or a bad thing. A construction boom that creates thousands of desirable new houses is a good thing; a construction boom that replaces thousands of old houses destroyed by a hurricane consists of running as fast as possible just to stay in one place. The GDP counts them equally.

Partly because of these deficiencies and others, some European governments, and some municipalities like the city of Somerville, Massachusetts, have begun compiling figures intended to measure something like "Gross National Happiness." Unfortunately, happiness is even more difficult to measure than goods and services (see the discussion on pages 152–154).

It is said that figures don't lie, but liars figure. Perhaps a more serious problem is that honest people figure carelessly. The antidote is careful attention to exactly what is being measured, and how it differs from what you would really like to measure if you could.

The Consumer Price Index measures the price of a particular basket of goods; that is not the same thing as the income necessary to maintain a particular level of happiness. The unemployment rate measures the number of people not working; that is not the same thing as the number of people who are unhappy. Annual income statistics measure the distribution of current incomes; that is not the same thing as the distribution of lifetime incomes. The GDP measures the value of all goods and services

that are traded in the marketplace; that is not the same thing as
the value of all goods and services that are produced, or of those
that are desirable.

Some of these discrepancies are simple problems of measurement, as when the GDP omits household production. Others are
more subtle, as when the income gap appears exaggerated because
those with unusually high or low current incomes are unlikely to
remain at those extremes.

By training, economists are sensitive to problems of measurement and statistical fallacies. By cultivated instinct, we correct for
them as best we can.

CHAPTER 14

THE POLICY VICE

Do We Need More Illiterates?

The economist's greatest passion is not to change the world but to understand it. Yet every human heart conceals a secret desire to improve its surroundings. Scratch an economist and you'll find a reformer.

For economists, policy is a vice, but a delicious one, and we indulge in it as you might indulge in a hot fudge sundae or an ill-advised affair, succumbing to its seductive and unhealthy pleasures while nurturing our disdain for colleagues who fall prey to the same temptation. We are passionate in our insistence that policy is unworthy of our attention, and in the attention that we give to it.

While economists take up positions on nearly every side of every issue, we share certain perspectives. The economic way of thinking emphasizes the importance of incentives, the gains from trade, and the power of enforceable property rights as forces for good. It embraces the confidence that perfect markets generally yield desirable outcomes and an instinct to make outcomes more desirable by making markets more nearly perfect.

When we are told that we should subsidize the aerospace industry because we'll need their facilities in the event of war, economists are likely to be skeptical. In ordinary circumstances, entrepreneurs can foresee the probability of war as accurately as government of-

ficials can. If there is a one-third chance of a major war in five
years, then there is a one-third chance that a factory capable of
producing fighter aircraft will be a very profitable thing to own.
Why shouldn't that prospect provide sufficient incentive to keep
the factory in business?

Of course, there will be fewer such factories when the chance
of war is one-third than when it's one-half, but that is presumably
the outcome that would also be chosen by a wise government. It
makes good sense to invest fewer resources to defend against a less
probable event.

The proper incentive is missing only if investors expect the government to follow historical precedent and impose price controls in
time of war.* If we are concerned about our defense preparedness,
the problem arises not from too *little* interference with the market
(in the form of subsidies) but from too *much* interference (in the
form of controls). The best prescription for military preparedness
might be a constitutional amendment guaranteeing freedom from
price controls.†

When pundits gripe, rightly or wrongly, about the quality of
American cars, economists wonder what all the fuss is about. After
all, *somebody* has to specialize in making lower quality cars. Why
shouldn't it be Americans?

---

* In World War II price controls were administered by the Office of Price Administration (OPA). I have been present at discussions where serious attempts were made to assess
the OPA's damage to the Allied cause, measured in terms of the equivalent number of
German panzer divisions. The estimates tended to be large.

† This is surely not a complete analysis of the problem. For example, investors' attitudes
toward risk might not coincide with the attitudes that are in some sense socially appropriate regarding an event such as a major war. I am not sure whether or not there is a
convincing case along these lines. But the argument in the text certainly represents the
sort of first pass at this issue that a typical economist might attempt.

There are markets for automobiles at every point along the price-quality spectrum. There is no special glory in success at the high end of that spectrum and no shame in success at the low end. I would far prefer to have founded the Walmart chain than a high-quality apparel store with a single retail outlet.

Quality need not be correlated with profit. Quality is costly to produce. Some consumers prefer to pay more for better—and expensively manufactured—products; others prefer to pay less for inferior—and cheaply manufactured—alternatives. There is honor in serving either market well.

American cars might or might not be of lower quality than their foreign counterparts, but if they are there is probably a good reason for it. Here's one possible reason: There are gains from having each type of production concentrated in a single place; it doesn't matter which is done where; and some historical accident has placed the lower-quality plants in the United States. Here's another: Americans design low-quality cars because the best American minds are employed more productively elsewhere; American cars are worse because American bioengineering is better. Here's a third: Detroit autoworkers, being wealthier than their counterparts abroad, are quite sensibly unwilling to exert as great an effort for a given wage. It's neither unusual nor dishonorable to adjust your priorities to reflect your income bracket.

A common response to these observations is that it would be all well and good to sacrifice quality in exchange for keeping costs down, but American manufacturers sacrifice quality *without* keeping costs down: It takes as many hours to build an American luxury car as to build a Japanese equivalent with a better maintenance record. To this there are two counterresponses. First, worker hours are a poor measure of overall costs. If one hour of a Detroit worker's time produces less than one hour of a Tokyo worker's time, it might be because Detroit wisely spends less on worker training or on devising methods to coordinate various aspects of its operations.

Second, *measured* worker hours are a poor measure of *actual* worker hours. If the Detroit worker spends 15 minutes out of every hour drinking coffee, then it takes only three-fourths as much time to build an American car as naive statistics might suggest.*

Economists exempt themselves from the common chorus of despair because they recognize the gains from trade. One product is made in Detroit; another is made in Tokyo. Whether you buy a Ford Fiesta or a Lexus 460, it doesn't matter where it comes from. Trade separates our consumption choices from our production choices. We can build cheap cars and drive expensive ones, if we build the cheap ones profitably.

When *ABC World News* runs a multipart series on the "problem" of illiteracy, the economist's first question is "What problem?" Of course illiteracy is a bad thing, but that doesn't mean we've got the wrong amount of it. Literacy is costly to produce and becomes costlier as it's extended to successively less receptive segments of the population. There is a right time to decide that additional resources devoted to reading programs would be better spent elsewhere.

You would think—or at least *I* would think—that the pundit who bemoans having the *wrong* amount of something would feel some obligation to divulge what he means by the *right* amount. None of the commentators on *ABC World News* seemed to feel that obligation. If they *had* told us what they meant by the right amount of literacy, they could have gone on to tell us what leads them to suspect that we have too little rather than too much of it.

An economist might be inclined to apply an efficiency criterion:

---

* An economist would have little sympathy for the counter-counterresponse that time spent drinking coffee is wasted. We drink a lot of coffee ourselves. I can imagine no reasonable basis for a blanket assumption that better cars are more important than better working conditions.

We should encourage further literacy until the additional costs begin to exceed the additional benefits. A journalist who objects to that criterion is well within his rights but is not thereby relieved of the obligation to reveal his alternative.

If efficiency is our guide, we might start with the expectation that markets already provide approximately the right literacy rate. The adult who learns to read captures many of the benefits, via higher wages and the satisfaction of being able to educate himself beyond the level of Charles Gibson or Diane Sawyer. Those benefits provide ample incentive to undertake any cost-justified self-improvement program.

Now that argument can easily be contradicted in several ways. It is fashionable to argue that educated citizens vote more wisely (though I am not aware of any study that establishes this) and thereby confer benefits on their neighbors beyond those that they capture for themselves. Or you could argue that better educated coworkers make the rest of us more productive. Whether that's in fact the case is an active and important area of research these days in economics; so far the results are mixed. Or maybe the illiterate, by virtue of their illiteracy, are unaware of life's possibilities and therefore make unwise choices that a well-crafted literacy program could efficiently alter. Or maybe people choose too much illiteracy because social welfare programs protect them from the consequences.

To investigate whether there is a literacy problem, *ABC World News* ought to have begun by asking whether there is any evidence that these or other considerations significantly distort the market's natural tendency to find the efficient outcome. If so, there is a case for nonmarket remedies. Now comes the crux of the entire matter: *How will we know when those remedies have gone too far?* How do we measure the benefits of literacy, how do we measure the costs of providing it, and how do we determine whether we currently have too much or too little? That is the central question, and the *ABC World News* crew ducked it completely. If these guys are literate, what is the point of literacy?

Responding to the quadrennial editorials demanding free network television time for presidential candidates, economists recognize that two quite separate propositions are being deceptively packaged as one. The first proposition is that more network television time should be devoted to political messages and less to the alternatives. The second is that television networks should be taxed more heavily.

If the goal is to provide more network time to the candidates, that time can be purchased with income tax dollars, or for that matter with a special tax on carrots, just as well as it can be confiscated from the networks. When a presidential candidate preempts an episode of *Celebrity Apprentice*, the social cost is a forgone episode of *Celebrity Apprentice*. That cost is the same whether it is borne by the general public, by carrot eaters, or by the owners of television networks.

"Should we, as a society, give up an hour of the Donald in order to see an hour of campaign ads?" is one question. "Who should bear the cost?" is quite another. They deserve to be debated separately.

When economists hear that the federal government, having decided to divest itself of the one-billion-cubic-foot National Helium Reserve, is selling off helium slowly to maintain a high price, economists are bemused.* A high price transfers income from citizens to the government. But the government has never lacked for mechanisms to accomplish such transfers. Why adopt a new mechanism with the primary effect of idling valuable resources?

Economists are sensitive to the effects of incentives. When a new

---

* This is not a joke. There really is a National Helium Reserve.

Civil Rights Bill imposes costs on businesses with 25 or more employees, we expect to see a lot of businesses contract to 24 employees. We are sensitive to questions of symmetry. Why does that same Civil Rights Bill forbid me to apply racial criteria when I choose an employ*ee* but allow me to apply racial criteria when I choose an employ*er*? If I turn down a job offer, should I be required to prove that my motives were not discriminatory? We are sensitive to analogies. Why am I permitted to apply racial criteria when I select a spouse but not when I select a personal assistant?*

Economists are sensitive to the gains from voluntary trade. Back in the days when airlines routinely "bumped" passengers from overbooked flights, it was an economist who advised them to pay volunteers to give up their seats.

Economists are sensitive to the power of property rights. When African elephants were hunted nearly to extinction, it was a team of economists (among others) who designed the CAMPFIRE program, under which villagers are given property rights to the herds, and hence incentives to preserve them. Ten years after the program was instituted, the elephant population had doubled.

Economists are sensitive to the problems that arise when people are unable to collect the fruits of their own labor. You can work for years to develop a major technological innovation, then watch the demand for your product fall to zero when a competitor makes a slight improvement on your design. Consequently you might not be willing to put in those years of effort to begin with, and neither your design nor the improvement ever gets developed. Ironically the solution might be either to subsidize inventors, so that you are compensated for the risk of being scooped, or to tax inventors, so that you have fewer rivals breathing down your neck.

---

* Of course, to raise a question does not imply that there can be no satisfactory answer. It *does* imply that the issue is worth thinking about.

There are many ways to be deprived of the rewards due your efforts. I am intrigued by the market for movie endings. Moviegoers want two things in an ending: They want it to be happy and they want it to be unpredictable. There is some optimal frequency of sad endings that maintains the right level of suspense. Yet the market might fail to provide enough sad endings.

An individual director who films a sad ending risks short-term losses, as word gets around that the movie is "unsatisfying." It is true that there are long-term gains, as viewers are kept off guard for future movies. Unfortunately most of those gains may be captured by other directors, because moviegoers remember only that the murderer *does* sometimes catch up with the heroine in the basement, but do not remember that it sometimes happens in movies with this particular director. Under these circumstances no individual director may be willing to incur costs for his rivals' benefit.

A solution is for directors to display their names prominently, so that viewers know when a movie was made by someone unpredictable. Viewers, however, may find it in their interests to protect themselves by covering their eyes when the director's name is shown. Perhaps this means the government should subsidize movies with sad endings!

I have a colleague who believes that almost anything you buy off the Internet arrives with too much packaging, because sellers don't account for the costs of disposal. My colleague wants to solve this problem with a tax on packing material. My first reaction is that at least in a world of private trash haulers (such as we have in my community), this should be a nonproblem: The haulers can charge me by weight or by volume or whatever else they care about; then I'll seek out products that are packaged more conservatively, which puts appropriate pressure on sellers. My colleague gently reminds me that the trash haulers do *not* in fact charge me by weight or by volume; I pay the same monthly fee whether my toter is empty, half-full, or overflowing. This is presumably because it's costly to measure my trash. I reply that if this were really an important problem, the haulers would find a way to solve it—say, by measuring my trash on three randomly selected occasions per year and setting my annual rate accordingly. My colleague fears that the haulers could cheat, measuring six times and reporting only the three biggest readings.

This particular colleague and I reach different conclusions about whether to tax packing material, as we have reached different conclusions on pretty much every other subject that's ever come up over the lunch table. Yet we have much in common. We agree that there is such a thing as too much packing material and such a thing as too little, and that either error can be costly. We agree that a perfectly functioning market would yield the best possible outcome, and we define "best possible" by the criterion of efficiency. We agree that markets can fail when information is hidden from one party, or when contracts cannot be enforced. My colleague and I have never voted for the same candidate, but I am sure that in the most important senses, my views are closer to his than to those of 99 percent of the people who always vote as I do.

We both approach the world as economists, and as economists resigned to—and sometimes even reveling in—the character defect that diverts us from pure science to policy analysis. An economist who has abandoned his resistance to policy *analysis* is liable to fall prey to the even more seductive and dangerous vice of policy *formulation*. Each day over lunch my colleagues and I design a better world. We are a merciless crew, and most of our ideas are thoroughly discredited before dessert is served. A few survive. In the next chapter I will share a few of those modest proposals.

CHAPTER 15

SOME MODEST PROPOSALS

The End of Bipartisanship

Only a crisis—actual or perceived—produces real change. When that crisis occurs, the actions that are taken depend on the ideas that are lying around. That, I believe, is our basic function: to develop alternatives to existing policies, to keep them alive and available until the politically impossible becomes the politically inevitable.

—MILTON FRIEDMAN

Driving through northwest Washington, DC, I remarked on the conspicuous opulence in that quarter of the city. My friend Jim Kahn, in the passenger seat, wondered how such great wealth could have accumulated in a city that is notorious for producing almost nothing of value. I was too quick with the obvious cynical response: Most of it is the moral equivalent of stolen, partly through direct taxation and largely through political contributions that constitute the collection arm of a vast protection racket.

But Jim was quicker than I and saw that, according to economic theory, my explanation was not cynical enough. In the presence of competition between the parties, *all* of those ill-gotten gains should be used to buy votes. If the Republicans are in power, pocketing $100 billion per year, then the Democrats can offer to duplicate Republican policies exactly, *plus* give away another billion per year to key constituents. Unchallenged, this strategy would enable them to buy the next election, pocketing a net $99 billion. But the Republicans would counter by offering to give away an extra $2 billion and settle for $98 billion for themselves. Our experience with competitive markets tells us that there is no end to this bidding war until all excessive profits are competed out of existence.

When an industry is dominated by two highly profitable firms, theory tells us that if there is no price war, there is probably collusion. In the case of the Republicans and Democrats, the requisite collusion is on display for all to see. It is called bipartisanship.

When Republican and Democratic legislators meet to "hammer out a compromise," they are engaging in an activity that could land any of their private-sector counterparts in jail. We do not allow the presidents of United and American Airlines to hammer out compromises regarding airfares. Why do we allow the majority and minority leaders of the Congress to hammer out compromises regarding tax policy?

Adam Smith observed that "people of the same trade seldom meet together, even for merriment and diversion, but the conversation ends in a conspiracy against the public, or in some contrivance to raise prices." That truth is the basis for the antitrust legislation that attempts to prevent such conspiracies and contrivances from getting off the ground. When the president of United runs into the president of American at a picnic, he is forbidden by law to say, "I will not undercut you on the Chicago-to–Los Angeles route provided that you do not undercut me on New York–to-Denver." Yet we allow Republican leaders to greet Democrats with offers like "I will support housing aid to your urban constituents if you will support agricultural programs for the farmers in my district."

When people get rich running airlines, I can surmise that it is because they have an extraordinary talent for delivering good air service. When people get rich in the political establishment, I am reluctant to surmise that it is because they have an extraordinary talent for delivering good government. Economics provides an alternative explanation: the absence of political antitrust legislation.

I propose that all political compromise—indeed all discussion

between candidates, officeholders, or officials of competing parties—be fully subject to the same provisions of the Clayton and
Sherman Antitrust Acts that regulate the activities of every private
business in America. I predict that political antitrust legislation will
confer on voters the same benefits that economic antitrust legislation confers on consumers. Once the wealth of northwest Washington is depleted by the resulting political price wars, politicians
might be forced to compete by offering more efficient government.

You are engaged to be married. Acting on your fiancé's promise of
eternal love, you turn away other suitors. In the event, you are left
waiting at the altar. The law provides recourse in the form of a suit
for breach of promise.

You cast your vote in a presidential election. Acting on the candidate's declaration "Read my lips: No new taxes," you pass up the
opportunity to vote for other candidates. In the event, your candidate wins and signs one of the largest tax increases in history. What
is your recourse?

You can, of course, vow never to vote for your candidate again, just
as you can vow never to reunite with your ex-fiancé. But why is the
promise itself not redeemable in a court of law? Why can't betrayed
voters file a class-action suit against the candidate who betrayed them?

Candidates looking to enhance their credibility might welcome
the opportunity to offer legally enforceable guarantees, just as home
buyers looking for mortgages welcome the opportunity to offer legally
binding promises to repay their loans. If the courts refused to enforce
those promises, you'd never get your mortgage in the first place.

Central banks (like the U.S. Federal Reserve) too could do better if their promises were enforceable. Theory and evidence suggest that when an expected inflation fails to materialize, aggregate
output can fall. By credibly promising not to follow inflationary

policies, the central bank could prevent costly expectations from forming in the first place.

What's true for central banks and home buyers is also true for politicians. A candidate whose no-tax pledge is met with skepticism gains no votes; a candidate who accepts personal liability for his no-tax pledge acquires valuable credibility.

My late and lamented colleague Alan Stockman once proposed that candidates be permitted to issue legally enforceable promises. It would be rash to hold politicians liable for every pledge they make in response to unexpected questions on the campaign trail, so let's restrict the program to those promises that the candidate explicitly declares to be legally binding.

You might argue that it is a bad thing to bind candidates to policies that might prove unwise under unforeseen circumstances. I reply that we accept that trade-off all the time. There might be unforeseen circumstances in which freedom of speech or the right to trial by jury or the separation of powers proves unwise, but we are prepared to accept that eventuality in return for the guarantee of certain liberties. Allowing politicians to make real commitments would foster public debate regarding which additional guarantees are sufficiently important to justify a further sacrifice of flexibility.

A politician's binding promise would be akin to a provisional constitutional amendment, in effect for the politician's term of office. It would be binding only on the candidate himself, so that, for example, a president who had promised to veto any tax increase might still have his vetoes overridden. The resulting limitations on policy options would be far less restrictive than the provisions of the U.S. Constitution, many of which seem to be generally regarded as desirable.

There are details to sort out. If a president reneged on a pledge to veto any tax increase, would we ignore his refusal and honor the original pledge, treating each new tax bill as automatically vetoed?

Or would we allow him to violate his promise and then hold him legally responsible via a class-action suit or an impeachment proceeding? Should we construct an escape clause, under which an officeholder, convinced that he had erred, could escape liability by resigning his office?

I support the Stockman proposal in any of these forms. The Constitution itself, in Section 10 of Article I, protects the right of individuals to enter into enforceable contracts. Why should politicians, uniquely among American citizens, be denied that fundamental freedom?

It is a recurring American nightmare: the accused criminal out on bail who commits a grisly murder while awaiting trial. The judge who signed the release order is second-guessed in the press and sometimes at the voting booth. Politicians decry the leniency of the justice system and call for stricter standards in the granting of bail.

There are two separate problems here. The first is to decide where we stand on the trade-off between public safety and the rights of the accused. How sure do we have to be about a prisoner's character before we're willing to accept the risk of having him out on bail? Reasonable people will disagree about their answers to this question. Ordinarily in our system, we consider such difficult trade-offs to be properly in the domain of the legislature.

The second problem, once the legislature has agreed on a standard, is to induce judges to abide by it. We can appoint watchdog agencies, but the watchdogs are likely to have far less information than the judge about the character of various defendants. They can therefore never be certain that the judge is really using all of his information to the best of his ability.

Economic theory tells us that when we can't monitor a decision maker, we should at least endeavor to present him with the right incentives. One way to incentivize judges is to make them personally liable for criminal damage done by the defendants they release.

Personal liability would at least give the right incentive in one direction: Judges would be loath to release those defendants whom they believe to be the most dangerous. Unfortunately they would be loath to release *any* defendants. So I propose a simultaneous countervailing incentive in the form of a cash bounty to the judge for each defendant he releases.

Whether judges would release more or fewer defendants than they do today would depend on the size of the cash bounty, which could be adjusted to reflect the priorities of the legislature. But whether we want judges releasing 1 percent or 99 percent, we can at least agree that those 1 percent or 99 percent should not be chosen randomly. We want judges to focus their full attention on the potential costs of their decisions, and, while of course there are many judges who strive to be diligent in any case, personal liability has a way of concentrating the mind.

I make no plea for greater strictness or for greater leniency. I plead only that we recognize the nature of the trade-off. My proposal's second advantage is that it would encourage clarity. Through ongoing debate about adjustments to the cash bounty, legislators would be forced to take unambiguous stands on fundamental issues of safety versus freedom. Rather than being able to hide their views in complex and mutually contradictory legislation, they would have to face the voters and defend an unambiguous position, which the voters could then accept or reject.

You might object that we should not trivialize a complex issue by asking legislators to commit themselves to a single number. I respond that they commit themselves to a single number already. The current network of laws does select some specific point on the scale between strictness and leniency. We just aren't told exactly what it is. Why should the complexity of an issue be an excuse for being coy about the choices that have been made?

My proposal would encourage judges to be more diligent and force legislators to be more straightforward.* I'd like to see it tried.

You download a picture that is unsavory but perfectly legal. Six months later a new law prohibits having such pictures on your hard drive. A zealous prosecutor attempts to indict you.

The Constitution takes a dim view of such proceedings. You have a fundamental right to know the consequences of your actions at the time you undertake them. Therefore Article I grants you absolute immunity from *ex post facto* proceedings such as this. Any court would instantly dismiss the prosecutor's case.

You purchase an asset that produces a stream of dividends that are taxed at 25 percent. Six months later a new law raises the tax rate to 35 percent. A zealous Internal Revenue agent attempts to collect from you.

You go to tax court, arguing that you have a fundamental right to know the consequences of your actions at the time when you undertake them. Because you bought your asset under the reasonable expectation that the dividends would be taxed at 25 percent, that is all you should be required to pay. The judge finds your argument ludicrous and attaches your wages.

I'd like to understand what differentiates these cases. One argument is that you bought the asset with full awareness that tax laws sometimes change. On the other hand, you downloaded the picture with full awareness that criminal laws sometimes change. So I'm not sure there is any meaningful distinction here.

---

* In my book *More Sex Is Safer Sex*, I've argued for a similar incentive program for members of the jury.

A subtler distinction is that an unexpected tax increase serves the purpose of collecting government revenue, whereas an *ex post facto criminal* prosecution serves no purpose whatsoever. The new law is able to deter future downloads by promising to punish those who disobey it in the future. The strength of that deterrence is independent of whether we punish those who disobeyed it in the past.

But *ex post facto* prosecutions *do* serve the purpose of deterring behavior that is likely to become the subject of criminal legislation in the near future, and presumably governments do want to deter such behavior. Those who would legislate against certain websites would presumably be happy to see those websites lose visitors even in advance of the legislation.

I asked my friend the law professor whether he could articulate the deep philosophical principle that proscribes *ex post facto* prosecution but allows tax rates to rise. He told me that my question presupposed a falsehood: "You want a distinction based in legal theory—but there is no such thing as legal theory." He told me not to waste my time scrutinizing the law for consistency.

As is my habit with lawyers, I ignored him. I admit to a gut feeling that the proscriptions of the Constitution are wise and that at the same time there should be flexibility in the tax laws. But I propose that serious thought be given to the source of that gut feeling and the question of whether it is really justifiable. Whatever justification we find will probably have significant policy implications. If we find none, the policy implications are even greater.

Every now and then I read a magazine article suggesting that the justice system turn criminals over to their victims for punishment. I suspect that such a system would have a bias toward leniency. Victims are often aware that their losses are irreparable and feel uncomfortable extracting revenge for its own sake. Their discomfort might even be great enough to preclude punishments that are not purely vengeful, such as putting your prisoner to work on the equivalent of a chain gang and attaching his wages.

If I'm right, then deterrence would be hampered and criminal activity would increase. But there is a market solution to this imperfection.

I predict that if markets were permitted to function, people would sell their punishment rights in advance to firms with show-no-mercy reputations and advertise what they'd done. The contract with the firm could be made irrevocable, so that criminals know there is no possibility of a reprieve from the victim.

One advantage would be that punishment firms would have every incentive to put prisoners to work as productively as possible; after all, the firm gets to collect what the prisoners produce. The present system puts investment bankers to work in the prison laundry.

I am not sure whether this justice system would be better than the present one, though my pro-market bias leads me to view it favorably. I *am* quite sure that *if* we adopt the more common proposal of allowing victims to mete out justice, then we should also allow the right of punishment to be bought and sold.

When Jonathan Swift advocated using babies as a food source, he titled his essay "A Modest Proposal" and did not intend it to be taken seriously. Although the proposals in this section may seem as offbeat as Swift's, I *do* intend them to be taken seriously. Enhanced competition, enforceable contracts, appropriate incentives, attention to consistency, and market forces generally serve us well, and I believe we should be ever on the lookout for new settings where we can employ them.

There is nothing in economic theory to suggest that existing political institutions are even close to optimal, in any sense of the word. If the best policy proposal seems bizarre, it might be only because we are unused to seeing anything like the best policy proposal in action.

Each of these proposals has serious flaws. That is no argument against them. Some standard is required for determining how their flaws compare to those of the status quo. Initially much analysis is called for—and we'll learn something from that analysis, even if the proposals are rejected. But eventually there is no substitute for the daring experiment.

IV

How Markets Work

CHAPTER 16

WHY POPCORN COSTS MORE AT THE MOVIES

And Why the Obvious Answer Is Wrong

It's one of the recurring problems of modern economics, one that has occupied great minds and boosted great careers: Why is popcorn so expensive at the movie theater?

Actually I'm not sure popcorn *is* so expensive at the movie theater. Five dollars a bag sure *seems* expensive, but maybe the owner has a lot of hidden costs that you and I don't see.* Still, there's no evident reason why costs should be so much higher in the theater than they are at the candy store, where you can buy the same size popcorn at one-third the price. So it seems a worthwhile exercise to assume the theater's markup really is enormous and to look for an explanation.

You might think the explanation is obvious: Popcorn is expensive because, once you're in the theater, the owner has a monopoly. If there were only one candy store in town, and if that were the only place to buy popcorn, a bag would cost $5 at the candy store. When you're trapped in the theater, the concession stand might as well be the only candy store in town.

---

* My former student Jeff Spielberg suggests that $4.50 of that $5 might be a fee for cleaning up after you.

But once you're in the theater, the owner has a *lot* of monopolies. He is the only supplier of rest rooms, for example. Why doesn't he charge you a monopoly price to use them? He has monopolies on the rights to proceed from the box office to the outer lobby, from the outer lobby to the inner lobby, and through the double doors. Why are there no toll booths? Once you're past those double doors, why is there no monopoly price to take a seat?

The answer, of course, is that instead of charging $10 at the box office and $2 to take a seat, it's simpler to just charge $12 at the box office. Whatever the owner thinks he can extract from you, he might as well extract it all up front.

As with seating, so with popcorn. When I go to the movies, I pay $10 for a ticket and $5 for popcorn. I'd be equally happy paying $11 for a ticket and $4 for popcorn, or paying $15 for a ticket and getting my popcorn for free.

Those options are pretty much interchangeable, but only up to some limit. If the ticket costs $6 and the popcorn costs $9, I might just buy the ticket and skip the popcorn. The owner would prefer not to risk that sad outcome. Since he's not sure where my cutoff is, he's best advised to price the popcorn at cost and take his monopoly profit at the box office.

Better yet, by keeping the popcorn cheap, the owner might induce me to take two or three bags instead of one. If I think those bags are worth more than their price, he can tack my extra willingness to pay onto my box office fee.

So here's my advice to the owner: If it costs you 50 cents to make a bag of popcorn, charge me 50 cents a bag. I'll buy (say) two bags for a dollar. If you think I would have happily paid another six dollars for those two bags, add the extra six dollars to my ticket price; I'll happily pay this for the right to come in and buy cheap popcorn. Charging more at the concession stand can only be a mistake; it might deter me from buying that second bag.

If I'm your only customer, that's surely your best strategy. Likewise if all your customers are exactly like me. If the customers differ slightly, you might need to make some slight adjustments. If some of us value popcorn a little less than others, and if you want to keep all of our business, you should probably add only $5.75 to the ticket price instead of $6. But you'll still want to keep the popcorn pretty cheap.

On the other hand, if your customers are extremely diverse, you've got a problem. Now the box office price that extracts most of my willingness-to-pay might drive away half your clientele. Time to rethink the problem from scratch. It's at least possible—though far from certain—that expensive popcorn will be part of the solution to this problem.

Moral: If the customers are all very similar, then a high popcorn price makes no sense. Therefore *any correct explanation of an observed high popcorn price must rely on diversity among the customers.* Or in other words, *If your explanation mentions monopoly power without mentioning diversity, it can't be right.*

What, then, *is* the right explanation? That's a surprisingly hard problem. So let's warm up with some easier pricing puzzles.

First, why do senior citizens get so many discounts? The stock answer is that they live on small fixed incomes. That answer founders on the fact that, at least in the United States, senior citizens have, on average, the highest net worth of any age group. A better answer is that senior citizens have a lot of free time to go shopping for bargains. If you don't give them a good price, they'll mosey across town looking for a better one.

There is a grocery chain in Philadelphia that advertises, "If you find anything in the dairy case that's past its expiration date, we'll give you a fresh one for free." For several years my father's self-appointed full-time job was traveling from store to store combing through the dairy cases. On a good day he'd come home with two fresh yogurts and a hunk of cheese. This, of course, was after he'd retired. You don't see many 40-year-olds in that line of work. A man who will spend three hours to earn a free yogurt is a man who's likely to do a lot of comparison shopping. That's why my father gets discounts that 40-year-olds can't get.

Of course, some 40-year-olds have more free time than others, and ideally the stores would like to target them for discounts as well. That's why they often make you earn your discounts by jumping through time-consuming hoops, like clipping coupons or mailing in rebate forms. That way the discounts are claimed primarily by customers with a lot of time on their hands—the same customers who would otherwise spend that time driving across town to get a better price.

If the goal were simply to lure more customers, stores wouldn't print coupons; they'd just lower their prices. The goal, instead, is to lure a particular *kind* of customer while still requiring others to pay full price. If everyone clipped coupons, they'd serve no purpose. If a random sample of the customer base clipped coupons, they'd still serve no purpose. The reason coupons serve a purpose is that Bill Gates is too busy to clip them, but my father is not.

Many jewelers will give you a discount on a new watch if you trade in your old one. Why? The obvious answer is that they resell the trade-ins, but the obvious answer is wrong. In fact they discard the trade-ins, apparently because it's too much trouble to sort out the good ones. Instead the goal is to offer a targeted discount. The most desperate customers—the ones who have just lost their watches—pay full price.

When furniture stores offer free delivery, who accepts the offer? Answer: customers with enough flexible free time to wait at home for the delivery truck. In other words, the same customers with enough flexible free time to shop elsewhere for a bargain. The discount (free delivery is a form of discount) is claimed primarily by the most price-sensitive customers.

Economists, who like jargon, have invented the term *price discrimination* for the ancient practice of targeting discounts to price-sensitive buyers. Examples abound. Dell Computer recently listed an ultralight laptop for $2,307 on its web page for sales to small businesses. On the web page for sales to health care companies, the same machine was listed at $2,228, and on the page for sales to state and local governments, the price was $2,072. The annual subscription fee for the *Proceedings of the National Academy of Sciences* is $650 a year for a small college library, or $6,600 for a large university. That tells you who Dell and the National Academy of Sciences believe is most sensitive to prices.

Colleges and universities, incidentally, are themselves among the most successful price discriminators on earth. At some colleges almost every student gets an individualized aid package, which is another way of saying that each student is quoted an individualized price. MIT recently sent a letter to parents announcing that it would be increasing both its tuition and its scholarship aid. I wonder whether the parents would have reacted differently if the letter had more transparently announced a new policy of escalated price discrimination.

Colleges are good at this partly because they have access to so much specialized information about their customers. So do Internet marketers. When you buy an airline ticket online, the seller is likely to know a lot about your recent browsing habits, including how many times you've searched for the same ticket. That information allows them to estimate your willingness-to-pay, and can affect the price you're quoted. If you want to see a different price, try clearing your browser cache.*

---

* In response to the constant flow of new information about demand, American Airlines changes 500,000 prices per day.

Car dealers strive mightily to price-discriminate. When you go to buy a car, the salesperson is likely to ask a question like "How much do you want to pay?" (Personally, I always answer "zero.") What he really means to ask is "What's the most you're *willing* to pay?" If he could rely on you to answer honestly, that would be your price. In practice, he connives to estimate the true answer by engaging you in conversation about the other cars you're considering, what you do for a living, and the size of your family. Then he does the best he can.

For a seller, price discrimination can mean the difference between prosperity and failure. But it's not always an easy trick to pull off. First you need a gimmick that prevents full-price customers from claiming the discount. Sometimes a newspaper coupon or a mail-in rebate or a watch trade-in program does the trick. Sometimes sellers get a bit more creative.

The first printer I ever owned was a Hewlett-Packard laser printer, which I bought in the 1990s for $1,500. I had a choice between two models: the Laser Printer and the Laser Printer E. They were basically identical except that the Laser Printer was both faster (ten pages a minute instead of five) and more expensive.

Why is the faster printer more expensive? The obvious answer is that it costs more to make a faster printer, but the obvious answer is wrong. The Laser Printer and the Laser Printer E came off the same assembly line. *After* the fully identical working printers were assembled, Hewlett-Packard set some of them aside, slapped on a label that said "Laser Printer E," and inserted an extra chip to *slow them down.*

It might seem like an odd thing to do, crippling your own product in order to make it less appealing to customers. But there was method to Hewlett-Packard's apparent madness. They believed, quite reasonably, that those customers who are most desperate for a printer (and will therefore pay full price if asked) are, by and large, the same customers who care a lot about speed.* Those customers pay top dollar for the faster printer, while others, who might otherwise have walked away, have a cheaper option available.

Hewlett-Packard's optimal strategy is "Pay $1,500 if you're willing to; $1,000 otherwise." Unless the customers are pathological truthtellers, this strategy doesn't work. The closest approximation HP could come up with was "Pay $1,500 if you care a lot about speed; $1,000 otherwise." As long as those who care a lot about speed are mostly the same people who are willing to pay $1,500, the strategy more or less works.

Hewlett-Packard did not invent this strategy. In the 19th century French railroads offered seats in first-, second-, and third-class carriages. In order to convert a second-class carriage to a third-class carriage, they removed the roof.

Likewise hardcover books are more expensive than paperbacks not because of any significant difference in production costs—in fact the production costs don't come close to accounting for the diference—but because publishers believe that much of the time those readers who are willing to pay the most for a book are the same readers who want their books to last a long time and/or the same readers who aren't willing to wait for the paperback. Again the ideal strategy would be "Pay more if you're willing to"; the tolerable approximation is "Pay more if you want a sturdier (or more immediately available) product."

A successful price discriminator needs some kind of a gimmick, be it a newspaper coupon or a trade-in program or a product that comes in crippled versions, that makes discounts alluring only to those customers who are unwilling to pay full price. But finding that gimmick is only half the battle. The next skirmish is preventing resales.

---

* This is no logical necessity. It's possible (though perhaps unlikely) that the customers most desperate for a printer are those who care the *least* about speed. If this were the case, HP's strategy would have failed.

If your local baker offers a senior citizen discount on apple pies, he's got to worry that you'll send in your grandmother to shop for you. Worse yet, your grandmother could come in, buy up all the $10 pies at the special senior citizen price of $8, and set up shop next door, reselling the pies for $9 apiece.

Barbers, by contrast, don't have this problem. When your barber offers a senior citizen discount, he doesn't have to worry that you'll send in your grandmother to get her hair cut for you. That's why we generally expect more price discrimination at barber shops than at bakeries. Likewise sending your grandmother to the movies so she can come home and tell you what happened is usually less satisfying than watching the movie yourself. That's why movie theaters can price-discriminate.

In the 1940s the Rohm and Haas chemical company developed a substance called methyl methacrylate (better known as Plexiglas). They priced it at $22 a pound for dentists (who needed it to make dentures) and 85 cents a pound for industrial users, who had many good substitutes. Sure enough, before long the industrial users were buying up the product and reselling it to dentists. To combat this problem, Rohm and Haas toyed with the idea of adding a touch of arsenic to each industrial batch, making it unsuitable for use in dentistry. (One internal memo called this "a very fine method of controlling the bootleg situation.") Liability concerns intervened, and this solution was never implemented. Instead, Rohm and Haas did the next best thing: They actively encouraged a *rumor* that they'd been adding arsenic.

So if you want to price-discriminate, you need not just a gimmick for targeting discounts but also a strategy for preventing resales. And you need one more thing: a dollop of monopoly power. Without that, your competitors will steal all your high-paying customers and leave you with only the discount trade.

Wheat farmers, for example, are notorious for their complete lack of monopoly power. That's why you've never heard of a wheat farmer who offers senior citizen discounts. Indeed suppose Farmer Jones hangs out a sign that says

WHEAT
$4 for the general public
$3 for senior citizens

Within minutes, we can expect Farmer Brown next door to hang out a sign that says

WHEAT
$3.75
I don't care how old you are.

That way Brown steals all of Jones's high-paying customers. After all, we know that Jones can cover his costs selling wheat at $3 a bushel; otherwise he wouldn't be selling to anyone, even senior citizens, at that price. That means he's making a lot of excess profit on all those $4 bushels, and if there's one thing we know about excess profits, it's that they tend to be competed away.

Of course, that's not the end of the story. Jones now lowers his general-public price to $3.50, and the story continues until the price gap has disappeared completely.

Jones's price discrimination can survive only if Brown can't steal his customers. That's the same thing as saying it can survive only if Jones has some monopoly power—which in this case he doesn't.

Neither, you would think, do most dry cleaners. There are, after all, six apparently identical dry cleaners within walking distance of my house. Yet dry cleaners appear to price-discriminate. They have signs that say

Dry Cleaning
Women's shirts cleaned and pressed—$5
Men's shirts cleaned and pressed—$3

For years this drove me nuts. Everything I think I know about economics—and everything I teach my students—tells me that competitors can't price-discriminate. Yet every day I walked past six dry cleaners who seemed to prove me wrong. As a professional economist, it made me ashamed to accept a paycheck.

If it weren't for the monopoly issue, the price discrimination story would make reasonable sense. You'd need to believe both that men are more price-sensitive than women (maybe because men care less whether their clothes are clean) and that many men are either unable or unwilling to pass off their wives' pink floral blouses as their own. I'm willing to believe those things.

But whence the monopoly power? When every dry cleaner is charging $3 for men and $5 for women, what stops any one dry cleaner from charging $4.50 for everyone, stealing all the female business, and, well, cleaning up?

Brand loyalty could explain it. If customers are reluctant to switch dry cleaners, then each one becomes a mini-monopolist and price gaps need not get competed away. I find that implausible, but maybe I'm just overgeneralizing from my own cheerful willingness to switch dry cleaners whenever I see an opportunity to save a buck.

The alternative is that maybe, despite appearances, this isn't price discrimination after all. Maybe men get a better price not because they're more price-sensitive but because they're cheaper to serve.

That's all very satisfying until you start trying to think of reasons why men should be cheaper to serve. True, men's shirts are more often made of cotton and women's blouses are more often made of silk. But if that's the right story, you'd expect the window signs to say "$3 for cotton; $5 for silk," not "$3 for men; $5 for women."

For many weeks my colleagues and I batted this conundrum around the lunch table at the (now sadly defunct) Hillside Restaurant in Rochester, New York. Is this price discrimination or isn't it? We returned to the topic so often that Bonnie Buonomo, the restaurant manager, got sick of overhearing us and did what none of us had thought to do: she called some dry cleaners. They gave her three answers:

- Dry Cleaner Number One said that it's more expensive to clean women's shirts because they absorb perfume. All the others rejected this theory.
- Dry Cleaner Number Two said that this was store policy and if Bonnie didn't like it, she was free to take her business elsewhere.
- Dry Cleaners Number Three, Four, and Five all said that men are cheaper to serve not because of the cleaning, but because of the pressing. First, men's shirts are pretty much all the same shape and so can be pressed by machine; women's blouses usually need individual attention. Second, men's shirts are usually worn under jackets, so it's no great tragedy if you miss a small wrinkle. Women's blouses, which are worn in the open, need more scrupulous care.

I don't know that this is the final word on the subject, but it makes enough sense that I've gone back to collecting my paycheck without compunction (though my wife points out rather forcefully that perhaps I should have signed my next paycheck over to Bonnie, who made the phone calls).

Other puzzles seem harder. Canadian restaurants near the border sometimes accept U.S. currency at above-market exchange rates. Is this price discrimination in favor of Americans? If so, why should Americans, who are likely to be traveling far from home, be more price-sensitive than Canadians, who can always cook in their own kitchens? But if not, what is the alternative explanation? Do Americans spend less time at the table than Canadians? Do they demand less service?

In many cities taxis charge one rate for a couple traveling together and a higher rate for two strangers going to the same destination. Price discrimination? If so, why do the discounts go to people traveling in pairs? Is it because they might otherwise talk each other into trying the subway?

Some cases are easier to crack. The salad bar costs less if you order an entrée. Price discrimination? More plausibly it's because people who order the entrée make fewer return trips to the salad bar. Ice cream shops charge less per scoop when you buy two scoops instead of one. Price discrimination? More plausibly it's because neither preparing the cone, opening the freezer, nor ringing up the cash register, all of which take valuable time, has to be repeated for the second scoop.

And what about those supermarket coupons? The usual story is that clippers get a price break because they have a lot of free time and therefore shop for bargains. When I included that example in the college textbook I was writing, one reviewer suggested an intriguing alternative: Coupon clippers, because they have more free time, tend to shop in the middle of the day when the store is uncrowded and the checkout clerks are idle. That makes them cheaper to serve, and that—as opposed to price discrimination—is why they get discounts.

I applaud the spirit that concocted this story, but I am skeptical. If grocery stores want to reward people for shopping at uncrowded times, they could simply announce a 10 percent discount for anyone who shops at those times—no coupons necessary. On the other hand, I suppose that time-of-day discounts could become a logistical nightmare. What do you do with the customer who complains that he would have checked out at 2:59 rather than 3:01 if only he had gotten competent service at the meat counter?

Should Amazon sell cheap Kindle e-readers to increase the demand for e-books, or cheap e-books to increase the demand for Kindles? Should Gillette sell cheap razors to increase the demand for razor blades, or cheap razor blades to increase the demand for razors? Should Disneyland charge low gate fees to get you into the park, where they can sell you expensive ride tickets, or cheap ride tickets to make the park more attractive, so they can charge more at the gate?

If customers were all identical, the solutions would be easy. Sell the e-books, the razor blades, or the ride tickets at cost so people will buy a lot of them. This enhances the customers' experience and increase their total willingness-to-pay, all of which you can extract upfront.

If customers were all *nearly* identical, the solution would be very similar. But if customers differ substantially, the solution falls apart. Disney sells cheap ride tickets so Alice will be willing to pay $100 at the gate. But a $100 admission fee drives away Bob, Charlie, and Doris. To keep their business, Disney lowers the admission fee to $25. Now what's the point of letting Alice buy cheap ride tickets?

When customers are diverse, it's hard to soak them at the admission booth, because the fee that soaks one will wash away another. But that's okay, because when customers are diverse, you should be thinking about something else entirely, namely: What's the best way to price-discriminate?

The answer, of course, is to give discounts to price-sensitive customers like Bob, Charlie, and Doris, while forcing Alice to pay a high price for her Disneymania. One way to accomplish that is to sell expensive ride tickets and let everyone in for free (or nearly so). That way Bob, Charlie, and Doris can buy two or three ride tickets, head home, and have an inexpensive day at the park, while Alice, who feels compelled to ride every ride, spends a lot of money along the way.*

Executive summary for Disney: With similar customers, price the rides low and the admission tickets high. With diverse customers do the opposite.

Likewise for Gillette: With similar customers, price the blades low and the razors high. That way they shave more often and you maximize their total willingness-to-pay. With diverse customers, price the blades high and the razors low. That way you effectively charge full price to the heavy shavers while light shavers, who might otherwise look for a cheaper product, get a discount.†

Now, then, why is popcorn so expensive at the movies?

As with Gillette and Disney, the key must lie in the diversity of the customer base. But moviegoers are diverse in more ways than shavers or theme park visitors. Gillette's customers differ in how much they value a shave. Disney's differ in how much they value a thrill ride. But the theater's customers differ *both* in how much they value the movie *and* in how much they value the popcorn.

Still, this much remains true: If the customers are identical (or

---

* This assumes that most customers are either enthusiasts like Alice, who ride lots of rides and are willing to pay dearly for the experience, or casual daytrippers like Bob, who ride very few rides and won't visit Disneyland unless the price is right. In principle, there could also be customers who buy very few tickets (like Bob) but are willing to pay handsomely for the experience (like Alice), or customers who buy a lot of tickets once they're in the park (like Alice) but are unwilling to pay much for the experience (like Bob). If so, this complicates the analysis considerably. This might be why Disney has a history of experimenting with a great variety of pricing structures.

† High blade prices effectively charge a higher price to heavy shavers, and therefore constitute a form of price discrimination. As with any price discrimination, this strategy can survive only in the presence of some monopoly power. In this case the monopoly power comes partly from brand loyalty to Gillette and partly from the patents Gillette holds.

nearly so) the best policy is surely to price the popcorn at cost so people will buy a lot—and to tack the value of what they're getting onto the admission fee.

With customer diversity, the problem is trickier. Here the owner wants to price discriminate. Ideally the policy would be something like "$15 if you're a movie lover who's willing to pay that much, or $9 if that's what it takes to get your business." The owner approximates this strategy with something like "$15 total if you're a popcorn buyer; $9 otherwise," or in other words, "$9 at the box office; $6 for a bag of popcorn."

The goal is to soak the movie lovers. The actual policy is to soak the popcorn buyers. That makes sense if (and only if!) the movie lovers and the popcorn buyers just happen to be, by and large, the same people.

On the other hand, it would make no sense at all in a world where, for example, movie lovers and popcorn *haters* just happened to be, by and large, the same people. In that world, owners would look for a way to charge more to the popcorn haters, something like "Free popcorn, and $5 off your admission fee if you agree to eat three bags." That way, the popcorn-hating movie lovers pay full price.

So why is popcorn priced the way it is? According to theory, it should be priced high at times and places where a love of popcorn is highly correlated with a love of movies, and low at times and places where the correlation is reversed. Instead, we see it priced high pretty much everywhere and always. Apparently, then, we live in a world where popcorn lovers and movie lovers just happen to be everywhere and always the same people (at least by and large) —the kind of world, in other words, where high popcorn prices make sense. That, perhaps, is the whole story. But I am instinctively dissatisfied with any explanation that employs the phrase "just happen to be." I'd prefer something a little more compelling, but, as economists know well, you can't always get what you want.

CHAPTER 17

COURTSHIP AND COLLUSION

The Mating Game

In the tenth century B.C., the Queen of Sheba (near what is now Yemen) had monopolized the shipment of spices, myrrh, and frankincense to the Mediterranean. When King Solomon of Israel threatened to invade her market, the book of Kings tells us that "she came to Jerusalem, with a very great train, with camels that bear spices, and very much gold, and precious stones," as a prelude to striking a deal. Twenty-eight centuries later, the first modern economist, Adam Smith, observed that "people of the same trade seldom meet together, even for merriment and diversion, but the conversation ends in a conspiracy against the public, or in some contrivance to raise prices"—or, in this case, to keep prices high.

Collusion, like sex, is ancient and ubiquitous. It should come as no surprise that two such popular enterprises have been pursued in tandem.

In the markets for sex and marriage, men compete among themselves for women, and women compete among themselves for men.* But men compete differently than women do, in part because men

---

* This is not an exhaustive catalogue of sexual competition; I am restricting this discussion to heterosexual couplings, which seem sufficiently common to merit some attention.

are more inclined to seek multiple partners. The reasons for this in-clination are rooted perhaps partly in biology (it can be good repro-ductive strategy to scatter your seed widely if your seed is regenerated every day, and equally good reproductive strategy to focus your atten-tion on a single partner if you can't give birth more than once a year), and perhaps partly in social conditioning. There are, of course, many people of both genders who fail to fit the pattern, but there is at least a germ of truth in the observation that a woman seeks one man to fill her every need, while a man seeks every woman to fill his one need.

In societies that allow polygamy, it is almost invariably men who take multiple wives, rather than the reverse. Males drunk on testoster-one might imagine that their lives would be better in such societies, but if the fantasy were realized most of the fantasizers would be disap-pointed. For each man with four wives, there must be three with no wives at all. You can change the laws of marriage, but you can't repeal the laws of arithmetic.

If, in modern mainstream America, each man were free to seek four women, the competition for women would be intense. Even those men who came out victorious would pay dearly for their victories. Women would be doubly fortunate: They would have more suitors, and their suitors, each trying to stand out from the crowd, would be more attentive and deferential. On dinner dates the woman would be more likely to pick the restaurant and the man more likely to pick up the tab. Married men, sensitive to their wives' continuing opportunities, would do more housework.*

Perhaps if polygamy were legal, most or even all women would still insist on monogamous marriages and we would pair up in pretty much the same combinations as we do today. Even so, it would be a very different world. Today when my wife and I argue about who

---

* In some primitive polygamous societies, and in some religious communities, things work out very differently. There women have little say in their choice of marriage part-ners—and therefore don't reap the benefits of competition.

should do the dishes, we start from positions of roughly equal strength. If polygamy were legal, my wife could hint that she's thought about leaving me to marry Michael and Leah down the block—and I might end up with dishpan hands. Wives would have more power in deciding all of the big and little conflicts that arise in marriage: how many children to have, what city to live in, who cooks dinner, and, on quiet evenings in front of the television, who operates the remote control.*

Men in a polygamous society are like spice merchants perpetually resisting encroachments from competitors. Merchants respond by agreeing to divide the territory. Somewhere back in history, the masculine gender did the same. By custom and by law, men have managed to enforce a collusive agreement to limit their attentions to one woman apiece. There is a lot of cheating on that agreement, but that is just what economic theory predicts.

In fact the antipolygamy laws are a textbook example of the theory of cartels. Producers, initially competitive, gather together in a conspiracy against the public or, more specifically, against their customers. They agree that each firm will restrict its output in an attempt to keep prices high. But a high price invites cheating, in the sense that each firm seeks to expand its own output beyond what the agreement allows. Eventually the cartel crumbles unless it is enforced by legal sanctions, and even then violations are legion.

That story, told in every economics textbook, is also a plausible story of male producers in the romance industry. Initially fiercely competitive, they gather together in a conspiracy against their "customers"—the women to whom they offer their hands in marriage. The conspiracy consists of an agreement under which men restrict

---

* The same phenomenon occurs in nonpolygamous situations and regardless of gender. An increase in the population of single women might seem to be a matter of indifference to those married men who don't engage in extramarital affairs. On the contrary, it allows those men to issue more credible threats about dissolving one marriage for another and therefore gives them more power within their families. *All* men benefit when more single women are available.

their romantic endeavors in an attempt to increase the bargaining position of men in general. But the improved position of men invites cheating, in the sense that men try to court more women than allowed under the agreement. The cartel survives only because it is enforced by legal sanctions, and even so violations are legion.*

Cartels have changed very little in the past 3,000 years, but they've gotten slicker about public relations. When the Overlap Group, consisting of MIT and the Ivy League universities, was caught conspiring to keep tuition rates high and financial aid offers low, their defense was at least creative: The goal, they said, was to prevent financial considerations from unduly influencing students when they choose a college. If the major auto manufacturers had been caught colluding to keep prices high, they might not have thought to argue that they'd served a noble purpose by preventing financial considerations from unduly influencing consumers when they choose a car.

With the same effrontery that led Overlap to maintain that it exists solely as a favor to its victims, men have maintained that antipolygamy laws are designed to somehow protect women. But a law that prohibits any man from marrying more than one woman is not different in principle from a law that prohibits any firm from hiring more than one worker. I suppose that if such a law were enacted, firms would argue that it was designed to protect workers. Who would believe them?

Theory suggests that when an enforcement mechanism is available, any group of competitors will attempt to collude. The observation is not limited to competitors of a particular gender. As men conspire against women, so women conspire against men.

---

* Note the exact parallel with the breakdown in the agreement among birds of paradise in chapter 8.

When firms discover an innovative but costly way to improve their products, they might profitably conspire to withhold the innovation from the marketplace. Such conspiracies usually founder on the ambitions of maverick firms that see huge profit opportunities in being the market's only innovator. The cartel's best hope for survival is a law that bans the innovation, and substantial resources are devoted to lobbying for such laws.

Modern technology offers women a variety of innovative but costly ways to attract men. One of these innovations is the silicone breast implant.* The costs to women include not only out-of-pocket expenses but a variety of health risks.

It can be advantageous for women to withhold such products from the marketplace. In doing so, they act like the major auto companies agreeing to stifle a new technology that would serve their customers well. In ordinary circumstances, each automaker would be left wondering who was going to violate the agreement first. But if they can arrange to have the innovation outlawed, auto executives can sleep more soundly at night.

Likewise, women cannot simply agree among themselves to avoid cosmetic surgery. Aside from the logistical problems of arranging a contract among 100 million parties, cheating would be uncontrollable. The best hope, then, is to ban the products.

In 1992, silicone breast implants became illegal in the United States, largely because of political pressure from feminist groups. The ban remained in place until 2006.† At first blush it seems inexplicable that a political lobby committed to a woman's absolute right

---

* I'm well aware that not all men find implants attractive. You, presumably, are well aware that many men do.

† Depo-Provera shots, which protect against pregnancy for three months at the risk of serious side effects, were banned until 2004, partly at the urging of the same feminist groups. Insofar as effective birth control is (among other things) an attractant to men, the argument here applies to Depo-Provera as well as breast implants.

to choose an abortion could seek to deny that same woman the right to choose her bra size. If women are rational, intelligent creatures capable of weighing the health risks (not to mention other weighty issues) of terminating a pregnancy, then one might expect that they are capable of weighing the health risks of a silicone implant.

The theory of cartels suggests that the feminists were right and the plausible objections I have just voiced are wrong. Producers *can* be made better off by laws that limit innovation. The Ford Motor Company is capable of deciding for itself whether to adopt a new automotive technology but might still want the technology banned—not to protect it from *itself* but to protect it from its competitors. If Ford could be the only innovator on the block, it would be happy; given the realities of competition, it would prefer to see the innovation disappear.

And likewise for women. Any woman who wanted silicone breast implants and could be assured of having the only implants in America would be happy. Given the reality—that if implants are legal her competitors will acquire them too—she might prefer an absolute ban.

The best argument for keeping new technologies legal is not that they benefit manufacturers but that they benefit their customers. Analogously, the best argument for keeping cosmetic breast implants legal is not that they guarantee freedom for women but that they gratify men. The economically correct argument is the most politically *in*correct argument imaginable.

A careful cost-benefit analysis would probably conclude that the recent legalization of breast implants is a good thing, because the benefits to men exceed the costs to women*—though if you took the cost-benefit exercise seriously there would be several other

---

* I infer this not from any direct estimates of the costs or benefits but from the fact that some women willingly bear the costs of implants in exchange for capturing part of the benefits in the form of increased attention from men.

factors to consider. First, some women want implants for reasons other than their effect on men; that goes on the benefit side and strengthens the argument for legalization. Second, implanted breasts might confer benefits on casual observers that are not captured by the owners of those breasts; chalk up one more benefit. But in the opposite direction, men might care not about breast size per se, but about *relative* breast size; that is, they don't care how big their mates' breasts are, as long as they're the biggest in the room. If so, artificial breast enhancements amount to a socially wasteful arms race (like the elaborate plumage on birds of paradise), so it can be efficient to tax or even ban them.

Likewise with steroids: If women enjoy having bulked-up partners, or if sports fans enjoy seeing a lot of home runs, that's a good argument for allowing steroids. If men like being bulked up for its own sake, or if passing strangers enjoy the show, that's another good argument. On the other hand, if women or sports fans just want their partners or their heroes to be more bulked up or to hit more home runs than the next guy, then it might be best for everyone to put an end to the arms race. We should still expect plenty of cheating, though—and as sports fans know, we get it.

When Chicago area butchers wanted to spend evenings at home with their families, they convinced the city council to outlaw meat sales after 6:00 P.M. (The law has since been repealed.) A simple agreement among the butchers to close early would have invited cheating by creating an irresistible temptation to be the only evening butcher in town.

A naive observer might think that butchers could not possibly benefit from a law restricting their freedom to choose their own hours—just as that same observer might think that men could not possibly benefit from a law restricting their freedom to pursue multiple marriage partners, or women from a law restricting their free-dom to pursue cosmetic surgery. But an agreement, even when it is mutually beneficial, needs to be enforced.

A century ago in China, goods were transported by barges pulled by teams of six men who were well rewarded if they arrived at their destination on time. Because each man calculated that success de-pended largely on the efforts of the other five, teams were plagued by chronic shirking. If everyone else is pulling hard, the team will make it anyway, so why pull hard? If *nobody* else is pulling hard, the team *won't* make it anyway, so why pull hard? Everyone makes the same rational calculation, everyone shirks, the goods arrive late, and nobody gets paid.

Barge teams quickly evolved a mechanism for averting such unfortunate outcomes: The six team members collectively hired a seventh man to whip them.

Pressing the government into service as an enforcer is not so different from hiring an enforcer with a whip. (There is, however, a significant difference between the bargemen and the butchers: When bargemen conspire to work harder, they form a victimless conspiracy. When butchers conspire to offer less service, they con-spire against the public.)

The mating game is a game that everyone can win. Even so, there is room for conflict about how to divide the spoils. With so much at stake, it is not surprising that coalitions form, break apart, and call on governments to resurrect them. Games breed strategic behavior. That includes the game where some believe that every strategy is fair.

CHAPTER 18

CURSED WINNERS
AND GLUM LOSERS

Why Life Is Full of Disappointments

Economic theory predicts that you are not enjoying this book as much as you thought you would. This is a special case of a more general proposition: *Most* things in life don't turn out as well as you thought they would. While psychologists, poets, and philosophers have often remarked on this phenomenon, few have recognized that it is a necessary consequence of informed, rational decision making.

Choosing a book is a process fraught with risk and uncertainty. Fortunately, your lifetime of experience as a reader is a valuable guide. It enables you to form some expectation of each book's quality. Your expectations are sometimes very wrong, but on average they are far better than random guesses.

Some books are better than you expect them to be and others are worse, but it is unlikely that you err in one direction much more often than the other. If you consistently either overestimated or underestimated quality, you would eventually discover your own bias and correct for it. So it is reasonable to assume that your expectations are too low about as often as they are too high.

This means that if you chose this book randomly off the shelf, it would be as likely to exceed your expectations as to fall short of them. But you didn't choose it randomly off the shelf. Rational consumer that you are, you chose it because it was one of the few available books that you expected to be among the very best. Unfortunately that makes it one of the few available books whose quality you are most likely to have overestimated. Under the circumstances, to read it is to court disappointment.

The logic of probable disappointment haunts every aspect of life in which we choose among alternatives. Even when your judgments *in general* are free of bias, your judgments about *those activities that you choose to engage in* are usually too optimistic. Your assessments of potential marriage partners might be exactly right on average, but the one who seems the perfect match is the one whose flaws you are most likely to have overlooked.

Things are even worse when you buy a good at auction. When you are the high bidder, you can be certain of one thing: Nobody else in the room thought the item was worth as much as you did. That observation alone implies that you've probably overestimated its true worth. Economists, ever dismal, call this phenomenon the *winner's curse*.

Imagine that you are a knowledgeable real estate developer submitting a sealed bid on a parcel of land. Your expert judgment tells you that if you could acquire this land for $50,000, you would make a handsome profit. You might think that under the circumstances you'd be happy to win that land at auction for $50,000. But if you *do* win the auction at that price, you learn that your competitors' expert judgments led all of them to less optimistic assessments than your own. Unless you are quite sure that your own information is better than anybody else's, you are likely to wonder if $50,000 is such a bargain after all.

When you are deciding how much to bid for a piece of land, the right question is not "Given what I know now, would I be happy to buy this land for $50,000?" Instead the right question is "Given what I know now, and assuming also that no other developer was willing to bid $50,000, would I *still* be happy to buy it for

$50,000?" These are very different questions. Those who frequently buy goods at auction must learn to appreciate that difference and to adjust their bids accordingly.

On the other hand, there are circumstances where the winner's curse is not an issue. Some auctiongoers are quite certain of how much they are willing to pay for an item, without any regard for what others may know or think. If you are bidding on an antique brass candelabrum, and you have examined it closely, and you know exactly how you plan to use it, and you don't care whether it is attractive to others, and you are certain that you will never want to resell it, then buying the candelabrum for $1,000 is an equally good bargain regardless of what the other bidders may think. In such cases there is no winner's curse. There is still the possibility of disappointment—the candelabrum might not look as good on your mantelpiece as you thought it would—but there is not the *probability* of disappointment that constitutes a true winner's curse. After all, it's equally possible that the candelabrum will look *better* than you imagined, and the fact that you have won the auction does nothing to diminish this possibility.

The presence or absence of a winner's curse is of immediate concern to the buyer, who must account for it in his bidding strategy. It is therefore of indirect concern to the seller, who cares very much how buyers behave. But the seller's role is not limited to hoping that buyers will bid high. The seller is also a strategic player in the auction game. He gets only one move, but it is the most important: He sets the rules.

There are many types of auction. The most familiar is the common English auction, where bidders offer successively higher prices and drop out until only one remains. There is the Dutch auction, where an auctioneer calls out a very high price and successively lowers it until he receives an offer to buy.* There is the first-price

---

* This, at least, is the traditional definition of a Dutch auction. eBay and other online auction sites have muddied the definitional waters by using the phrase "Dutch auction" to mean several different things.

sealed-bid auction, where each buyer submits a bid in an envelope, all are opened simultaneously, and the high bidder gets the item for the amount of his bid. There is the second-price sealed-bid auction, where the high bidder gets the item but pays only the amount of the *second*-highest bid. There are third-, fourth-, and fifth-price sealed-bid auctions. And there are more exotic possibilities. In the Glum Losers auction, the high bidder gets the item for free and everybody else pays the amount of his own bid.

The seller can choose among these or any other rules that he manages to dream up. Ideally his goal is to maximize the selling price. In practice, he rarely has enough information to achieve that goal. If two bidders are both willing to go very high, an English auction can force them to compete with each other, pushing the price up as high as possible. If only one bidder is willing to go very high, an English auction is disastrous for the seller: Everyone else drops out early and the potential high bidder gets a fabulous bargain. Because bidders are unlikely to reveal their bidding strategies in advance of the auction, the seller can never know for certain on any given night whether an English auction is preferable to, say, a Dutch auction.

Even to decide between a first-price and a second-price sealed-bid auction can be difficult for the seller. On the one hand, in a first-price auction he collects the high bid, while in a second-price auction he collects only the amount of the second-highest bid. On the other hand, bidders generally submit higher bids in a second-price auction. They submit even higher bids in a third-price auction. Which is best for the seller? Again the answer depends on who shows up to bid, and what the bidders' strategies are.

Given his limited information, the seller is in no position to choose the rule that will maximize the selling price at any one auction. But he *can* hope to choose the rule that will maximize the *average* selling price over *many* auctions. At some auctions English rules yield the highest prices, while at others Dutch rules yield the highest prices. Which rules yield the highest prices on average?

At this point economic theory makes its entrance, to announce an astonishing truth: Under certain reasonable assumptions (about which I will soon say more), and as a matter of mathematical fact, all of the auction rules I've mentioned yield the same revenue to the seller on average over many auctions. If I regularly sell merchandise at English auctions, while you sell at Dutch auctions, your brother sells at first-price sealed-bid auctions, your sister sells at second-price sealed-bid auctions, and your crazy Uncle Fester sells at Glum Losers auctions, and if we all sell merchandise of comparable quality, then in the long run we must all do equally well.

This result applies as well to a vast number of other auction rules—in fact to any rule you can imagine that does not involve some entrance fee to the auction hall or its equivalent.

I haven't told you how I know that sellers using vastly different rules all do equally well on average, because the argument is technical and I haven't yet figured out how to translate it into simple English. (Probably this means that I don't yet understand it well enough.) But there is no doubt that the argument is correct.

A result like this is a great joy to a theorist. It is surprising, elegant, and emphatic. There is no need to mince words or to introduce qualifications. We need not make long and ugly catalogues ("The English auction is superior under any of the following seven conditions, while the Dutch auction is superior under any of the following six other conditions"). We can state our conclusion in no more than five words—"All rules are equally good"—and we can prove it incontrovertibly to anyone with an undergraduate's knowledge of advanced calculus. The best thing about it is that almost nobody would have guessed it. If theory never did more than confirm what we already know, there would be no need for it.

And yet . . . It remains disturbingly the case that real-world auctioneers show marked preferences for some rules over others. Cattle and slaves have always been sold in English auctions, tulips in Dutch auctions, and oil drilling rights in sealed-bid auctions. If all rules are equally good for the seller, why do sellers insist on one rule rather than another?

An economist might feel some temptation to respond that auctioneers are not economists and so are likely to live in ignorance of the latest breakthroughs. Not only do many auctioneers fail to subscribe to the *Journal of Economic Theory*, but all too often their advanced calculus has grown sufficiently rusty that it would be difficult for them to stay abreast of the field even if they made an honest effort. But the economist's temptation is best resisted. It is a fair assumption that people who run auctions for a living know what they are doing, and that if there is some discrepancy between their behavior and the prescriptions of the economic theorist, then it is the theorist who is missing something. Our job as economists is not to tell auctioneers how to run their business. It is to assume that they *know* how to run their business and to figure out why their strategies are the right ones.

On the one hand, we have an argument that under certain assumptions, the choice of auction rule is a matter of indifference. On the other hand, we have the behavior of auctioneers, from which we infer that the choice of auction rule is a matter of considerable concern. The inescapable conclusion is that those "certain assumptions" do not always apply. So it is time to be explicit about what they are.

The most important assumption is that there is no winner's curse. More precisely, the argument assumes that a bidder does not change his mind about the item's value when he learns that another bidder disagrees with him. If you are bidding on a van Gogh to hang on your wall, you might be willing to pay $50 million regardless of what anyone else thinks; if you are bidding on the same painting in anticipation of a large profit at resale, you are likely to be chagrined when you learn that none of the other dealers in the room bid more than $10 million. The equivalence of auction rules holds in the first case but not in the second.

In fact when bidders care about one another's opinions, the seller is well advised to choose the English auction. Going into the auction, there may be only one bidder willing to pay above $10 million. When others observe his willingness to go high, they may reason that he knows something and decide to compete with him. A sealed-bid auction precludes this outcome. So does a Dutch auction—by the time the high bidder reveals his enthusiasm, the auction is over.

English auctions are by far the most common and appear to be the form most favored by auctioneers. The theory suggests that the only reason auctioneers would have such a preference is that bidders respond to information about one another's assessments. This means in particular that bidders are subject to the winner's curse. So while the curse is initially no more than a theoretical possibility, the prevalence of English auctions suggests that it is a pervasive phenomenon.

Although the argument for the equivalence of auction rules assumes away the winner's curse, this is not the only direction in which it may depart from reality. Another key assumption is that buyers do not have large fractions of their wealth riding on the outcome of the auction. This assumption is important, because in its absence, buyers bid more conservatively, which affects the entire analysis. In that case, the seller should prefer a first-price sealed-bid auction to an English auction. Because buyers are loath to risk losing, and because a sealed bid gives them only one chance to win, they tend to shade their bids upward, profiting the seller.

Another questionable assumption in the standard theory is that the population of bidders does not change when the rules change. In reality a Dutch auction might draw an entirely different class of bidders than an English auction. Some future theorist will earn fame by figuring out how to incorporate this effect into the analysis.

Rather than venture into such uncharted territory, let me take a side path to explore another issue that confronts the seller. Sellers frequently know more about their merchandise than buyers do and can acquire reputations for honesty by always revealing everything they know, good or bad. Does honesty pay?

Honest John holds used-car auctions on a regular basis. He makes it a point always to announce everything that he knows about the cars he sells. If a car burns oil, or if it's been in an accident, Honest John will tell you. People bid lower when John announces that the car on the block is a lemon, but they bid higher at other times because they know that if John were aware of any problems, he would tell them.

John earns less on the lemons than he would if he were secretive, but he earns more on the good cars. These effects can cancel, leaving John no better or worse off than his counterpart, Silent Sam, in the next town, who reveals nothing. So far, we have found no good argument for Honest John's honesty. But John has one additional advantage over Sam: His policy partly alleviates the threat of the winner's curse and so gives buyers an *additional* reason to bid high. In the long run, John is sure to do better than Sam.

To put this another way, the winner's curse is initially the buyer's problem but becomes the seller's problem also because buyers defend against it by shading their bids downward. It is therefore a good idea for the seller to help buyers ward off the curse. A history of honest dealings can be an effective talisman.

The news that honesty is the best policy would not surprise your grandmother, any more than the news that life is full of disappointments. Like auctioneers, grandmothers have a lot of instinctual knowledge that economists work hard to acquire.

CHAPTER 19

RANDOM WALKS
AND STOCK MARKET PRICES
A Primer for Investors

When I was young and first heard that stock market prices follow random walks, I was incredulous. Did this mean that Google might as well replace its corporate officers with underprivileged eight-year-olds? My question was born of naiveté, and of considerable ignorance. I've learned a lot in the interim. One thing I've learned is that a random walk is not a theory of prices; it is a theory of price *changes*. In that distinction lies a world of difference.

My original (entirely wrong) conception invoked a roulette wheel as its central image. One day the little ball lands on 10, and the stock price is $10; the next day it lands on 8, and the price falls to $8, or it lands on 20 and the stockholders get rich. Blinded by that false vision, I could not see why it mattered if Google appointed a president who cared more about paper dolls than balance sheets. If fate dictated a $20 stock price, then fate would have its way.

The *right* image also invokes a roulette wheel, but in a very different way. The wheel is marked with both positive and negative numbers. Each day the wheel spins, and the little ball's destination determines not today's price, but the *difference* between yesterday's price and today's. If the current price is $10 and the ball lands on –2, then the price falls to $8; if instead it lands on 5, then the price rises to $15.*

With a random walk *every change is permanent.* Today's price is the sum of all the (positive and negative) changes that have come before, and each of those changes is determined by a separate spin of the wheel. If today's spin yields –15, then all future prices will be $15 lower than if today's spin had yielded 0. The effect is entirely undiminished by the passage of time.

If Google brings in Mrs. Grundy's third-grade class to serve as its board of directors, the wheel comes up –20 and the stock price falls from $25 to $5. But future price *changes* continue according to their original destiny. If one-fourth of the spots on the wheel are +.25, then the stock price goes up by 25 cents on one-fourth of all future days; if three-eighths of the spots are marked –.20, then the stock price goes down by 20 cents three-eighths of the time. *Those* numbers don't change. The only change is that the stock price itself is permanently $20 lower than it might have been.

You might object that the $20 drop is itself unprecedented and clearly not from the usual roulette wheel. I reply that the roulette wheel is large, with many spots, and only one of those spots is labeled –20; that is why it doesn't come up very often. But the spot always existed, because there always was the same small probability that Google would do something very foolish.

Which brings me to another of my early misconceptions. I had misinterpreted the word *random* to mean "unrelated to anything else in the world," which is why I thought that the random walk theory denied that Google's behavior could affect its stock price.

---

* An even more accurate image is that the roulette wheel determines not the actual price change but the *percentage* price change; when the ball lands on –2, the stock price falls 2 percent, and when the ball lands on 5 the stock price rises 5 percent. The image I've adopted in the text is slightly easier to think about and close enough to true that nothing interesting will be lost in the discussion.

But one random event can be perfectly correlated with another. Great corporate blunders arrive randomly, and the corresponding stock price changes arrive along with them.

Economists believe that stock market prices behave a lot like random walks most of the time. That is, we believe that price *changes* (not *prices*) usually have the same statistical characteristics as the series of numbers generated by a roulette wheel. If *prices* were random, as I once erroneously believed, then today's price would be useless as a predictor of tomorrow's. Because price *changes* are random, the opposite is true. Today's price is the *best possible* predictor of tomorrow's. Tomorrow's price is today's price, plus a (usually small) random adjustment.

Imagine a simple game of chance. Start with $100 and spin the roulette wheel—the one with both positive and negative numbers—repeatedly. If you spin 5, collect $5; if you spin –2, pay $2 to the house. Your balance follows a random walk. As with any random walk, the present is an excellent predictor of the future. If your balance is low after 10 spins of the wheel, it is likely to remain low after 11.

But while the present value of a random walk foretells a lot about the future, its *past* values are of no additional use. Once I've had a look at the wheel and your current balance, I know all that a mortal can know about your probable destiny. You might have a gripping story to tell about how rich (or poor) you were five minutes ago, but hearing it adds nothing to the accuracy of my forecast.

So it is with stock market prices. Google's current share price is an excellent predictor of its future price. But the history that led to the current price is quite irrelevant.

Commentators report that because a particular stock, or the market as a whole, has recently fallen, it is likely to undergo a "correction" upward in the near future. Or that because it has recently fallen, it is likely to continue downward in the near future. Or that because it has recently risen, it is likely to fall soon or to rise further. But if stock prices are like random walks, as economists believe they usually are, then future price changes are quite independent of past history. The current price predicts the future price. The commentators notwithstanding, past price changes predict nothing.

Those who play the market like to believe that they are more sophisticated than those who play casino games. Yet only the most naive roulette player would suggest that because his cash balance has fallen over the past several plays, it is now due for a "correction" upward. Experienced gamblers know what to expect from a random walk.

When I was young, I harbored many misconceptions (not all of them related to finance). Another was that in the presence of a random walk, there can be no role for investment strategy. I don't know where I got this idea, except perhaps that I knew there is no role for strategy in a random *lottery*, and I came to attribute that to some mystical property of the word *random*. In any event, I was wrong.

First, different stocks are attached to different roulette wheels. Some grow predictably (their wheels have the same number in nearly every spot where the ball might land), while others fluctuate wildly (their wheels have many different numbers, some quite large in both the positive and negative directions). Choosing the right wheel is a matter of taste and of judgment.

Second, and more interesting, the same wheel can control more than one stock. The daily weather is like the spin of a roulette wheel. Sometimes the ball lands on a spot marked "rainier," whereupon Consolidated Umbrellas goes up 5 points and General Picnic

Baskets goes down 5. Other times the ball lands on a spot marked "sunnier," whereupon Consolidated goes down 10 and General goes up 10. A savvy investor who buys stock in *both* Consolidated Umbrellas *and* General Picnic Baskets can shield himself from fluctuations, as one asset's losses are offset by the other's gains. Careful diversification can create a low-risk portfolio that earns more on average than any single low-risk asset.

Typically even the best diversification is imperfect. The wheel has a spot marked "earthquake," and when the ball lands there Consolidated Umbrellas and General Picnic Baskets *both* fall. On the other hand, those are precisely the occasions when the stock of American Home Construction Services rises, and the strategic investor might want to add a few shares of American to his portfolio as a form of earthquake insurance.

If asset prices behave as economists believe they do, most investors should focus not on picking the right assets but on constructing the right portfolios. The question "Is Consolidated Umbrella a good buy?" is meaningless except in the context of an existing portfolio. In conjunction with General Picnic Baskets, Consolidated can compose a well-diversified portfolio. In conjunction with International Raincoats, Consolidated composes a portfolio with a lot of unnecessary risk, courting disaster if the sun comes out.

To earn large rewards, you must accept risk. (This is a moral that runs at large, extending beyond the world of high finance.) The trick is to accept no more risk than is necessary. The method is to diversify by recognizing assets that tend to move in opposition and by using this information judiciously. That is very different from the traditional prescription to "pick winners," which economists believe is rarely possible. But it requires no less savvy. With or without random walks, financial markets continue to reward hard work, talent, and occasionally luck.

*   *   *

Strategy matters. Unfortunately financial counselors don't always distinguish between strategy and superstition. They engage, for example, in a bizarre ritual called "dollar-cost averaging," which will make as much sense to your great-grandchildren as the Salem witch trials make to you.

The "idea" of dollar-cost averaging is to purchase an asset in fixed dollar amounts at regular intervals—say, $1,000 worth of General Motors stock each month for a year. That way, it is argued, you buy less when the price is high (only 50 shares when the price is $20) and more when the price is low (100 shares when the price falls to $10).

"Buy more when the price is low" sounds deceptively appealing, but it also suggests that we pause to consider the question "Low compared with what?" A price is attractive not when it is low compared with the past, but when it is low compared with the expected future. Unfortunately a random walk is *never* unusually low compared with the expected future. The price is as likely to go down $1 when it starts at $10 as when it starts at $100. Would a wise roulette player ever believe that he could improve his fortunes by betting more when his balance is low?

A low current stock price forecasts a low future price. If today's price is low, there is a good reason to buy *more* (it's cheap) and also a good reason to buy *less* (it's likely to *stay* cheap). The two reasons cancel out and make "buying more when the price is low" no more attractive than "buying more when the price is high."

Dollar-cost averaging is a very bad strategy against a random walk. Imagine walking into a casino where 10 identical roulette wheels are to be spun simultaneously. You have $55,000 to bet. You can, if you choose to, bet $1,000 on the first wheel, $2,000 on the second, $3,000 on the third, and so on. (These numbers add up to

$55,000.) But that is an unnecessarily risky way to play roulette; over a third of your wager is riding on the ninth and tenth wheels. The low-risk strategy is to bet $5,500 on each wheel, so that no spin is more important than any other.

Having money in the stock market for 10 months is like betting on the spins of 10 roulette wheels. If you dollar-cost average, adding $1,000 to your investment each month, then you have $1,000 riding on the first spin, $2,000 on the second, $3,000 on the third, and so on.* But we've just agreed that this is a great mistake. The wise gambler bets $5,500 on each wheel. In terms of investment strategy, this means that you should invest $5,500 the first month; then adjust your holdings up or down as necessary so that your stock is always worth $5,500. (If the value falls to $5,000, invest another $500; if it rises to $6,000, sell $500 worth of stock.)

Under either strategy, you have $5,500 at risk in the average month. Either strategy yields the same expected return. But dollar-cost averaging introduces an extra element of unnecessary risk. If the stock goes up in six out of ten months and down the same amount in the other four, the investor with a constant $5,500 holding is a guaranteed winner. The dollar-cost averager, who has less invested in the early months than in the late ones, has to worry about *which* six months are good and which are bad. If the good months are the early ones, the dollar-cost averager is a loser.†

Anxiety about whether your stocks will rise is part of being an

---

* This is an approximation to the truth; you won't have exactly $2,000 riding on the second spin because by the second month your initial investment will be worth something other than exactly $1,000.

† This advice ignores a few incidentals like tax consequences and broker's fees, which tend to discourage a lot of buying and selling. In real life it might be best to invest $5,500 at the beginning and make adjustments less often than I've suggested. But the perfect strategy is surely much closer to keeping a constant investment than it is to dollar-cost averaging.

investor. By contrast, anxiety about *when* they will rise is easily avoidable. Dollar-cost averaging is a good way to lose more sleep than necessary.

Until now my case against dollar-cost averaging has been based on the random walk hypothesis. But even when stock prices *fail* to follow random walks, I cannot imagine *any* belief about price behavior that would justify dollar-cost averaging. Suppose, for example, that your belief is the naive one I held when I was young, that stock *prices* (as opposed to price *changes*) fluctuate randomly according to the spins of a mythical roulette wheel. In that case, your goal should not be to buy a lot of stock when the price is low and somewhat less when the price is high—it should be to buy a lot of stock when the price is low and *none at all* when the price is high.

The next time somebody advises you to dollar-cost average, ask him what he believes about the behavior of stock prices. Don't accept a meaningless answer like "They fluctuate"; pin him down on exactly *how* they fluctuate. Are they random walks, with price changes drawn randomly each day? Are the prices themselves drawn randomly each day? Do they follow a trend, with deviations from the trend drawn randomly? Are they chosen randomly from different roulette wheels on different days, and if so, what is the procedure by which the day's wheel is chosen? Chances are, the question will be new to him. In that case, it is better to pour boiling oil in your nostrils than to take this person's investment advice. If he *does* have an answer, it is almost surely inconsistent with his advice to dollar-cost average.

For over 25 years now, the high priest of dollar-cost averaging has been Bob Brinker of radio's *Moneytalk,* an inexhaustible source of unexamined platitudes. Call Mr. Brinker for advice, and he'll tell you to dollar-cost average. I tend to view this apocalyptically, as a sure sign that Western civilization has decayed beyond resurrection.

The advice you get from *Moneytalk* would not survive five minutes of critical examination, yet it is dispensed as from an oracle weekly. If Mr. Brinker had ever taken a moment to test his advice against some simple numerical examples, he would know it was wrong. Presumably he has too little respect for his listeners to bother.

Random walk theory implies that you can never improve your prospects via a strategy that relies on examining past price behavior. It is, however, silent on the issue of what can be gained by examining other variables.

In principle, one "roulette wheel" could determine both the weather and the price of Consolidated Umbrellas, with a time lag between them. First the sky darkens; 24 hours later Consolidated's share price responds. A savvy investor who noticed this pattern could make a fortune. By observing variables other than past price history, you might beat a random walk.

Having raised the hope that investors can achieve unlimited wealth by observing simple correlations, I am sorry to report that most economists consider such a prospect quite unlikely. It is reasonable to expect that more than one investor will notice the relationship between the weather and Consolidated's share price. As soon as the weather turns, those investors rush to buy stock, and, in competing with one another, they drive the price up almost instantly. The predicted future price rise takes place in the present instead of the future, and the typical investor is unable to purchase any shares while there is still time to realize a profit.

Nothing in this story requires that all or even most investors are on to the secret. It requires only that a small number of investors be alert enough to spot a profit opportunity and to exploit it fully.

The hypothesis that markets behave in this way is called the *efficient markets* hypothesis. According to the efficient markets hypothesis, no investment strategy based on the use of publicly available information can successfully beat the market.

The efficient markets hypothesis and the random walk hypothesis are closely related, and they are often confused with each other. But the hypotheses are quite distinct. The random walk hypothesis says only that you can't get rich by observing price histories; the efficient markets hypothesis says that you can't get rich by observing anything that is publicly available.

There is overwhelming empirical evidence for the random walk hypothesis as a description of most stock price behavior most of the time. The apparent exceptions are small, and, more important for the practical investor, nobody has figured out a way to exploit them for profit. The vast majority of economists find this evidence convincing, and among this vast majority there are at least several who are smart, skeptical, and not easily bamboozled.

By contrast, the efficient markets hypothesis, because it makes an assertion about *all* publicly available information, is much harder to test. The best evidence in its favor is that professional investors have consistently failed to outperform the market (with a small number of exceptions comparable to what you'd expect on the basis of random chance). Indexed mutual funds, which buy and hold broad stock market portfolios, consistently do as well as managed funds, which try to pick winners—and the indexed funds charge lower fees.*

Professors of finance have identified a number of so-called anomalies in stock prices, claiming, for example, that stock prices are more likely to rise in January or on Mondays. But of course, given enough data, it's always possible to identify a spurious pattern

---

* If you average the returns on all existing funds, you'll get an upward-biased estimate of the returns on all funds, because your average will fail to include funds that did poorly and were shut down. In comparing the performances of indexed and managed funds, it's important to correct for this bias.

or two—and in fact these anomalies have tended to disappear as
quickly as they're "discovered." The economist and portfolio manager Richard Roll summarizes it this way:

> I have personally tried to invest money, my clients' money and
> my own, in every single anomaly and predictive device that
> academics have dreamed up, and I have yet to make a nickel
> on any one of these supposed market inefficiencies. If there's
> nothing investors can exploit in a systematic way . . . then it's
> very hard to say that information is not being properly incor-
> porated into stock prices.

Surprisingly little of this has penetrated the reporting of financial news. When a stock price begins to fall after having recently
risen, the radio commentators report that the fall is due to "profit
taking." When the Dow-Jones average begins to approach a previous high, we hear about its efforts to break through a "resistance
area" and hear predictions that if it succeeds in breaking through,
then it will continue to rise through a period of "clear sailing"—unless, of course, there is profit taking.

Economists have the same feelings about much financial reporting that many people have about horoscope columns. They find it
entertaining, and they tell themselves that it is intended only for
amusement. But deep down, they wonder how many readers take
it seriously, and they shudder.

CHAPTER 20

IDEAS OF INTEREST

Armchair Forecasting

Each profession has its drawbacks. Doctors get emergency calls in the middle of the night. Mathematicians spend months stuck in blind alleys. Poets worry about where their next check is coming from. And economists get asked to forecast interest rates.

I have a colleague who deals with this most onerous of questions by adopting the deliberative demeanor of a very wise man, pausing for effect, and then pronouncing, "I think they'll fluctuate."

Although I can't forecast next year's (or even tomorrow's) interest rate precisely, I do know something about how those interest rates will be determined. In fact interest rates are far more predictable than, say, stock market prices. Theory and evidence tell us that stock market prices follow random walks, so past price behavior has no predictive value. Interest rates, by contrast, tend to bounce back toward their historic levels, so that if they're low today, they're likely to rise, and if they're high today, they're likely to fall. And a few key insights, which I'll share in this chapter, allow us to say quite a bit more.

First, let's recognize that there are many different interest rates, depending on who's borrowing, who's lending, and the projected time until the loan is repaid. But these rates tend to move up and down in tandem, so if we can forecast one of them, we can forecast most of them. For concreteness, when I talk about "the" interest rate, you can interpret that as the three-month Treasury bill rate (that is, the rate the U.S. government pays when it borrows money to be repaid in three months).

Next let's clarify an ambiguity: When economists talk about interest rates, they frequently make an adjustment for inflation. If you lend at 8 percent in an era of 3 percent inflation, your buying power grows by just 5 percent per year; the first three cents that you earn on every dollar goes just to maintaining the real value of your principal. The quoted value of 8 percent is called the *nominal* interest rate; the inflation-corrected rate of 5 percent is called the *real* interest rate.

Bowing to the inevitability of the pun, I pronounce that only the real interest rate is of real interest. An investment that earns 10 percent in an era of 7 percent inflation is neither more nor less desirable than one that earns 8 percent in a time of 5 percent inflation, or 3 percent in a time of 0 percent inflation. In each case the real rate is 3 percent. The real interest rate is the nominal interest rate minus the inflation rate.*

In what follows, when I say "interest rate," I mean the real interest rate. That said, we are almost ready to return to the question of how interest rates are determined—as soon as we dispose of one confusing falsehood.

Whatever you might have heard, there is no useful sense in which the (real) interest rate is the "price of money." Almost nobody ever borrows in order to hold money. People borrow to expand their businesses, to buy cars or houses, and to finance college educations or extravagant lifestyles. Bank loans are initially disbursed as dollars, but those dollars are typically spent and deposited back into the banking system within hours. We pay interest not so we can

---

* George Bush *père*, the most economically illiterate of modern presidents, once proudly proclaimed his inability to grasp this distinction in a nationally televised debate.

have money; we pay it so we can have cars and houses. More precisely, we pay it so we can have our cars and houses now instead of later. So you should think of the interest rate as measuring the price of *current goods* (relative to future goods).*

That simple observation has an important consequence. Because the interest rate is the price of current goods, it must ultimately be determined by the supply and demand for current goods.

From reading the financial pages, you might have gotten the idea that interest rates are determined by central bankers who control the money supply. But central bankers cannot dictate either the supply or the demand for cars and houses. It would take a power beyond all human understanding to have a lasting impact on a market price without being able to influence either supply or demand.

They can, however, make a good attempt. Suppose the central bank (which, in the United States, is called the Federal Reserve) wants to lower the interest rate from 3 percent to 2 percent. They do that by announcing a willingness to lend at 2 percent, which of course forces other lenders to follow suit.

This can work for a while, but it can't work forever. Here's why: When the central bank announces its bargain rate of 2 percent, a whole lot of eager borrowers turn up to take advantage. To satisfy them, the central bank must create a lot of new money, which tends to drive up prices throughout the economy. Then, because people are borrowing not to hold money but to buy goods, and because those goods have just gotten more expensive, they'll want even *more* money, which the central bank must create, driving up prices still further, and off we go round a vicious circle that in principle leads to the sort of hyperinflation that no central banker this side of Zim-

---

* More precisely, the price of current goods in terms of future goods is equal to *1 plus* the interest rate. When the annual interest rate is 5 percent (that is, .05), then in order to have an extra dollar's worth of goods today, you must forgo 1.05 dollars' worth of goods next year.

babwe is willing to countenance. At some point, then, the central
bank must surrender and allow the interest rate to rise.*

The only reason the central bank can hold out for any appre-
ciable time is that it sometimes takes a while for prices to adjust to
changes in the money supply. The length of the adjustment period,
and the reasons for it, are matters of ongoing research and considerable dispute.

Great events are linked to interest rate movements through the
choices of ordinary citizens. The good news is that, as an ordinary
citizen yourself, you have some of the insight necessary to develop
a good feel for the magnitudes of those effects.

Suppose, for example, that the president and Congress agree to
spend $24 billion this year in a one-year program to develop an
attack helicopter that will not fly. What's important here are not
the billions of dollars, but the real resources—steel, labor, and en-
gineering effort—that those dollars represent. Those real resources,
having been diverted to the building of helicopters, are newly unavailable for the building of cars, kitchen appliances, and personal
computers. There must, then, be fewer of those (and other) things,
by about $24 billion worth.

With fewer goods available, the average consumer must end up
buying fewer goods; this is a law not of economics but of arithmetic. If the value of available goods falls by $24 billion in a world of
6 billion people, the average person must consume about $4 less.
Of course some people's consumption will fall much more than
others. If you're the average American, you're about eight times
as rich as the average Earthling, so maybe your consumption will

---

* Rather than making loans to all comers at the rate of 2 percent, the central bank can—
and frequently does—make loans only to banks, which in turn relend these funds. But
the fundamental issues remain the same.

fall by about $32; if there are four people in your household, your household consumption falls by roughly $125.*

Initially, of course, nobody chooses to delay purchasing a garbage disposal just because the president did something stupid. We continue to demand what we demanded all along, even though the supply has shrunk. As a result the price of current goods—that is, the interest rate—is bid up until your typical family *chooses* to cut this year's consumption by $125.

If I want to know how that $24 billion attack helicopter will affect the interest rate, I ask myself this question: How high would the interest rate have to go before *my* family chose to cut this year's expenditures by $125? If I answer honestly, and if my household is fairly typical, then I can make at least a ballpark prediction.

Things would be quite different if the president and Congress had announced an agreement to waste $24 billion *every* year, as opposed to this year only. In that case, I expect my tax burden to rise substantially, which makes me feel poorer, which can be enough on its own to discourage me from buying that garbage disposal. Now there's no need for the interest rate to rise.†

The main idea is this: The interest rate has to be whatever is nec-

---

* Like all of the other numbers in this example, this is a wild-ass guess; I certainly don't know that being eight times as rich means you'll make eight times the sacrifice. The point here is not to make a precise prediction but to illustrate a way of thinking. I should also point out that for the sake of simplicity, I'm ignoring a few important factors. First, rising interest rates discourage investment projects and thereby free up some resources for immediate consumption; steel that would have been used to build factories is used instead to build cars. Second, rising interest rates encourage work (it's more fun to earn income when you can put it into a high-interest savings account), which means more goods are produced. Third, it's possible to increase current output by putting unemployed resources to work. For all three reasons, world consumption falls not by $24 billion, but by somewhat less. So a better wild-ass guess might be not $125, but, oh, say $80.

† A one-time wasteful project also makes me slightly poorer, but not nearly as much as a wasteful project that continues forever.

essary to convince the average family to consume its average share of the goods that are available for consumption. If the supply of goods falls, as when the government wastes resources, the interest rate must rise. If the supply of goods rises, as when there is an unusually good harvest, or when the government provides useful services that are worth more than their cost, the interest rate must fall.

As supply can change, so can demand. Suppose the average family finds a reason to become more optimistic about the future. Maybe new developments in technology herald increased productivity, or climatic changes herald better harvests, or a new administration takes office promising policies that are widely perceived to ensure an era of prosperity.

Generally speaking, people who expect to be richer in the future respond by consuming more in the present. If you're told today that you're in for a big raise next month, you probably won't wait till next month to start celebrating. Among college students, economics and philosophy majors have similar current incomes, but it's the economics students who drive cars, because it's the economics students who expect to have jobs someday.

So when the future looks brighter, everyone decides to consume more in the present. But here's the rub: There are no additional goods *available* in the present. In the short run, there are a certain number of cars, a certain number of houses, a certain number of ice cream cones, and a certain number of seats at the theater. It's simply not possible for everyone to consume more; in fact the average family must go right on consuming the average allotment.

So what convinces people to abandon their new spending plans? The answer is that when they all attempt to borrow to finance those plans, they collectively bid up the interest rate. The interest rate rises until the average family's original spending plans are restored.

When I read about a new technological breakthrough, I expect productivity to increase, the future to be brighter, people to demand more goods in anticipation of becoming wealthier, and the current interest rate to rise. How much will it rise? As always, I try to answer this question by thinking about my own family. First, I wonder how much our future incomes will go up. Then I ask how much I'm likely to increase my current spending once I've digested this information. If the answer is $100, I ask how high the interest rate must rise to convince me to *cut* my spending by $100, restoring the *status quo ante*.*

Now the answers to all of these questions are, of course, highly speculative, and their relevance depends very much on how typical I really am. My speculation is sure to be inexact. But there is great comfort in taking a question that seems to concern forces both mysterious and invisible ("How does technology affect interest rates?") and converting it to a question about the behavior of people like me.

Of course, there are economists who are unsatisfied with that kind of introspection and want to go further, by making careful statistical measurements of how people have responded to similar developments in the past, and finding sophisticated techniques for converting observations of the past into predictions for the future. Those economists surely make considerably more accurate estimates than whatever I come up with from my armchair, trying to imagine how I would act in various hypothetical circumstances. More power to them, but I like my armchair.

A famous professor of finance once lectured a group of successful investors on how markets behave. His talk painted a profound vision of how the world works but offered little in the way of prac-

---

* As in the previous footnote, these calculations should be tempered by considerations involving investment and labor supply. If firms building new computers divert resources away from the production of consumption goods, the average family's consumption may be forced to go *below* what was originally planned.

tical investment advice. The audience, which had come seeking not wisdom but wealth, grew restless. When the professor invited questions, the first was overtly hostile and entirely predictable: "If you're so smart, how come you're not rich?" The professor (who was in fact the richest person in the room, but that's another story) responded, "If you're so rich, how come you're not smart?"

Economists study interest rates because interest rates are a pervasive social phenomenon and economists aspire to understand everything about human society. I hope that here and there in this book I have conveyed something of the sheer joy of understanding. Still, it must have occurred to some readers to wonder whether this kind of analysis can be a road to both wisdom *and* wealth. Let me try to address that question.

Harry Truman used to say his administration needed a one-armed economist, because the economists around him were incapable of completing a sentence without adding the phrase "on the other hand." Truman wouldn't like where this discussion is headed. On the other hand, he did appreciate honesty, and I will be as honest as I can.

With no more theory than I've presented here, you really *can* begin to estimate how interest rates are likely to respond to a bumper crop or a natural disaster, to a wasteful or enlightened government policy, or to good or bad news about what the future holds.

On the other hand, that knowledge alone won't make you rich. The consensus among economists is that interest rates adjust to news in effectively no time at all. When the president announces the new missile project, you can begin to reason, "Now let's see; this means that there will be fewer consumption goods, so . . . ," but by the time you've gotten up to the semicolon, the interest rate has completed its upward adjustment. Once the news arrives, it's too late to take advantage of it.

But there is a third hand. Just possibly you have some knowledge or some talent or some instinct that makes you smarter than the average bear when it comes to predicting what the president is going to announce at tomorrow's news conference, or whether the hurricane raging toward the coast is going to dissipate before it hits land, or when someone in Cupertino is going to announce a technology for attaching a computing device directly to your brain. If you are so blessed, and if you have a basic understanding of how interest rates behave, then you can really make predictions and you probably *can* get rich.

If you do get rich, I'll be pleased to hear about it. Send me a note. I'll be in my well-worn armchair, thinking about things.

CHAPTER 21

THE IOWA CAR CROP

A thing of beauty is a joy forever, and nothing is more beautiful than a succinct and flawless argument. A few lines of reasoning can change the way we see the world.

I found one of the most beautiful arguments I know while I was browsing through a textbook written by my friend David Fried-man. While the argument might not be original, David's version is so clear, so concise, so incontrovertible, and so delightfully surpris-ing, that I have been unable to resist sharing it with students, rela-tives, and cocktail party acquaintances at every opportunity. The argument concerns international trade, but its appeal is less in its subject matter than in its irresistible force.

David's observation is that there are two technologies for pro-ducing automobiles in America. One is to manufacture them in Detroit, and the other is to grow them in Iowa. Everybody knows about the first technology; let me tell you about the second. First you plant seeds, which are the raw material from which automo-biles are constructed. You wait a few months until wheat appears. Then you harvest the wheat, truck it to California, load it onto ships, and sail the ships westward into the Pacific Ocean. After a few months the ships reappear with Toyotas on them.

International trade is nothing but a form of technology. The fact that there is a place called Japan, with people and factories, is quite irrelevant to Americans' well-being. To analyze trade policies, we might as well assume that Japan is a giant machine with mysterious inner workings that convert wheat into cars.

Any policy designed to favor the first American technology over the second is a policy designed to favor American auto producers in Detroit over American auto producers in Iowa. A tax or a ban on "imported" automobiles is a tax or a ban on *Iowa-grown* automobiles. If you protect Detroit carmakers from competition, then you must damage Iowa farmers, because Iowa farmers *are* the competition.

The task of producing a given fleet of cars can be allocated between Detroit and Iowa in a variety of ways. A competitive price system selects that allocation that minimizes the total production cost.* It would be unnecessarily expensive to manufacture all cars in Detroit, unnecessarily expensive to grow all cars in Iowa, and unnecessarily expensive to use the two production processes in anything other than the natural ratio that emerges as a result of competition.

That means that protection for Detroit does more than just transfer income from farmers to autoworkers. It also raises the total cost of providing Americans with a given number of automobiles. The efficiency loss comes with no offsetting gain; it impoverishes the nation as a whole.

There is much talk about improving the efficiency of American car manufacturing. When you have two ways to make a car, the

---

* This assertion is true, but not obvious. Individual producers care about their individual profits, not about economywide costs. It is something of a miracle that individual selfish decisions must lead to a collectively efficient outcome. In my chapter "Why Prices Are Good," I indicated how economists know that this miracle occurs. In the present chapter I will pursue its consequences.

road to efficiency is to use both in optimal proportions. The last thing you should want to do is to artificially hobble one of your production technologies. It is sheer superstition to think that an Iowa-grown Prius is any less "American" than a Detroit-built Volt. Policies rooted in superstition do not frequently bear efficient fruit.

In 1817 David Ricardo—the first economist to think with the precision, though not the language, of pure mathematics—laid the foundation for all future thought about international trade. In the intervening 150 years his theory has been much elaborated but its foundations remain as firmly established as anything in economics. Trade theory predicts, first, that *if you protect American producers in one industry from foreign competition, then you must damage American producers in other industries*. It predicts, second, that *if you protect American producers in one industry from foreign competition, there must be a net loss in economic efficiency*. Ordinarily textbooks establish these propositions through graphs, equations, and intricate reasoning. The little story that I learned from David Friedman makes the same propositions blindingly obvious with a single compelling metaphor. That is economics at its best.

The Pitfalls of Science

CHAPTER 22

WAS EINSTEIN CREDIBLE?

The Economics of the Scientific Method

In 1915 Albert Einstein announced his general theory of relativity and some of its remarkable implications. The theory "predicted" an aberration in the orbit of Mercury that had been long observed but never explained. It also predicted something new and unexpected concerning the way light is bent by the sun's gravitational field. In 1919 an expedition led by Sir Arthur Eddington confirmed the light-bending prediction and made Einstein an international celebrity.

Both the explanation of Mercury's orbit and the successful prediction of light bending were spectacular confirmations of Einstein's theory. But only the light bending—because it was unexpected—made headlines.

Imagine for the moment that Eddington had undertaken his expedition in 1900 instead of 1919. The facts of light bending would have been as well established—and as mysterious—as the orbit of Mercury, long in advance of Einstein's work. Einstein would have lost the psychological impact that comes from predicting the unexpected. He might never have established his remarkable hold on the public imagination and on the grooming habits of a generation of physicists. But putting aside the issue of Einstein's personal glory, we can ask, What would have been the fate of relativity theory itself? Would the scientific community have been slower to embrace it? And if so, would that response have been justifiable?

Conversely, we can imagine that the aberration in Mercury's orbit had gone unnoticed until Einstein predicted it, and that subsequent observations had confirmed the prediction. Would the psychological impact of a second unexpected prediction have established relativity theory even more securely? And should it have?

Certainly a new explanation for an old fact (like Mercury's orbit) and a successful prediction of a new fact (like the bending of light) should both count in a theory's favor. The more psychologically spectacular case, the successful new prediction, is sometimes called *novel* evidence for the theory. The question is: Should novel evidence count more heavily in a theory's favor than nonnovel evidence? Or, more succinctly: Does novelty matter?

As far back as the 13th century, Roger Bacon prescribed an early version of what has come to be known as the *scientific method*: Theorize first (using experience and existing evidence as a guide), then test your theory against experiments and other observations. By the 16th century the scientific method had been endorsed by several prominent philosophers and scientists, most notably Francis Bacon and René Descartes. Today science students absorb it as gospel.

The scientific method, which we can summarize as "Theorize first; look later," assigns a central role to novel confirmation. But there is an alternative method: Make all your observations first and do all your experiments first, then devise a theory consistent with the outcomes: "Look first; theorize later." The alternative method dispenses with novel confirmation entirely.*

---

* Of course, there's a huge spectrum in between these two extremes. Scientists observe both before and after theorizing, but some make more of their observations in advance than others. By pretending that some scientists make *no* observations before theorizing while others make *all* their observations before theorizing, we are trying to throw the main issues into sharp relief.

Why, if at all, should we prefer one method to the other? When my colleagues James Kahn and Alan Stockman and I got interested in this question several years ago, all we could find in the science textbooks was a mandate to follow in the paths of Roger and/or Francis Bacon, without any clear indication of *why*. Then we turned to the philosophy journals, where the role of novel confirmation in science is still hotly debated. But the arguments we found in those journals didn't satisfy us very much.

So we decided to approach this question from scratch. We thought that as economists, we might have something new to contribute. After all, the work of science is to draw (tentative) conclusions in the face of incomplete information. That's an issue economists know something about.

Eventually we did come up with some new ways of thinking about this subject, which were published in both the *Journal of Economic Theory* and the *British Journal for the Philosophy of Science*. We certainly don't claim to have had the last word on the subject. We *do* claim that unlike almost anybody else addressing this subject in the past 400 years, we have spelled out clear assumptions and the logic that follows from those assumptions. We hope and expect that others, with different assumptions, will do the same.

I'll start with a highly stylized example. Boris and Natasha are squirrel scientists at Wossamotta University. One day they hear on the news that following a spell of cold wet weather, a lot of squirrels have been found dead on the nearby island of Moosylvania. They go off to their separate labs, hoping to solve the mystery of what killed the squirrels.

Boris begins by performing a series of autopsies. His autopsies reveal that the squirrels died of heart failure. But why? Boris meditates on this a while, drawing on his general knowledge of squirrel biology. Eventually he theorizes that for reasons A, B, and C, cold weather is likely to cause heart failure in squirrels.

Natasha, by contrast, does not stop to perform autopsies. Instead she starts in right away to construct a theory. After meditating on the circumstances, and drawing on her general knowledge of squirrel biology, she eventually theorizes that for reasons D, E, and F, wet weather is likely to cause heart failure, and therefore death, in squirrels. Next, being schooled in the scientific method, she sets out to test her theory. She notes that if her theory is correct, then a series of autopsies should reveal that the squirrels died of heart failure. She performs the autopsies and her prediction is confirmed.

So was the culprit cold, as Boris says, or rain, as Natasha says? Eventually some non-PETA-approved experiments might settle this issue, but in the interim, whom should we believe? If we want to save the remaining squirrels, should we work to keep them warm or to keep them dry?

Only Natasha followed the textbook version of the scientific method. She first theorized, then used her theory to make the novel prediction that autopsies would show heart failure as the cause of death, and then tested that prediction by making some observations. Boris did no such thing; he made all his observations before he ever theorized. Is that a reason to prefer one theory over the other? Here we have two theories, each consistent with all the observations. The theories, and the arguments for and against them, stand on their own. Why should it matter how the theories were constructed?*

If Boris and Natasha are equally good at what they do, and if you're aware that they're equally good at what they do, we (that is,

---

* Our model, of course, oversimplifies the scientific process. But it does capture important features of the real world. At the point when they construct their theories, some scientists are aware of more relevant facts than others.

Kahn, Stockman, and I) could think of no reason why you should have more faith in one theory than the other.* In other words, novelty doesn't matter.

Although this argument against the relevance of novelty appears simple and airtight, it is, in our experience, rejected by the great majority of working scientists, who argue that anyone can take existing facts and concoct some sort of theory to "explain" them, so that a novel prediction is the one true hallmark of scientific accomplishment. They have a powerful intuition that novelty *does* matter, and the challenge is to give a full account of why.

Here's the beginning of an answer: Natasha, unlike Boris, has proven her ability to construct a theory with fewer observations to guide her. (Of course, both Natasha and Boris are guided partly by the myriad observations that they and others have made in the past, but still, Natasha got by with one fewer observation—and a critically important one—than Boris did.) Maybe that means Natasha is smarter than Boris, or at least has more insight into this particular sort of problem. Maybe that's a reason to trust her more.

In fact it might be *two* reasons to trust her more. First, she managed to construct a theory that fits the facts before she even knew all the facts. Second, she was willing to invest her time and effort into constructing that theory, which suggests a degree of self-confidence that might boost our faith in her even further, at least if we believe that self-confidence often reflects actual abilities.

---

* Suppose—and we realize that we're making vast simplifying assumptions here—that there are 10 potential theories that conform to the known facts about the squirrel deaths, all of them equally plausible and equally easy to find. Suppose one of these 10 theories is correct. Then the probability that Boris has found the correct theory is 1/10. Ditto for Natasha. Therefore there's no reason to prefer one to the other. Subtler but similar arguments apply if some theories are easier to find than others, or if you toy with the assumptions in a great variety of other ways.

To assess that argument—to decide whether Natasha's research strategy reflects true self-confidence—we need to know more about why she chose this particular research strategy in the first place. In other words, we need to know more about her incentives.

Here's one of many possible scenarios (again highly stylized): Suppose we learn that at Wossamotta U., scientists who routinely theorize first and make successful novel predictions are paid $100,000 a year, while those who make unsuccessful novel predictions are paid $20,000. Suppose that those who routinely fit their theories to existing observations and never attempt novel predictions are paid $50,000. Then Natasha, the novel predictor, puts her income on the line. Because she's willing to gamble on her own talents, it might be rational for the rest of us to gamble along with her by accepting her theory. By contrast, Boris, who has chosen the safe $50,000, leaves us wondering whether we are being asked to have more confidence in him than he has in himself.

With a different pay structure, we'd be led to different conclusions. Now we are really on the economist's turf. Instead of just hypothesizing a pay structure, we'd like to *predict* the pay structure, and how scientists respond to that pay structure, and the inferences an observer can draw from those responses.

That's a hard problem, because all these phenomena feed back into each other. The pay structure affects incentives; incentives affect research strategies; research strategies affect the inferences administrators can draw about who's especially smart; those inferences affect the perceived value of different research styles; that perceived value affects the pay structure. All of these things are determined simultaneously via competition among scientists, among research institutions, and among the patrons and beneficiaries of science. The problem is to understand the interlocking effects and predict how they all sort out.

Stockman, Kahn, and I didn't know how to solve that problem, so we retreated to an easier problem. Instead of asking what *does* happen, we asked what *should* happen. That is, we imagined a national science czar, charged with designing a system that induces scientists to behave efficiently. We asked what system that czar should design.

The two problems are not unrelated. We know of many examples in economics where actual market outcomes, the things that *do* happen, correspond with efficient outcomes, the things that *should* happen. Perhaps the market for science is one of those examples. If so, the solution to the easy problem automatically tells us the solution to the hard problem. That, or at least some approximation to that, is our hope. Even if that hope is dashed, our efforts won't have been entirely wasted. We can always go into business advising future science czars.

So let's imagine a czar who can order scientists either to *look first*, like Boris, or to *theorize first*, like Natasha.

The downside of *theorize first* is that it can be wasteful. Scientists pour too much time and too many resources into blind alleys. As it happens, Natasha's colleague Mr. Peabody is another theorize-firster. After a week of hard work, he came up with the theory that for reasons G, H, and I, cold wet weather causes squirrels to die of aneurysms. If Mr. Peabody had looked first, like Boris, he'd have known that the squirrels died of heart failure and wouldn't have wasted his week.

But the upside of *theorize first* is that while theories like Mr. Peabody's get rejected by the evidence, those that survive, like Natasha's, have passed a test that indicates their proponents might be smarter than average. The czar can justifiably have extra confidence in those theories. By contrast, if everyone *looks first*, no theory is ever rejected (at least not until some future moment when more facts become available), so the czar has no idea which theories to believe.*

---

* A real-world czar, of course, is likely to have plenty of external evidence about who the smartest scientists are and whose theories to believe. But additional evidence is always valuable. And of course, the czar's beliefs are only provisional, until future researchers bring new insights to bear. But sometimes you really need to know who to believe provisionally. If you're trying to save the squirrels, you need some belief about what's likely to be killing them.

That, then, is the trade-off: Under *theorize first*, there are fewer surviving theories, but we can have more confidence in them. Under *look first*, all theories survive, but we're not sure which to believe.

Now we introduce one more twist: We suppose that the scientists themselves know something about how smart they are.* The czar would like them to reveal this information. In fact he'd like them to reveal it for two reasons. First, it helps him decide whose theories to believe. Second, it allows him to pay more for smart scientists than for dumb ones, encouraging more smart people to become scientists in the first place, while discouraging those whose talents lie elsewhere.

What's the best way to sort out the smart from the dumb? The simplest method is to ask. Unfortunately scientists are generally reluctant to reveal that they're dumb, especially when their salaries are on the line. So what's needed is an incentive for scientists to tell the truth.

Here's a solution, along lines I've already hinted at: The czar sets up two separate research institutions: the Look-First Institute and the Theorize-First Institute. At Look-First, all scientists always look first and all are paid $50,000 per year. At Theorize-First, all scientists always theorize first. Those whose theories are subsequently confirmed get paid $100,000 per year; those whose theories are subsequently rejected get paid $20,000.

If these salaries are chosen correctly, then smart scientists—those who are confident of their ability to make successful novel predictions—will take jobs at Theorize-First, where they anticipate high re-

---

* We use the word "smart" to mean that the scientist has a better-than-average chance of producing theories that both conform to known facts and turn out to be useful. We use the word "dumb" to mean the opposite. A scientist might be classified as smart if he or she has a particular insight into the problem at hand, or a particularly strong motivation for solving it. Of course, with these definitions, the same scientist might count as smart when working on one problem and dumb when working on another.

wards. Dumb scientists, who know that their novel predictions often fail, accept the guaranteed $50,000 at the Look-First Institute.*

What's cool here is that scientists *voluntarily* reveal information that is useful to the czar, even though they initially have no reason to do so.

Of course, some smart scientists get unlucky in this scheme and end up earning only $20,000 per year. But smart scientists earn more on average than dumb scientists do, and relatively more of them are attracted into scientific careers. Moreover the czar knows whose theories to trust when he wants to, say, start a program to save the lives of squirrels. The scientists at Look-First make contributions that are politely acknowledged but never acted upon.

There are several remarkable features to this solution. First, smart scientists waste a lot of time and effort by theorizing first. If they looked first, they'd avoid blind alleys. (Therefore, if left to their own devices, they'd all choose to look first.) Unfortunately, if we allow them to look first, their careers become less risky, whereupon dumb scientists start to infiltrate their ranks. (It is, after all, only the prospect of a rejected theory that scares dumb scientists away from applying for jobs at the Theorize-First Institute). By requiring smart scientists to risk wasting their time, the czar can discover who's smart and who's dumb. The information is worth the waste.

Second, dumb scientists are paid to do research that's known in advance to be worthless.† Nevertheless it's important to keep paying them their guaranteed salaries, so they won't try to pass themselves off as smart. To me as a veteran academic, this rings somewhat true.

---

* The salaries in this paragraph are for illustration. To set the salaries properly, the czar must weigh several considerations. First, they must be set in such a way that scientists will sort themselves appropriately, so that the smart will go to Theorize-First and the dumb will go to Look-First. Second, they must be set with an eye to how many people of each type they are likely to draw into science.

† Keep in mind that our model is highly stylized, so that where the model predicts research that's entirely worthless, the real-world correlate might be research that's not terribly valuable.

In a given year, my department devotes vast resources to evaluating the qualifications of hundreds of job candidates. One reason we have to sort through only hundreds and not thousands is that some of the less qualified applicants accept reasonably well-paying jobs at Wossamotto U.* (And maybe we provide the same service to Harvard that Wossamotto supplies to us.)

Likewise the editors of the highest quality research journals are deluged with submissions. One way to keep the workload manageable is to consider only manuscripts produced by theorize-firsters, who, if the czar has set the right pay structure, are known to be relatively smart.

It's worth noting that if scientific research were left to the private sector, no firm would be willing to play the crucial role of hiring dumb scientists who produce useless theories. Yet it can be socially important to have such firms in order to keep dumb scientists from passing themselves off as smart. So the theory suggests that the government ought to play a significant role in organizing scientific activity—because only a government would be willing to fund research that has no social value whatsoever!

Third, it's possible to show that because of the czar's imperfect information and the constraints he faces, the world will always have too few smart scientists and too many dumb ones, relative to what you'd get in a world where abilities are perfectly observable. True to life? Readers familiar with the structure of modern science can decide for themselves.

The smart scientist/dumb scientist model is surely not the only possible justification, or perhaps even the best one, for caring about novel

---

* The outcome is even better if the dumb scientists can be assigned some useful tasks, such as teaching undergraduates.

prediction. I suspect, however, that it is the only argument that has ever been spelled out in such detail. It would be a good thing for alternative theories to be spelled out in equal detail so that we could seriously discuss their merits. Somehow the debate about novelty has gone on for centuries without any of the participants feeling obliged to specify a model of scientific behavior. Beware of great thinkers who advertise their conclusions without revealing their assumptions. I like economics because it insists on a higher standard.

CHAPTER 23

NEW IMPROVED FOOTBALL

How Economists Go Wrong

Once upon a time, in a century not too long before our own, there was an economist who wanted to understand football. So he decided to observe the great coaches and to learn from them.

Each time he watched a game, the economist painstakingly recorded all of the plays that were called and all of the surrounding circumstances that might have been relevant. Each night he performed sophisticated statistical tests to reveal hidden patterns in the data. Eventually his research began to pay off. He discovered that quarterbacks often throw the ball in the direction of a receiver, that the ball carrier usually runs in the direction of the opposing team's goalpost, and that field goals in the final minute are most often attempted by teams that are one or two points behind.

One day the commissioner of the National Football League became concerned about punting. He had come to believe that teams punt far too often, and that their behavior is detrimental to the game. (Exactly why he thought this has never been determined, but he was quite sure of himself.) The commissioner became obsessed with the need to discourage punting and called in his assistants for advice on how to cope with the problem.

One of those assistants, a fresh MBA, breathlessly announced that he had taken courses from an economist who was a great expert on all aspects of the game and who had developed detailed statistical models to predict how teams behave. He proposed retaining the economist to study what makes teams punt.

The commissioner summoned the economist, who went home with a large retainer check and a mandate to discover the causes of punting. Many hours later (he billed by the hour) the answer was at hand. Statistical analysis left no doubt: Punting nearly always takes place on the fourth down.

But the economist was trained in the scientific method and knew that describing the past is less impressive than predicting the future. So before contacting the commissioner, he put his model to the acid test. He attended several football games and predicted in advance that all punting would take place on fourth down. When his predictions proved accurate, he knew he had made a genuine scientific discovery.

The commissioner, however, was not paying for pure science. Knowledge for its own sake might satisfy a philosopher, but the commissioner had a practical problem to solve. His goal was not to understand punting but to eradicate it.

So the commissioner sent the economist back to his computers to formulate a concrete policy proposal. After a few false starts, the economist had a brainstorm. What if teams were allowed only three downs?

To test his idea, the economist wrote a computer program to simulate the behavior of teams in a game with three downs. The program was written to fully incorporate everything the economist knew about when teams punt. Simulation after simulation confirmed his expectation: Because punting takes place on fourth down only, nobody punts in a game without fourth downs.

The commissioner was impressed by the weight of the evidence and held a press conference to announce a change in the rules of football. From now on, only three downs would be permitted. The commissioner announced his confidence that the days of excessive punting were behind us. But the reality was otherwise. Teams began punting on third down, and the commissioner stopped listening to economists.

Our economist-hero was well within the mainstream of mid-20th-century policy analysis. In the years following World War II economists learned statistics. The new subject of econometrics made it possible to detect deep patterns in economic data and to test whether those patterns were likely to be repeated. Economists scrutinized consumption behavior, investment decisions, farm output, labor supply, sales of financial assets, and everything else they could think of. And the enterprise succeeded beyond their dreams. The data revealed striking consistencies that were used to predict the future with remarkable accuracy.

A contemporary American might find it difficult to imagine a time when macroeconomic predictions were frequently correct. But that brief golden era did exist. A half century later, the natural question is: What went wrong?

What went wrong appears to be that governments started taking economists seriously, and that this development undermined everything. Let's follow the trail of one particular economist, formerly a consultant to the National Football League and now employed by the U.S. government to help formulate economic policy.

The goal, at the urging of several farm state senators, was to boost cornflake consumption. The first task was to determine the facts. After many months of poring over data, the economist found the statistical regularity he was looking for: The average family spends $10 a month on cornflakes. This behavior is remarkably consistent. For example, small changes in after-tax income have almost no effect on cornflake sales.

Ever the skeptical scientist, the economist was unwilling to rely exclusively on historical data. Instead he put his theory to the acid test of prediction. He forecast that over the next several months, families would continue spending about $10 a month on cornflakes. His forecasts were repeatedly confirmed. His sense of triumph recalled that glorious day in his youth when he had first detected the fourth down–punting connection.

The economist's superiors were pleased with his finding, and even more pleased when he made it the basis of a policy proposal: Let the government provide each American family with an additional $5 worth of cornflakes every month. This should boost corn flake consumption by 50 percent. Financing the program will require a small tax increase, but we know that small tax increases don't affect cornflake sales.

But a strange thing happened. When the government started giving away cornflakes, shoppers reacted like football players given only three downs to gain 10 yards: They changed their strategies. As soon as people realized that the government was delivering cornflakes to their doorsteps, they cut their grocery store purchases in half.

Our economist-hero is no exaggerated fiction but a true representative of his generation. In the 1950s and 1960s his path was the path to fame and glory. Less than 40 years ago, Robert E. Lucas Jr. (now of the University of Chicago) issued the first widely recognized warning that human beings respond to policy changes, and that this simple observation renders traditional policy analysis completely invalid. Even today college students taking their first economics course are taught to assume that when the government provides cornflakes, people go on buying cornflakes just as before. (Of course, the textbooks express this assumption in terms of algebra rather than cornflakes, to ensure that students will not understand what it means.)

Unfortunately for policy analysts, people are not simple automatons. They are strategic players in a complicated game where government policies set some of the rules. The behaviors that economists can observe—the decision to buy a car or a house, to quit one job or to take a new one, to hire additional workers or to build a new factory—are bits of strategy. As long as the rules stay fixed, we can reasonably expect the strategies not to change very much, and we can accurately extrapolate from past observations. When the rules change, all bets are off.

Our economist-hero would have been well advised to devote less effort to his statistics and more to pure theory. Guided by the right theory of football—which is that each team attempts to score more points than the other—he could have accurately predicted how players would respond to a new set of rules. Guided by the right theory of cornflakes—which is that families buy cornflakes *in order to eat them* and won't buy more than they want to eat—he might have realized that letting the government do people's shopping would not make them any hungrier.

Of course, some theories are wrong, and economists who subscribe to those theories do not predict accurately. But an economist with a theory has at least a *chance* that his theory is the right one. An economist who relies on nothing but statistical extrapolations might do just fine under a fixed policy regime, but when it comes to predicting the effects of a policy *change*, he has no chance at all.

The area where macroeconomists have failed most spectacularly is in the relationship between employment and inflation. Back in that golden era of the 1950s and 1960s, economists observed a powerful correlation: Times of high inflation are times of low unemployment, and vice versa. By the late 1960s this observation had survived rigorous statistical testing and was generally accepted as a scientific truth. Accepting that truth as a basis for policy, politicians attempted to manipulate the inflation rate as a means of controlling unemployment. The result was a decade of stagflation: high inflation and high unemployment combined. Then in the 1980s inflation fell dramatically, and, after an initial severe recession, employment opportunities expanded at unprecedented rates. The old statistical regularities seemed to have been turned on their heads.

What had changed? The government, on the advice of economists, had adopted new policies that changed the rules of the economic game. As a result, the players—firms and individuals—had adopted new strategies that economists failed to foresee. In 1971 (and therefore with considerable foresight into the events of the 1980s) Robert Lucas wrote a careful account of how and why people might behave differently when authorities manipulate the inflation rate.

The Lucas story starts like this: Willie Worker is currently unemployed not because he has literally *no* job opportunities, but because his opportunities are so unattractive that he prefers unemployment. Willie's best wage offer is $15,000 a year, which would barely cover the cost of getting to work. At anything less than $20,000, Willie won't take the job.

One night, while Willie sleeps, there is a massive inflation, causing all prices and all wages to double. The employer who offered $15,000 yesterday offers $30,000 today. That's still not good enough, though. In a world of doubled prices, Willie doesn't want to work for less than $40,000. He remains unemployed.

Now let me change the story only slightly. The morning after the night of the great inflation, Willie is awakened by a phone call from an employer offering $30,000. At this point, Willie has not yet read the morning papers and is unaware that prices have changed. He happily reports for work. Only on his way home, stopping at the supermarket to spend his first paycheck, does Willie discover the cruel truth and begin composing a letter of resignation.

This highly stylized fable captures a potentially important aspect of reality. One way that inflation can increase employment is by fooling people. It makes job opportunities look more attractive than they really are and entices workers to accept jobs they would reject if they knew more about the economic environment.

We can tell pretty much the same story from the employer's viewpoint. Suppose you own an ice cream parlor, selling ice cream cones at $1 apiece. If you could sell them for $2 apiece, you would expand your operation, but you've learned by experimenting that $2 is more than the traffic will bear.

If all prices and wages—including all of your costs—were to double, then you'd be able to sell cones for $2, but that $2 would be worth no more than $1 was worth yesterday. You would continue as before.

But suppose that prices and wages double without your noticing. You notice only that your customers suddenly seem willing to pay more for their ice cream cones. (Probably you first discover this when traffic picks up because your $1 cones have begun to seem like quite a bargain to customers whose wages have doubled.) You expand your operation and hire a lot of new workers. Even after you discover your mistake, part of the expansion is irrevocable: The new freezers are in place, the new parking spaces are under construction, and you might want to keep at least some of those new employees.

The Lucas story implies not that *inflation* puts people to work but that *unanticipated inflation* puts people to work. In this story, fully anticipated inflations do not affect anyone's behavior. If this is the right story, then a (highly stylized) history of modern macroeconomics would go something like this: Inflations fool workers into accepting more jobs and employers into hiring more workers. Governments notice that inflation is consistently accompanied by high employment and decide to take advantage of this relationship by systematically manipulating the inflation rate. Workers and employers quickly notice what the government is up to and cease to be fooled. The correlation between inflation and unemployment breaks down precisely *because* the government attempts to exploit it.

Throughout the two decades following World War II fluctuations in the inflation rate were largely unanticipated. There was no distinction between *inflation* and *unanticipated inflation*. If economist A asserts that *inflation* puts people to work and economist B asserts that *unanticipated inflation* puts people to work, then nothing in the historical data can distinguish between their hypotheses. Anything that goes to confirm economist A's theory will go to confirm economist B's theory, and vice versa. Both theories will predict equally accurately *until the rules change*. But *after* the rules change, when the government starts systematically manipulating the inflation rate in foreseeable ways, one theory will continue to be correct, while the other goes drastically wrong.

Many economists are deeply unsatisfied with this story and ask embarrassing questions like "Why can't the ice cream store owner learn the inflation rate from the *Wall Street Journal* before he embarks on a massive expansion program?" In response, Lucas and others have constructed increasingly elaborate versions of the original story, and also a host of competing stories.

Today there are many different models of macroeconomics. Some incorporate parts of the original Lucas story; others dispense with it completely. But they all have this much in common: They tell precise stories about individuals making decisions under changing and uncertain conditions, and they use substantial mathematics to keep track of how everyone's decisions affect everyone else's. These models are usually called *dynamic stochastic general equilibrium* models (DSGE for short).* DSGE models vary greatly in the stories they tell and the predictions they make, but they provide a

---

* The word "dynamic" means that decisions made today affect outcomes tomorrow, and the people in the stories must account for this. The word "stochastic" means that the people in the stories face uncertainty. The phrase "general equilibrium" means that we track all the interactions among all the decision makers.

common language that allows macroeconomists to pinpoint *why* they've reached different conclusions. Because they focus on motivations rather than just behavior, DSGE models look nothing like the macroeconomics of 50 years ago.

An economist who understands *why* teams punt *knows* what will happen if you change the rules; an economist who understands *why* people buy cereal *knows* what will happen if you give out free cornflakes; and an economist who understands *why* people accept certain job offers *knows* what will happen if you manipulate the inflation rate. That's why we need stories—ideally, stories that are simple enough to understand, but complicated enough to bear some relation to the true story of the world we inhabit.

Almost all of modern macroeconomics consists of attempts to tell better stories and to develop new mathematical techniques that let us keep track of what's going on when the stories get complicated. As a predictive science, macroeconomics has a long way to go, but, at the beginning of its fifth decade, it has learned from the mistakes of its elders and has found a new and promising path.

VI

The Pitfalls of Religion

CHAPTER 24

WHY I AM NOT AN ENVIRONMENTALIST

The Science of Economics versus the Religion of Ecology

This essay was written 20 years ago and appeared in the first edition of *The Armchair Economist*. Since then it's been widely quoted, not always with disapproval. It is republished here with only minor changes to bring it up to date.

Despite the provocative title, I am, of course, an environmentalist in many senses of the word. Like you, I care about the quality of my environment. I prefer my air and water to be clean and my physical surroundings to be beautiful. I also prefer my computer to be fast, my car to be comfortable, and my shower spray to be strong. All of those things are part of my environment. I am enough of an economist to know that having more of one thing often means having less of another, but that doesn't stop me from wanting it all.

Like you, I believe we ought to care (or at least act as if we care) about costs we impose on our fellow Earthlings. In ordinary circumstances, that means not littering, keeping your lawn presentable, and perhaps worrying about your carbon footprint. Like you, I recognize that people don't always live up to this standard, and that wise government policies can sometimes improve their behavior—though of course there's plenty of room for disagreement about specific cases.

In all of those senses, I am an environmentalist. The sort of environmentalist I am *not* is the sort who respects a preference for clean air but disdains a preference for fast cars. Different people prioritize different things, and sometimes our priorities clash. That means we have a problem to solve. But it's rarely useful to recast a clash of priorities as a battle between Good and Evil. This, of course, is an economics lesson, which is why it's appropriate for this book.

When I talk about "environmentalists" in this chapter, I'm referring specifically to the sort of environmentalists who have not learned this lesson. Perhaps it would have been better to call them something like "ideological environmentalists" and to have titled this chapter "Why I Am Not an Ideological Environmentalist." But since the essay is already well known under its original (and catchier) title, I'm leaving it as is, trusting that no careful reader will mistake the meaning.

At the age of four, my daughter earned her second diploma. When she was two, she graduated with the highest possible honors from the Toddler Room at her nursery school in Colorado. Two years later she graduated from the preschool of the Jewish Community Center, where she matriculated on our return to New York State.

At the graduation ceremony, titled Friends of the Earth, I was lectured by four- and five-year-olds on the importance of safe energy sources, mass transportation, and recycling. The recurring mantra was "With privilege comes responsibility," as in "With the privilege of living on this planet comes the responsibility to care for it." Of course, Thomas Jefferson thought that life on this planet was more an inalienable right than a privilege, but then he had never been to preschool.

I'd heard some of this from my daughter before and had gotten used to the idea that she needed a little deprogramming from time to time. But as I listened to the rote repetition of a political agenda from children not old enough to read, I decided it was time for a word with the teacher. She wanted to know which specific points in the catechism I found objectionable. I declined to answer. As environmentalism becomes increasingly like an intrusive state religion, we dissenters become increasingly prickly about suggestions that we suffer from some kind of aberration.

The naive environmentalism of my daughter's preschool is a force-fed potpourri of myth, superstition, and ritual that has much in common with the least reputable varieties of religious fundamentalism. The antidote to bad religion is good science. The antidote to astrology is the scientific method; the antidote to naive creationism is evolutionary biology; and the antidote to naive environmentalism is economics.

Economics is the science of competing preferences. Environmentalism goes beyond science when it elevates matters of *preference* to matters of *morality*. A proposal to pave a wilderness and put up a parking lot is an occasion for conflict between those who prefer wilderness and those who prefer convenient parking. In the ensuing struggle, each side attempts to impose its preferences by manipulating the political and economic systems. Because one side must win and one side must lose, the battle is hard-fought and sometimes bitter. All of this is to be expected.

But in the 40 years since the first Earth Day, a new and ugly element has emerged in the form of one side's conviction that its preferences are Right and the other side's are Wrong. The science of economics shuns such moral posturing; the religion of environmentalism embraces it.

Economics forces us to confront a fundamental symmetry. The conflict arises because each side wants to allocate the same resource in a different way. Jack wants his woodland at the expense of Jill's parking space, and Jill wants her parking space at the expense of

Jack's woodland. That formulation is morally neutral and should serve as a warning against assigning exalted moral status to either Jack or Jill.

The symmetries run deeper. Environmentalists claim that wilderness should take precedence over parking because a decision to pave is "irrevocable." Of course they are right, but they overlook the fact that a decision *not* to pave is *equally* irrevocable. Unless we pave today, my opportunity to park tomorrow is lost as irretrievably as tomorrow itself will be lost. The ability to park in a more distant future might be a quite inadequate substitute for that lost opportunity.

A variation on the environmentalist theme is that we owe the wilderness option not to ourselves but to future generations. But do we have any reason to think that future generations will prefer inheriting the wilderness to inheriting the profits from the parking lot? That is one of the first questions that would be raised in any honest scientific inquiry.*

Anyway, if environmentalists were as passionate as they claim to be about conserving resources for future generations, I'd expect more of them to oppose the taxation of capital income, the Social Security system, and other policies that encourage overconsumption in the present. The absence of these issues from the environmentalists' agenda suggests that their stance on future generations is the rhetoric not of principle but of convenience.

Another variation is that the parking lot's developer is motivated by profits, not preferences. To this there are two replies. First, the developer's profits are generated by his customers' preferences; the ultimate conflict is not with the developer but with those who prefer to park. Second, the implication of the argument is that a pref-

---

* A related point: There seems to be general agreement that it is better to transfer income from the relatively rich to the relatively poor than vice versa. It seems odd, then, to ask present-day Americans to make sacrifices for the benefit of future generations who will almost surely be richer than we are.

erence for a profit is somehow morally inferior to a preference for a wilderness, which is just the sort of posturing that the argument was designed to avoid.

It seems to me that the "irrevocability" argument, the "future generations" argument, and the "preferences not profits" argument all rely on false distinctions that wither before honest scrutiny. Why, then, do some environmentalists repeat these arguments? Perhaps honest scrutiny is simply not a part of their agenda. In many cases, they *begin* with the postulate that they hold the moral high ground and conclude that they are thereby licensed to disseminate intellectually dishonest propaganda as long as it serves the higher purpose of winning converts to the cause.

The hallmark of science is a commitment to follow arguments to their logical conclusions; the hallmark of certain kinds of religion is a slick appeal to logic followed by a hasty retreat if it points in an unexpected direction. Environmentalists can quote reams of statistics on the importance of trees and then jump to the conclusion that recycling paper is a good idea. But the opposite conclusion makes equal sense. I am sure that if we found a way to recycle beef, the population of cattle would go down, not up. If you want ranchers to keep a lot of cattle, you should eat a lot of beef. Recycling paper eliminates the incentive for paper companies to plant more trees and can cause forests to shrink. If you want large forests, your best strategy might be to use paper as wastefully as possible—or lobby for subsidies to the logging industry. Mention this to an environmentalist. My own experience is that you will be met with some equivalent of the beatific smile of a door-to-door evangelist stumped by an unexpected challenge but secure in his grasp of Divine Revelation.

This suggests that environmentalists—at least the ones I have met—have no real interest in maintaining the tree population. If they did, they would seriously inquire into the long-term effects of recycling. I suspect that they don't want to do that because their real concern is with the ritual of recycling itself, not with its consequences. The underlying need to sacrifice, and to compel others to sacrifice, is a fundamentally religious impulse.

Environmentalists call on us to ban carcinogenic pesticides. They choose to overlook the consequence that when pesticides are banned, fruits and vegetables become more expensive, people eat fewer of them, and cancer rates consequently rise.* If they really wanted to reduce cancer rates, they would weigh this effect in the balance.

Environmentalism has its apocalyptic side. Species extinctions, we are told, have consequences that are entirely unpredictable, making them too dangerous to risk. But unpredictability cuts both ways. One lesson of economics is that the less we know, the more useful it is to experiment. If we are completely ignorant about the effects of extinction, we can pick up a lot of valuable knowledge by wiping out a few species to see what happens. I doubt that scientists really *are* completely ignorant in this area; what interests me is the environmentalists' willingness to *plead* complete ignorance when it suits their purposes and to retreat when confronted with an unexpected consequence of their own position.

In June 2009 the Wildlife Conservation Society announced the discovery of a tiny new species of monkey in the Amazon rain forest and touted it as a case study in why the rain forests must be preserved. My own response was rather in the opposite direction. The fact that I've lived half my life without knowing about these monkeys tells me that I wouldn't have missed them much if they'd gone extinct. They're cute monkeys, and I liked seeing them on YouTube, but beyond that they've done very little to enrich my life.

Of course these monkeys might do the world a lot of good I

---

* I owe this observation to the prominent biologist Bruce Ames.

don't know about, either now or in the future. They also might do the world a lot of harm I don't know about. There are certainly species we'd be better off without; consider the malaria parasite.

There are other species I care more about, maybe because I have fond memories of them from visiting the zoo or from childhood storybooks. Lions, for example. I would be sorry to see lions disappear, to the point where I might be willing to pay up to about $50 to preserve them. I don't think I'd pay much more than that. Would you? If lions mean less to you than they do to me, I accept our difference and will not condemn you as a sinner. If they mean more to you than to me, I hope you will extend the same courtesy.

In the current political climate, it is frequently taken as an axiom that the U.S. government should concern itself with the welfare of Americans first; it is also frequently taken as an axiom that air pollution is always and everywhere a bad thing. You might, then, have expected a general chorus of approval when the chief economist of the World Bank suggested that it might be a good thing to relocate high-pollution industries to Third World countries. To most economists, this is a self-evident opportunity to make not just Americans but *everybody* better off. People in wealthy countries can afford to sacrifice some income for the luxury of cleaner air; people in poorer countries are happy to breathe inferior air in exchange for the opportunity to improve their incomes. But when the bank economist's observation was leaked to the media, parts of the environmental community went ballistic. To them, pollution is a form of sin. They seek not to improve our welfare, but to save our souls.

There is a pattern here. Suggesting an actual *solution* to an environmental problem is a poor way to impress an environmentalist, unless your solution happens to feed his sense of moral superiority. Subsidies to logging, the use of pesticides, planned extinctions, and exporting pollution to Mexico are outside the catechism; subsidies to mass transportation, the use of catalytic converters, planned fuel economy standards, and exporting industry from the Pacific Northwest are part of the infallible doctrine. Solutions seem to fall into one category or the other not according to their actual utility but according to their consistency with environmentalist dogma.

In the last weeks of his reelection campaign for president, George Herbert Walker Bush, running as the candidate of less intrusive government, signed with great fanfare a bill dictating the kind of showerhead you are permitted to buy. The American Civil Liberties Union took no position on the issue. I conjecture that if the bill had specified allowable prayer books instead of allowable shower-heads, then even the malleable Mr. Bush might have balked—and if he hadn't, we would have heard something from the ACLU. But nothing in the science of economics suggests any fundamental difference between a preference for the Book of Common Prayer and a preference for a powerful shower spray. Quite the contrary: The economic way of thinking forces us to recognize that there *is* no fundamental difference.

The proponents of showerhead legislation argue that a law against extravagant showers is more like a law against littering than like a law against practicing a minority religion: It is designed to prevent selfish individuals from imposing real costs on others. If that was the argument that motivated Mr. Bush, then—not for the first time in his life—he had fallen prey to bad economics.

There are good economic reasons to outlaw littering and other impositions (though even this can be overdone; walking into a crowded supermarket is an imposition on all the other shoppers, but few of us believe it should be outlawed). But in most parts of the United States, water use is *not* an imposition for the simple reason that you *pay* for water. It is true that your luxuriant shower hurts other buyers by driving up the price of water, but equally true that your shower helps *sell-*

ers by exactly the same amount that it hurts buyers. You would want to limit water usage only if you cared more about buyers than sellers—in which case there are equally good arguments for limiting the consumption of *everything*, including energy-efficient showerheads.

Like other coercive ideologies, environmentalism targets children specifically. After my daughter progressed from preschool to kindergarten, her teachers taught her to conserve resources by rinsing out her paper cup instead of discarding it. I explained to her that time is also a valuable resource, and it might be worth sacrificing some cups to save some time. Her teachers taught her that mass transportation is good because it saves energy. I explained to her that it might be worth sacrificing some energy in exchange for the comfort of a private car. Her teachers taught her to recycle paper so that wilderness is not converted to landfill space. I explained to her that it might be worth sacrificing some wilderness in exchange for the luxury of not having to sort your trash. In each case, her five-year-old mind had no difficulty grasping the point. But I feared that after a few more years of indoctrination, she would be as uncomprehending as her teachers.

In their assault on the minds of children, the most reprehensible tactic of environmental extremists is to recast every challenge to their orthodoxy as a battle between Good and Evil. The Saturday morning cartoon shows depict wicked polluters who pollute for the sake of polluting, not because polluting is a necessary byproduct of some useful activity. That perpetuates a damnable lie. American political tradition does not look kindly on those who advance their agendas by smearing the character of their opponents. That tradition should be upheld with singular urgency when the intended audience is children. At long last, have the environmentalists no decency?

Economics in the narrowest sense is a science free of values. But economics is also a way of thinking, with an influence on its practitioners that transcends the demands of formal logic. With the diversity of human interests as its subject matter, the discipline of economics is fertile ground for the growth of values like tolerance and pluralism.

In my experience, economists are extraordinary in their openness to alternative preferences, lifestyles, and opinions. Judgmental clichés like "the work ethic" and the "virtue of thrift" are utterly foreign to the vocabulary of economics. Our job is to understand human behavior, and understanding is not far distant from respect.

Following our graduation day confrontation, I sent my daughter's teacher a letter explaining why I had declined her invitation to engage in theological debate. Some of the opinions in that letter are more personal than professional. But the letter is above all a plea for the level of tolerance that economists routinely grant and expect in return. Therefore I will indulge myself by reproducing it, as an example of how the economic way of thinking has shaped one economist's thoughts.

Dear Rebecca:

When we lived in Colorado, Cayley was the only Jewish child in her class. There were also a few Moslems. Occasionally, and especially around Christmas time, the teachers forgot about this diversity and made remarks that were appropriate only for the Christian children. These remarks came rarely, and were easily counteracted at home with explanations that different people believe different things, so we chose not to say anything at first. We changed our minds when we overheard a teacher telling a group of children that if Santa didn't come to your house, it meant you were a very bad child; this was within earshot of an Islamic child who certainly was not going to get a visit from Santa. At that point, we decided to share our concerns with the teachers. They were genuinely apologetic and there were no more incidents. I have no doubt that the teachers were good and honest people who had no intent to indoctrinate, only a certain naiveté derived from a provincial upbringing.

Perhaps that same sort of honest naiveté is what underlies the problems we've had at the JCC this year. Just as Cayley's teachers in Colorado were honestly oblivious to the fact that there is diversity in religion, it may be that her teachers at the JCC have been honestly oblivious to the fact that there is diversity in politics.

Let me then make that diversity clear. We are not environmentalists. We ardently oppose environmentalists. We consider environmentalism a form of mass hysteria akin to Islamic fundamentalism or the War on Drugs. We do not recycle. We teach our daughter not to recycle. We teach her that people who try to convince her to recycle, or who try to force her to recycle, are intruding on her rights.

The preceding paragraph is intended to serve the same purpose as announcing to Cayley's Colorado teachers that we are not Christians. Some of them had never been aware of knowing anybody who was not a Christian, but they adjusted pretty quickly.

Once the Colorado teachers understood that we and a few other families did not subscribe to the beliefs that they were propagating, they instantly apologized and stopped. Nobody asked me what exactly it was about Christianity that I disagreed with; they simply recognized that they were unlikely to change our views on the subject, had no business trying to change our views on the subject, and certainly had no business inculcating our child with opposite views.

I contrast this with your reaction when I confronted you at the preschool graduation. You wanted to know my specific disagreements with what you had taught my child to say. I reject your right to ask that question. The entire program of environmentalism is as foreign to us as the doctrine of Christianity. I was not about to engage in detailed theological debate with Cayley's Colorado teachers, and they would not have had the audacity to ask me to. I simply asked them to lay off the subject completely, they recognized the legitimacy of my request, and the subject was closed.

I view the current situation as far more serious than what we encountered in Colorado for several reasons. First, in Colorado we were dealing with a few isolated remarks here and there, whereas at the JCC we have been dealing with a systematic attempt to inculcate a doctrine and to quite literally put words in children's mouths. Second, I do not sense on your part any acknowledgment that there may be people in the world who do not share your views. Third, I am frankly a lot more worried about my daughter's becoming an environmentalist than about her becoming a Christian. Fourth, we face no current threat of having Christianity imposed on us by petty tyrants; the same cannot be said of environmentalism. My county government never tried to send me a New Testament, but it did send me a recycling bin.

Although I have vowed not to get into a discussion on the issues, let me respond to the one question you seemed to think was very important in our discussion: Do I agree that with privilege comes responsibility? The answer is no. I believe that responsibilities arise when one undertakes them voluntarily. I also believe that in the absence of explicit contracts, people who lecture other people on their "responsibilities" are almost always up to no good. I tell my daughter to be wary of such people—even when they are preschool teachers who have otherwise earned a lot of love.

Sincerely,

Steven Landsburg

APPENDIX

Notes on Sources

This book contains many ideas and arguments that I learned, borrowed, or stole from other people. My memory is not good enough to accurately acknowledge them all. In this appendix I will do the best I can.

While I'm at it, I'll also mention a few additional ideas that seemed just a hair too subtle to go into the text.

1. THE POWER OF INCENTIVES

From August 2007 to August 2008, the average price of gas rose 35 percent (from $2.77 a gallon to $3.74), while fuel consumption fell by about 8.5 percent. In economic jargon the *elasticity* of the response was 8.5/35 or .25. Writing four years earlier in the journal *Transport Reviews*, Phil Goodwin, Joyce Dargay, and Mark Hanly reported a consensus estimate among economists that this elasticity was probably about .25. Hence the comment in the text that the 8.5 percent drop was "just about exactly the consensus forecast among economists."

Sam Peltzman's original work appeared in the *Journal of Political Economy* in 1975.

The observation about the efficacy of spears mounted on steering wheels was first made, to the best of my knowledge, by Professor Armen Alchian of UCLA.

Sobel and Nesbit's work on NASCAR safety appeared in the *Southern Economic Journal* in 2007. Pope and Tollison's paper on the HANS device appeared in the journal *Public Choice* in 2010.

Isaac Ehrlich's pioneering work was published in the *American Economic Review*, also in 1975. Ed Leamer's article on taking the "con" out of econometrics was published in the *American Economic Review* in 1983. There's a good survey of more recent literature at http://www.cjlf.org/deathpenalty/dpdeterrence.htm.

2. RATIONAL RIDDLES

In the text I've asked why people so often choose to bet on the same sports teams they're fond of, rather than betting against those teams to ensure a good outcome no matter what. I also offer a possible answer: Maybe fans are ensuring themselves against an expensive urge to celebrate when their teams win. Chuan-hau Yau, a student from Taiwan, has pointed out an intriguing subtlety: that fans have, to some extent, the option of ignoring games entirely. So the right question isn't "Why would you want to bet on the home team?"; instead it's "Why would you want to bet on the home team *in those games you've decided to watch*?" Those in turn are the games you particularly expect to enjoy, so they are by no means a random sample of games—which, at the very least, complicates the question. He also mentions the pleasure people get from the sense that they and their favorite teams are in the same boat.

Deirdre McCloskey's thoughts on scattering (and a great variety of other topics) can be found in the book *Measurement and Meaning in Economics: The Essential Deirdre McCloskey*, from Edward Elgar (2001).

André Weil's remarks on voting are taken from his autobiography, *The Apprenticeship of a Mathematician* (Birkhauser, 1992).

3. TRUTH OR CONSEQUENCES

The observations about smoking come from a paper by Eric Bond and Keith Crocker in the *Journal of Political Economy*, 1991.

The discussion of why employers give productive fringe benefits is inspired by the work of Paul Yakoboski and Ken McLaughlin. The discussion of why we don't buy our jobs (and of how to split a check) is inspired by work of Ken McLaughlin.

The idea of using Joseph Conrad to illustrate truth-revelation mechanisms is due to Gene Mumy.

The systematic study of executive compensation begins with the work of Jensen and Murphy, published in 1990 in both the *Journal of Political Economy* and the *Harvard Business Review*. For the state of what's currently known, see "CEO Compensation," NBER Working Paper #16585, by Caroly Frydman and Dirk Jenter of MIT and Stanford (November 2010).

4. THE INDIFFERENCE PRINCIPLE

Hanan Jacoby pointed out to me that sex scandals need not be bad for politicians.

The estimated costs and benefits of the Clean Air Act are from the EPA's "Second Prospective Study, 1990–2020," released in March 2011.

When I asked him why farmers are subsidized and grocers are not, Mark Bils upped the ante by asking me why motel owners are not paid to keep rooms vacant. David Friedman suggested the answer.

6. TELLING RIGHT FROM WRONG

When he read this book in manuscript form, my philosophical consultant Benjamin Sherman rose to the defense of my dinner companion who thought she could recognize fairness in the real world but not in the simplified world of Jack and Jill: "Quite plausibly we might be able to recognize clear-cut cases of fairness without knowing how to decide some tougher cases. Many theorists suggest our intuitions are more trustworthy in more familiar cases, and some theories of moral epistemology even suggest that our intuitions about cases are virtually always more reliable than abstract principles." Moreover, he observes, it's possible that my dinner companion's failure to settle the case of Jack and Jill might have resulted from my failure to fully specify the environment in which they live.

Fairness compels me to concede that he has a point. I'll aim to address this point (and others!) in blog posts at www.TheBigQuestions. com in the near future.

7. WHY TAXES ARE BAD

The fiction of Exxon and the mineral rights activists is designed to be stark, but in one important way it's a flawed example. I've assumed the "determined opponent" of drilling is willing to pay $3,000 to get his way. (We call that number his *willingness-to-pay*, or WTP.) Therefore I've given him 3,000 votes to cast against the drilling project. But there's an alternative measure of how much our determined opponent cares about the outcome, namely the minimum amount he'd accept in exchange for allowing drilling, if the decision were in his hands. That amount is called his *willingness-to-accept*, or WTA. Sometimes it's more appropriate to use one number, sometimes the other; there are many subtleties here (all of which have been well and thoroughly studied by economists). Fortunately the subtleties are often avoidable: For most people, most of the time, the WTA and WTP are very close, so it doesn't matter which one you use. (This is provable under very general assumptions.) Unfortunately this might be one of the rare exceptions. (The general assumptions are more likely to fail when people are particularly passionate about the issue at hand.)

The story of the lost dollar bill is a fiction but could have been a truth. When I presented David Friedman with the airline ticket conundrum from the end of the chapter, he immediately responded by telling me that if I believed in an efficiency standard for personal conduct, I was honor-bound not to retrieve the next dollar bill that I dropped.

9. OF MEDICINE AND CANDY, TRAINS AND SPARKS

Ronald Coase's historic paper first appeared in the *Journal of Law and Economics*, and has been widely republished.

10. CHOOSING SIDES IN THE DRUG WAR

Mr. Dennis's cost-benefit analysis appeared in the *Atlantic Monthly* back in November 1990. There are more recent examples of bad cost-benefit analyses, but none that manages quite so thoroughly to commit every conceivable error; therefore I've retained this one as the chapter's main example.

11. THE MYTHOLOGY OF DEFICITS

In the discussion of myth #5, I've observed that you can always effectively pay off your share of the national debt by putting an appropriate sum of money in an interest-bearing account, pretending it's gone forever, and using the interest to pay the excess taxes caused by the debt burden. Occasionally readers object that this won't work because the interest on your savings account is taxed. The mistake is to overlook the fact that interest on *everyone's* savings account is taxed, which brings in revenue to the government and therefore reduces the amount the government needs to collect from you—by an amount that precisely offsets the taxes on your savings account. If that went by too fast, you can either trust my assurance that this is a nonissue or read a more careful presentation at www.landsburg.com/riceq.pdf.

12. UNSOUND AND FURIOUS

James Kahn pointed out to me the irony of Al Gore's timing.

Andrew Martin's piece on locavorism appeared in the *New York Times* on December 9, 2007. Stephen Budiansky's far more thoughtful piece appeared on August 19, 2010.

13. HOW STATISTICS LIE

The observation about Star Market's misleading advertising is due to Walter Oi.

For data on income mobility, see the paper "Income Mobility in the United States: New Evidence from Income Tax Data" by Gerald Auten and Geoffrey Gee in the *National Tax Journal* (June 2009). The mobility from quintile to quintile is pretty much unchanged since the first edition of *Armchair*.

14. THE POLICY VICE

The *ABC World News* series "Living in the Shadows: Illiteracy in America" aired in February 2008, nearly 20 years after ABC ran a

similar report as part of its Sunday morning *David Brinkley Show.*
The *David Brinkley* report featured prominently in the first edition
of *The Armchair Economist.* I had planned to cut this material from
the second edition on the grounds that it was no longer timely, but
with "Living in the Shadows," ABC did me the favor of making it
timely again.

The observation that the possibility of "scoops" might justify
either taxing or subsidizing inventors is due to Marvin Goodfriend.

The colleague who worries about packing material is Bruce
Hansen, now of the University of Wisconsin.

15. SOME MODEST PROPOSALS

The epigraph is from Milton Friedman's *Capitalism and Freedom,*
first published in 1962 and still in print.

The remark about people of the same trade rarely meeting without getting around the topic of price-fixing is from Adam Smith's
The Wealth of Nations, first published in 1776 and also still in print.

I believe, but am not certain, that the idea of allowing people
to sell their punishment rights arose from a conversation with Alan
Stockman.

16. WHY POPCORN COSTS MORE AT THE MOVIES

The theory of two-part pricing (e.g., charging once for the razor
and again for the blades, or once for admission to Disneyland and
again for the ride tickets) sprang full-blown from the head of my
colleague Walter Oi, and was published in the *Quarterly Journal of
Economics* in 1971.

Robert Michaels of Cal State, Fullerton, pointed out to me that
free delivery of furniture is a form of price discrimination.

The prices for Dell computers were cited in the *Wall Street Jour-*

nal on June 8, 2001, and again by Andrew Odlyzko in a paper called "Privacy, Economics and Price Discrimination on the Internet." (This paper seems never to have been published, though it's not hard to find on the web.) Odlyzko also cites the examples of the laser printer E and the French railroad cars.

Preston McAfee told me how often American Airlines changes its prices.

For the full story of Rohm and Haas and its attempts to market methyl methacrylate, see George Stocking and Myron Watkins, "Cartels in Action" (The Twentieth Century Fund, 1946), and Thomas Nagle, *The Strategy and Tactics of Pricing,* 5th edition (Prentice-Hall, 2010).

The chapter addresses the question "How would a price-discriminating theater owner set prices?" It glosses over the question of why the theater owner can price-discriminate in the first place, that is, whence the monopoly power? Certainly some monopoly power comes from locational advantages, especially when first-run movies play at a limited number of theaters. But the economists Luis Locay and Alvaro Rodriguez have offered an alternative story that I think has the ring of truth: People go to movies in groups. Popcorn lovers often travel with companions who eat no popcorn. The usual argument says that under competition, you can't price-discriminate against popcorn eaters without losing them to another theater. The Locay-Rodriguez response is that popcorn eaters can't go to another theater without splitting up their social groups. If another theater offers cheap popcorn and high ticket prices, the nonsnackers in the group will vote to stay put. Locay and Rodriguez have constructed a complete argument demonstrating that under plausible hypotheses about the way groups make decisions, theater owners have a degree of monopoly power over popcorn lovers who travel with popcorn non-lovers, and can plausibly exploit this power by pricing popcorn high.

I like that story, but it does leave a thread hanging. It doesn't tell me why the popcorn lover fails to offer his friends a deal: Let's stick to theaters with low-priced popcorn, and I'll occasionally pay for your tickets.

17. COURTSHIP AND COLLUSION

The analysis of polygamy derives from the work of Gary Becker.

The footnote on page 218 is due to Mark Bils.

For the role of feminist groups in the Depo-Provera ban, see the column "Clinicians Clash with Consumer Groups over Possible Depo Ban" in the journal *Contraceptive Technology Update* (January 1995).

I learned about the Chinese bargemen from Walter Oi.

18. CURSED WINNERS AND GLUM LOSERS

The theory of disappointment is due to Jack Hirshleifer. I learned it from Alan Stockman.

There is an excellent overview of auction theory by R. P. McAfee and J. McMillan in the *Journal of Economic Literature*, 1987.

19. RANDOM WALKS AND STOCK MARKET PRICES

Over the past four decades, hundreds of empirical studies have confirmed the essential truth of the random walk hypothesis. The strongest challenge to that orthodoxy is to be found in the work of Andrew Lo and Archie Craig MacKinlay, of MIT and the University of Pennsylvania, reported in their book *A Non-Random Walk Down Wall Street* (Princeton University Press, 2001). Lo and MacKinlay assert that, contrary to the random walk hypothesis, past changes in stock market prices do have predictive power for near-term future changes. However, even if Lo and MacKinlay's statistical analysis is correct, nobody (or at least nobody who's talking) has found a way to make money off it—the deviations from random walks are too small, and the transactions costs you'd incur to take advantage of them are too large. Thus even if the *random walk* hypothesis turns out to be not quite correct, the *efficient markets* hypothesis—which says, in effect, that you can't make money off publicly available information—can still survive.

The remarks from Richard Roll occurred during an exchange with the economist Robert Shiller and are reported in the *Journal of Applied Corporate Finance*, Spring 1992.

For a good survey of the evidence, see Burton Malkiel's paper in the *Journal of Economic Perspectives*, Winter 2003.

23. NEW IMPROVED FOOTBALL

I learned the football analogy from Chuck Whiteman; I believe (but am not certain) that it originated with Tom Sargent.

Nobel prize winners Milton Friedman and Edmund Phelps (separately and simultaneously) were the first to suggest that inflation could affect unemployment by fooling people about the real value of their wages. Both papers appeared in 1968, Friedman's in the *American Economic Review* and Phelps's in the *Journal of Political Economy*.

Robert Lucas used the Friedman-Phelps insight as the basis for his pathbreaking work in the *Journal of Economic Theory* in 1972. Lucas's critique of econometric policy evaluation appeared in the *Carnegie Rochester Conference Series on Public Policy* in 1976.

24. WHY I AM NOT AN ENVIRONMENTALIST

Michael Darby, writing in the *Journal of Political Economy* in 1973, was, to my knowledge, the first person to mention in print that recycling is likely to lead to fewer trees. David Tatoutchoup and Gerard Gaudet (both of the University of Montreal) provide a substantially more detailed analysis in a 2009 research paper titled "The Impact of Recycling on the Long-Run Stock of Trees." See also the book *The Economics of Waste* by Richard Porter of the University of Michigan.

INDEX

ABOUT THE AUTHOR

Steven E. Landsburg is a professor of economics at the University of Rochester. He is the author of *The Armchair Economist, Fair Play, More Sex Is Safer Sex, The Big Questions,* two textbooks on economics, a forthcoming textbook on general relativity and cosmology, and over thirty journal articles on mathematics, economics, and philosophy. His current research is in the area of quantum game theory. For over ten years he wrote the monthly "Everyday Economics" column in *Slate* magazine, and has written regularly for *Forbes* and occasionally for the *New York Times*, the *Wall Street Journal*, and the *Washington Post*. He appeared as a commentator on the PBS/Turner Broadcasting series *Damn Right* and has made over 200 appearances on radio and television broadcasts over the past few years. He blogs at www.TheBigQuestions.com.